Britain, the US a Anti-Soviet Stance in the Cold War

This book shows how international trade was a key part of the classic Western policy of containment towards the Soviet Union in the Cold War in the late 1970s.

Trade and containment may summarise the new relation that communist China moulded with the capitalistic West in the late 1970s. Ideology had become less important and a rapprochement between the PRC (People's Republic of China) and the Western powers over trade, with the purpose of isolating and weakening the common Russian rival, was practically unavoidable. Within a relatively short span of time the balance of power in the Indo-Pacific area had been reversed. Simply put, Beijing's market was too big to be ignored and the Atlantic allies collaborated, sometimes even competing with each other, to allow China access to the centres of world finance. However, the Western powers had not realised that Beijing would never pursue alignment with them. On the contrary, the increased trading and financial linkage with capitalistic countries gave China room to manoeuvre, enabling it to play the Western states off against each other.

This book will be of much interest to students of Cold War Studies, Chinese history, foreign policy and international relations.

Bruno Pierri is an adjunct professor in the Department of Political and Social Sciences at the University of Bologna and has a PhD in History of extra-European countries from the University of Pisa, Italy.

Cold War History

Series Editors: Michael Cox
London School of Economics, UK
Odd Arne Westad
John F. Kennedy School of Government, Harvard University, USA

In the new history of the Cold War that has been forming since 1989, many of the established truths about the international conflict that shaped the latter half of the twentieth century have come up for revision. The present series is an attempt to make available interpretations and materials that will help further the development of this new history, and it will concentrate in particular on publishing expositions of key historical issues and critical surveys of newly available sources.

US Foreign Policy and the End of the Cold War in Africa
A Bridge between Global Conflict and the New World Order, 1988–1994
Flavia Gasbarri

European Socialist Regimes' Fateful Engagement with the West
National Strategies in the Long 1970s
Edited by Angela Romano and Federico Romero

NATO and the Strategic Defence Initiative
A Transatlantic History of the Star Wars Programme
Edited by Luc-André Brunet

Technological Innovation, Globalization and the Cold War
A Transnational History
Edited by Peter Svik and Wolfgang Mueller

British Nuclear Weapons and the Test Ban
Squaring the Circle of Defence and Arms Control, 1974–82
John R. Walker

Britain, the US and China's Anti-Soviet Stance in the Cold War
Containment and Trade, 1977–1980
Bruno Pierri

For more information about this series, please visit: https://www.routledge.com/Cold-War-History/book-series/SE0220

Britain, the US and China's Anti-Soviet Stance in the Cold War

Containment and Trade, 1977–1980

Bruno Pierri

Routledge
Taylor & Francis Group

LONDON AND NEW YORK

First published 2024
by Routledge
4 Park Square, Milton Park, Abingdon, Oxon OX14 4RN

and by Routledge
605 Third Avenue, New York, NY 10158

Routledge is an imprint of the Taylor & Francis Group, an informa business

© 2024 Bruno Pierri

The right of Bruno Pierri to be identified as author of this work has been asserted in accordance with sections 77 and 78 of the Copyright, Designs and Patents Act 1988.

All rights reserved. No part of this book may be reprinted or reproduced or utilised in any form or by any electronic, mechanical, or other means, now known or hereafter invented, including photocopying and recording, or in any information storage or retrieval system, without permission in writing from the publishers.

Trademark notice: Product or corporate names may be trademarks or registered trademarks, and are used only for identification and explanation without intent to infringe.

British Library Cataloguing-in-Publication Data
A catalogue record for this book is available from the British Library

ISBN: 978-1-032-48660-4 (hbk)
ISBN: 978-1-032-48661-1 (pbk)
ISBN: 978-1-003-39013-8 (ebk)

DOI: 10.4324/9781003390138

Typeset in Sabon
by MPS Limited, Dehradun

to C.G.

Contents

Acknowledgements

First of all, I would like to thank my parents and my sister for being so patient while the veranda at the sea-side was impossible to enjoy, as it was full of papers I was using to write this book. Moreover, I feel grateful to Professor Paolo Soave for having always believed in me, encouraging me to carry on despite all the academic difficulties he knows very well. I want also to mention my long-time friend, Professor Leila El Houssi, who gave me the idea of this monograph. Finally, I cannot forget my cousin Paolo and my close friends, the Dossenas, who witnessed the very first minutes of this work, and my colleague Roberta, with whom I finally revised my writing style.

Introduction

In his work, *On China*, Henry Kissinger quotes a 1985 CIA report describing how the People's Republic of China was getting closer to the Soviet Union through high-level meetings taking place after about two decades. Nevertheless, the former secretary of state minimised the consequences of such a manoeuvre, stating that there was no incentive to move away from Washington, as long as Moscow remained a nuclear power with precarious relations with Asian neighbour. In a few words, the relationship between the Atlantic country and the Far East giant was living a sort of transition from a Cold War balance to a global international order shaping new challenges. Everything seemed to suggest that the USSR was always regarded as the main security threat.[1] The other architect of the historic rapprochement with the People's Republic, Richard Nixon, shared such a vision. In fact, in 1982 he had written to President Ronald Reagan, encouraging him to favour a Chinese greater role in the so-called Third World. Simply speaking, the more successful Beijing, the less successful the Soviets. The point was that China and the United States had a common concern about the threat of Russian aggression, but what could draw the two powers closer together in the future was their economic interdependence.[2] A couple of years previously, in a TV interview Deng Xiaoping seemed to have confirmed this policy, as he had been able to distinguish between China's position towards Third World liberation movements and the relations with developed capitalist countries to carry out the struggle against superpower hegemonism. In fact, Beijing was always committed to fight against exploitation, imperialist oppression, colonialism and racism.[3] Another pivotal interview was the one given by Xue Muqiao, adviser to the State Planning Commission and director of the Research Institute of Economics. Actually, he said that the time had come to develop a market economy to suit at least the large-scale urban socialised production. In a few words, competition was no longer regarded as something negative, thus enterprises with different levels of mechanisation and scales of production were allowed to adopt different forms of management.[4] Further example of how communist China was on the way to access the world market economy is the "Resolution on Certain Questions in the History of our Party since the Founding of the People's Republic of China", issued in 1981 by

DOI: 10.4324/9781003390138-1

the Sixth Plenary Session of the 11th Central Committee of the Communist Party. This document repudiated the ultra-leftist measures of the Cultural Revolution, claiming at the same time the determination to remain independent and self-reliant.[5]

As we can see from these few lines, trade and containment may be the key words summarising the new relation that communist China moulded with the capitalistic West in the 1970s. Just to give an example, Chairman Mao Zedong had formulated a sort of global theory of containment towards the Soviet Union, saying that the countries threatened by Moscow were supposed to draw a horizontal line, from the United States, to Japan, Iran, Pakistan and Europe, as a sort of fence to commonly deal with what the Chinese leader called "the bastard".[6] As far as this was concerned, in an article published in 2010 Kuisong Yang and Yafeng Xia wrote that Mao was thinking of exploiting the Sino-American common thoughts about Soviet expansionism to involve a complex of countries in a strategic line. To sum up, on one hand the Chinese government always publicly opposed the hegemony of the two superpowers and backed revolutionary struggles around the world; on the other hand, Beijing was developing a policy of getting allied with Washington.[7] More recently, Jason M. Kelly stated that in the early 1970s the Chinese were by then determined to face new world challenges, such as the outlook of war with the Soviet Union, rapprochement with the United States, and above all a large gap between what the Communist Party had promised to achieve and what had been actually delivered. Hence, the leaders of the People's Republic were learning to consider more expansively how global markets might be exploited not only to pursue revolution, but also and mostly to achieve the long-term national goals that the revolution had sought in the first place.[8] Of the two imperialist superpowers, we can read in a 1977 Peking Review editorial, the Soviet Union was "... the more ferocious, the more reckless, the more treacherous, and the most dangerous source of world war". First of all, continues the article, Moscow had become an imperialist power imitating the United States, and therefore more aggressive and adventurous, as latecomer among imperialist countries. This implied that the Euro-Asian power had decided to harm the sovereignty of other countries and replace US influence. Moreover, being economically weaker, the Soviet Union was thought to be obliged to rely chiefly on military power in order to expand.[9]

Clues that things were being channelled along a pattern of economic development and international trade were already visible in 1975, when Deng Xiaoping returned from his exile after having been purged during the Cultural Revolution. In order to testify this statement, suffice it to quote Deng's remarks dating back to 26 September, entitled "Priority Should Be Given to Scientific Research", through which he emphasised several themes that he was going to develop in the following years, such as the need to improve science and technology and above all the development of individual talent and initiative as a way to follow a new economic order. To achieve such a task, special attention was to be paid to promoting competent individuals to leading positions.[10] In his recent biography of the Chinese leader, Michael Dillon reminds that these objectives had already been set at the fourth National People's Congress held in Beijing in January 1975. All sectors of the economy had been severely damaged during the previous years, but expenditure was still augmenting.[11] The weak and ill Zhou, deputised by Deng who was practically running the government, delivered the "Report on the Work of the Government", testifying that China's economy had to be developed in two stages: the former to build an independent and relatively comprehensive industrial and economic system within fifteen years; the latter to accomplish the comprehensive modernisation of agriculture, industry, national defence, and science and technology before the end of the century. Priority had to be acknowledged to agriculture as the foundation, followed by light industry and heavy industry, as a new political goal walking on two legs. The prime minister also underlined that the Soviet leadership had taken a series of measures to worsen the relations with the Asian communist giant. On the contrary, despite fundamental differences between China and the United States, the relations with the Anglo-Saxon power were thought to improve in the following years.[12]

Concerning this, Kissinger was very clear while talking to Mao in the same year, stating that the White House was trying to contain Soviet expansionism and that was why China had strategic priority for Washington.[13] This posture was not difficult to understand, as Deng himself stated that causes for another world conflict had to be found in (a) the development of the Soviet social-imperialist system of society; (b) Moscow's pursuit of global hegemony; and (c) the growth of the Soviet military and economic potential. On the other hand, the USSS had some weak points to exploit, such as lack of enough grain supplies and the backwardness of its industry and technology.[14] From an American point of view, by reading CIA reports it seems there was no particular concern about long-term improvement of Sino-Soviet relations, which did not necessarily mean communist unwillingness to deal with the West. However, adverse effects were always possible, such as Chinese decreased tolerance towards US military presence in the Far East, or the Kremlin's willingness to compete with the White House over the global scene.[15] In a nutshell, the US Intelligence might have wished to obstruct the dialogue between the two socialist countries in order to keep the reins of containment. As far as Asia was concerned, American analyses highlighted that the USSR was persisting in proposing an Asian collective security system in order to assert its credentials as a continental power. Such a proposal was believed to be an anti-Chinese device aimed either at forcing Beijing to accept a Soviet leading role in the continent, or at showing China as an ambitious and bellicose country.[16]

As a matter of fact, all these records show that ideology had become much less important in Chinese foreign policy and therefore a rapprochement between the Dragon and Western powers over a trading basis with the purpose to isolate and weaken the common Russian rival was practically unavoidable.

Succinctly, the then candidate to the Presidency, Jimmy Carter, on addressing the Chicago Council on Foreign Relations showed to follow the same pattern by stating that the United States had a great stake in a nationally independent, secure and friendly China. On the other hand, a Sino-Soviet reconciliation was thought to be inimical to international stability and American interests. Therefore, the future president believed that the Atlantic power should widen American-Chinese trade relations, as well as further consolidate a political relationship.[17] Tellingly, Washington's studies, a few months before Mao passed away, predicted that hatred and fear of the USSR almost certainly would always be China's main factor of foreign relations.[18] Pivotal to highlight is also what Zbigniew Brzezinski wrote when he was still professor of political science at Columbia University. In a nutshell, the future National Security Adviser predicted the emergence of a globalised society wherein cultural values and economic efficiency would be tightly linked in a globalised world without relevant borders. In order to cope with such new challenges, he argued that American foreign policy could no longer be limited to government-to-government relations, but rather required skills in intellectual scientific communications able to attract creative segments of other societies.[19]

As far as oil trade was concerned, according to Kazushi Minami, who published a remarkable article in "Diplomatic History" in 2017, there were three main reasons why this raw material helped set on track the relations between China and the West. In short, when Beijing started to sell oil to capitalist countries, Far Eastern reserves were seen as a potential alternative to Middle Eastern oil. Secondly, Western interests quickly shifted to Chinese imports of petroleum technology, especially offshore equipment. Finally, oil technology cooperation was seen as a way to prevent the Soviets from expanding their influence in the resource-rich developing world.[20] Such a policy is confirmed by what Michel Oksenberg – who later became one of Carter's main collaborators on Far Eastern issues – asserted in 1976 in Houston, Texas, when he said that natural resources, and oil in particular, could become the key for China to accelerate industrial growth by importing technology. Finally, in the same year Premier Hua Guofeng, assuming leadership after Mao's death, spoke about the so-called "Western-led Leap Forward", characterised by quick industrialisation with foreign inputs.[21] From the British point of view, in order for London not to be left out of the impending rush to the Chinese market, Downing Street had continuously delivered the message that, whatever the economic troubles of the previous years, the UK economy was now able to compete with the rest of the world for export business, always keeping Beijing informed about what British companies had to offer.[22] As Priscilla Roberts says, in spite of the fact that in the 1970s China and East Asia still occupied a very marginal position in London's estimates of national interests, British elites cooperated to ease the resumption of relations with the Asian power with the stake to promote Chinese economic reform and development, thus encouraging Beijing's integration into the international system.[23]

This decision was well motivated, if we think that in the following years Chinese exports grew strongly. Despite less favourable international market conditions in the early 1980s implying a reduction of imports, International Monetary Fund analyses expected a more liberal import policy contributing to accelerated introduction of new technology and competition in the domestic market.[24] Quite different is what Ann Lane writes on Sino-British relations in the Labour years. In fact, she states that China was not a major issue in British foreign policy during this span of time. Nevertheless, Beijing was willing to develop closer relations with the British armed services, thus a series of high-level diplomatic and military exchanges took place to encourage this pattern. On one hand, the British government was aware that the Chinese wanted to buy sophisticated military equipment; on the other hand, London's interest was moulded essentially by awareness of the need to establish friendly connections with China in view of developments in policies towards Hong Kong.[25]

By quoting these first few records, this work aims at showing how international trade was part of the classic policy of containment towards the Soviet Union, which by the late 1970s was clearly the common rival of both China and the Atlantic powers. To tell the truth, the Anglo-Saxon capitals sometimes criticised the Chinese for looking obsessed by the Russian threat, but archive documentation proves that the Western allies were clearly interested in fanning on the Sino-Soviet split to widen the breach within the communist world short of any large-scale war. Whilst in public statements Western leaders denied the intention to play the China card against the Soviet Union, evidence shows both Beijing and the North Atlantic partners often associated business issues to Cold War questions. As far as international trade was concerned, Deng Xiaoping had always declared that the purpose of the Chinese Communist Party was to learn from industrialised countries in order to acquire the necessary know-how to pursue economic independence and produce what China lacked, thus modernising both economy and society.[26] Succinctly, Deng sought to strengthen China without attracting too much attention, for he understood that it was not in the interest of the Dragon to develop a similar type of unstable relationship like the one between the two superpowers. As a matter of fact, Deng was convinced that a position of no threat was the best strategy to grow without raising unnecessary resistance.[27] The Long March veteran wanted his country to gradually turn into an insider of the existing international system and institutions dominated by the United States and the capitalist West.[28] The Chinese government under Deng's leadership dramatically reduced and finally stopped support to radical nationalist movements while adopting an open approach in external relations. As an outcome of this, interconnections between Beijing and the outside increased significantly, strengthening the interdependence between China and the rest of the world. With Deng Xiaoping altering the basic courses of the Dragon's external policies, the Cold War in Asia changed its paradigm almost one decade before the conclusion of the global dual confrontation.[29]

Just to quote a few numbers, China's foreign trade jumped by between fifty and one hundred per cent in the first half of the 1980s, with imports and exports tracking each other, so that in 1985 exports reached twenty-five billion dollars.[30] As a matter of fact, Deng's project implied not only an economic revolution, but also a political one, with the ideological model of the Maoist era replaced by something quite close to the developmental system of East Asian Tigers. On the other hand, for a long time Beijing's growth has been extremely resource-intensive. With the notable exception of rare earth minerals – China is responsible for more that ninety per cent of the world's supply of magnesium, cerium oxide, silicon, bismuth and many others, used in a range of products from mobile phones, hybrid cars, wind turbines – Beijing is becoming increasingly dependent on foreign countries for a huge quantity of raw materials, such as copper, iron ore, alumina, coal, steel, cotton.[31] To give an example of how the Asian power manages to expand its influence on a global scale, suffice it to say that the People's Republic of China (PRC) has been implementing a pragmatic economic diplomacy towards resource-rich countries. Though in extreme need of raw materials, Beijing also relies on external demand to absorb labour-intensive products. As a consequence of this, the Far Eastern power's total trade with these regions started to grow at a much faster speed than the one with the rest of the world.[32] In summary, while in the early 1980s China mainly played the role of economic suitor, by attracting foreign investors through special tax arrangements, a cheap labour force and a practically limitless domestic market, in the following decade a more confident Dragon began to act as a major player, able to more assertively negotiate the terms to best participate in the international community.[33]

The book is mainly based on British and American archival records, such as the documents collected at the National Archives in Kew, London, and the Department of State Record Group 59 papers located at the National Archives and Records Administration in College Park, Maryland. Pivotal to quote are also the collections in the Carter Presidential Library in Atlanta, Georgia. As far as American records are concerned, the author has also collected the *Foreign Relations of the United States* (FRUS) series and the *Public Papers of the Presidents of the United States*. Apart from this, a few web sites have given quite an important contribution to the reconstruction of this era. In particular, we are speaking about the CIA Foia Electronic Reading Room and the Cold War International History Project. As concerns Chinese records, we can quote two main history sources. The former is the Beijing Review (called Peking Review until 1979), which provides an insight knowledge of the Chinese government's view on economic and foreign policy questions, as well as the position of the main leaders of the country. The latter is the marxists.org archive with the selected works of Deng Xiaoping. Essential to mention are also the two books of Memoirs by President Carter, *Keeping Faith* and *White House Diary*. Obviously, Carter's main collaborators published their memoirs, highlighting how the National

Security Adviser, Zbigniew Brzezinski (*Power and Principle* the title of his work), disagreed with the Secretary of State Cyrus Vance (*Hard Choices*), who pursued a more prudent course of action towards the People's Republic, while keeping a more diplomatic and conciliatory stance towards the process of Détente with the Soviet Union. Last but not least, *Prisoner of the State* is the biography written by former Chinese Premier Zhao Ziyang when he was under house arrest and portraying economic freedom was accepted while resisting political change.

The monograph is quite innovative, at least as far as Italian historiography is concerned. As a matter of fact, in Italy there are not so many scholars dealing with this particular issue. From this point of view, an important and recently published work to quote is *Rekindling the Strong State in Russia and China*, edited by Antonio Fiori and Stefano Bianchini in 2020, which gives us quite a detailed analysis to understand the profound regeneration of the state in the two countries also affecting their global aspirations. In 2014, Fiori edited *The Chinese Challenge to the Western Order* with Matteo Dian, dealing with China's extraordinary rise as a possible crucial challenge for the contemporary international order, with a particular focus on how other great powers and Asian middle ones had reacted to such a change. As far as international scholarship is concerned, one of the first works to be produced on China's world posture after the death of Mao is the one edited in 1984 by Samuel S. Kim, *China and the World: Chinese Foreign Policy in the Post-Mao Era*. Some chapters of this work, in fact, cope with the relations between Beijing, Washington and Moscow, as well as with other Western countries, before and after the 1976–1978 breakthrough. Based on interviews and visits to factories is David Wen-Wei Chang's *China under Deng Xiaoping*, an attempt to assess the 1980s political history of China at the end of the decade stating that the regime had not yet abandoned its superficial adherence to Mao Zedong thought. More recently, two paramount volumes were published in 1994, that is to say *Deng Xiaoping and the Chinese Revolution*, by David S.G. Goodman, and *Burying Mao*, by Richard Baum. Goodman wrote a political biography describing Deng as a committed communist with a pragmatic view, while Richard Baum deals with the intriguing story of an escalating intergenerational clash of ideas and values between the aging revolutionaries of the Maoist era and their younger, more pragmatic successors. In 1995, Robert S. Ross wrote *Negotiating Cooperation*, dealing with the relations between China and the United States in the 1970s and 1980s. Ross examines several factors leading to the normalisation with the Atlantic power, including the perceived common threat from the Soviet Union. A very good appraisal of Deng's reform era is *Ideology and Economic Reform under Deng*, 1996, by Wei-wei Zhang, which explores the ideological transformation from the orthodox anti-market doctrine into a more elastic and pro-business one. In particular, the study is focused on the origin and evolution of the "Socialism with Chinese characteristics" doctrine and its impact on the reform programme. Robert Ross edited another study on the normalisation with William C. Kirby and

Gong Li ten years later, this time after the declassification of archive records. The thesis developed in this work is that Beijing's effort to grant its security towards the Soviet Union was regarded as a tactical necessity to promote Chinese military and economic interests. From their point of view, the Americans saw this relationship as a way to forestall the Soviets. Always dealing with this issue is *US-Chinese Relations: Perilous Past, Pragmatic Present*, by Robert G. Sutter, which offers an analysis of the relationship between the two powers over the last two centuries. Among the latest works, we can mention *Unlikely Partners*, 2017, by Julian Gewirtz, which gives a review of the competition for influence between reformers and conservatives during the Deng Xiaoping era. Two of the most recent works on China's foreign policy are *Deng Xiaoping and China's Foreign Policy*, 2018, by Ronald C. Keith, and *China and the World*, edited by David Shambaugh, 2020. The former explores how Deng established principles encouraging China to have a kind of foreign policy supporting economic development and stressing harmony in the world, rather than hegemony, thus trying over the years to normalise relations not only with the United States, but also with the Soviet Union. The latter covers China's contemporary position towards all major powers and across multiple arenas of international interactions. Among the very latest monographs, really interesting and with a global approach is the one by Lorenz M. Lüthi, *Cold War: Asia, the Middle East, Europe*, arguing that the cold war had ended first in the Middle East by the late 1970s, and then in Asia by the early 1980s, thus leaving the superpower confrontation as the only major conflict that remained by then.

As far as analyses of Chinese economy are concerned, remarkable studies are those by Barry Naughton, *Growing out of the Plan*, 1996, and *The Chinese Economy: Adaptation and Growth*, 2018. On the other hand, in 2014 Shu Guang Zhang published *Beijing's Economy Statecraft during the Cold War*, portraying Beijing's use of economic instruments as a way to pursue policy goals. Such a work therefore assesses how foreign economic policies played out in the PRC's relations with the United States, United Kingdom, as well as many other actors. Finally, being published in 2022, Priscilla Robert's edited book, *Chinese Economic Statecraft from 1978 to 1989*, so far is very likely the latest publication on this subject. In short, the authors cover topics such as efforts to steer an economic course tailored to "socialism with Chinese characteristics", beside China's dealings with international economic institutions and other powers like Japan, the United States and Europe. Pivotal works (some of which edited with Shambaugh) have also been written by Michael Yahuda on the international relations of the Asia-Pacific region. Since 1983, when he edited *Towards the End of Isolationism: China's Foreign Policy after Mao*, Professor Yahuda has been discussing Beijing's foreign policy, as well as its capacity to absorb advanced Western technology through the policy of "Open Door". Several updated editions of *The International Politics of the Asia-Pacific*, finally, cover this issue from the impact of the Cold War to the relations of major Asian powers with the Trump administration.

Among the many biographies of Deng Xiaoping, of paramount importance seems to be the one written by Michael Dillon in 2015, *Deng Xiaoping: The Man who Made Modern China*, which uses recently released Chinese sources underlining the contradictions between his desire for economic liberalisation and political conservatism. On the other hand, *Deng Xiaoping: A Revolutionary Life*, released in the same year by Alexander V. Pantsov and Steven I. Levine, showed what was defined the likely definitive biography of the Chinese statesman until Chinese Communist Party archives would become available, though adding very little to what Ezra Vogel had published four years previously. To quote other Chinese scholars, certainly essential is *Politics of Disillusionment: The Chinese Communist Party under Deng Xiaoping*, by His-Sheng Ch'i, which provides a first assessment of the era at issue. Besides, edited by Vogel and Levine in 2004 is *Deng Xiaoping Shakes the World*, that is Yu Gungyuan's eyewitness account of the 1978 Third Plenum and China's Party Work Conference, showing for the first time how the works of the Plenum were just ceremonial, while the key debates and consequent decisions took place at the Conference summoned a few days before the more famous event. Finally, we have to say that British historiography, and in general scholars studying the relations between Beijing and Washington, is more focused on the question of Hong Kong, which is also developed in Margaret Thatcher's *The Downing Street Years*. As far as the relations with Western Europe are concerned, therefore, suffice is to quote a few books, such as Nicola Casarini's *Remaking Global Order*, 2009, through which the author provides an examination of the evolution of contemporary European Union-China relations in the economic, technological and high politics fields. *China-Europe Relations*, edited in 2008 by David Shambaugh, provides what the Chinese perceptions are of Europe, as well as assessing the rapid growth of bilateral commercial and technological relations. The 2016 study by Martin Albers, *Britain, France, West Germany and the People's Republic of China, 1969–1982*, provides a good analysis of the little known history between Western Europe and its most important trading partner, showing how the China policies of those three countries helped Beijing get reintegrated into the international community. In a few words, at the end of the Cold War the Europeans were obliged to counterbalance their declining influence and promote their own national interests in Asia by supporting a rapid expansion of the trade with the People's Republic, thus substantially contributing to the success of the Dragon.

Notes

1 Henry Alfred Kissinger, *On China* (London: Allen Lane, 2011), 392–393.
2 *Ibidem*, 393.
3 'TV Interview with Deng Xiaoping', *Beijing Review*, 23/2 (1980), 18–23.

4 'Special Interview: More on Economic Reform', *Beijing Review*, 23/36 (1980), 18–23.

5 *Resolution on Certain Questions in the History of Our Party since the Founding of the People's Republic of China, Adopted by the Sixth Plenary Session of the 11th Central Committee of the CCP on 27th June 1981*, 2 July 1981, in The National Archives (thereafter NA), London, Kew, FCO 21/1905, *China Internal Political*, FE/6764/C/1 (B).

6 *Memorandum of Conversation*, 17–18 February 1973, Top Secret, Sensitive, Exclusively Eyes Only, in William Burr (ed.), *The Kissinger Transcripts: The Top Secret Talks with Beijing and Moscow* (New York, NY: The New Press, 1998), 86–101.

7 Kuisong Yang and Yafeng Xia, 'Vacillating between Revolution and Détente: Mao's Changing Psyche and Policy toward the United States, 1969–1976', *Diplomatic History*, 34/2 (2010), 408–409.

8 Jason M. Kelly, *Market Maoists: The Communist Origins of China's Capitalist Ascent* (Cambridge, MA and London: Harvard University Press, 2021), 11.

9 'Chairman Mao's Theory of the Differentiation of the Three Worlds Is a Major Contribution to Marxism-Leninism', *Peking Review*, 20/45 (1977), 10–41.

10 Deng Xiaoping, 'Priority Should Be Given to Scientific Research', 26 September 1975, in *The Selected Works of Deng Xiaoping*, Vol. 2 (1975–1982), https://dengxiaopingworks.wordpress.com/2013/02/25/priority-should-be-given-to-scientific-research/, accessed 29 July, 2021.

11 Michael Dillon, *Deng Xiaoping: The Man Who Made Modern China* (London and New York, NY: I.B. Tauris, 2015), 203–206.

12 Zhou Enlai, Report on the Work of the Government, 13 January 1975, in Documents of the First Session of the Fourth National People's Congress of the People's Republic of China, https://www.marxists.org/reference/archive/zhou-enlai/1975/01/13.htm, accessed 29 July 2021.

13 *Memorandum of Conversation between Mao Zedong and Henry A. Kissinger*, 21 October 1975, Secret/Sensitive, http://digitalarchive.wilsoncenter.org/document/118072, accessed 29 July 2021.

14 *Conversation between Federal Chancellor Schmidt and Chinese Deputy Prime Minister Deng Xiaoping in Beijing*, 31 October 1975, http://digitalarchive.wilsoncenter.org/document/119995, accessed 30 July 2021.

15 *National Intelligence Estimate: Possible Changes in the Sino-Soviet Relationship*, 25 October 1973, NIE 11/13/6–73, Secret, Controlled Dissem., https://www.cia.gov/readingroom/docs/DOC_0000273309.pdf, accessed 30 July 2021.

16 *National Intelligence Estimate: Soviet Military Policy in the Third World*, 21 October 1976, NIE 11-10-76, Secret, Noforn/Nocontract, https://www.cia.gov/readingroom/docs/CIA-RDP07S01968R000200450001-2.pdf, accessed 30 July 2021.

17 *Remarks by Jimmy Carter: Our Foreign Relations*, 15 March 1976, in Adam M. Howard (gen. ed.) and Kristin L. Ahlberg (ed.), *Foreign Relations of the United States* (thereafter FRUS) *1977–1980*, Vol. I, *Foundations of Foreign Policy* (Washington, DC; United States Government Printing Office, 2014), Doc. 4, 15–26.

18 *Paper Prepared in the Central Intelligence Agency: The Foreign Policies of China's Successor Leadership*, June 1976, PR 76 10053 Secret, Noforn, in Edward C. Keefer (gen. ed.) and David P. Nickles (ed.), FRUS 1969–1976, Vol. XVIII, *China 1973–1976* (Washington, DC; United States Government Printing Office, 2007), Doc. 148, 931–935.

19 Federico Pachetti, 'The Roots of a Globalized Relationship: Western Knowledge of the Chinese Economy and US-China Relations in the Long 1970s', in Priscilla

Roberts and Ode Arne Westad (eds.), *China, Hong Kong, and the Long 1970s: Global Perspectives* (Cham: Palgrave Macmillan, 2017), 188–189.

20 Kazushi Minami, 'Oil for the Lamps of America? Sino-American Oil Diplomacy, 1973–1979', *Diplomatic History*, 41/5 (2017), 961–962.

21 *Ibidem*, 971.

22 *British Embassy Peking - Her Majesty's Ambassador at Peking to the Secretary of State for Foreign and Commonwealth Affairs: Visit of the Chinese Minister of Foreign Trade*, 4 November 1977, in NA, PREM 16/1533, *The Visit to the UK by Mr. Li Ch'iang, the Chinese Minister of Foreign* Trade, Confidential.

23 Priscilla Roberts, 'Bringing the Chinese Back in: The Role of Quasi-Private Institutions in Britain and the United States', in Roberts and Westad (eds.), *China, Hong Kong*, 311.

24 *Staff Report for the 1983 Article IV Consultation, Prepared by the Staff Representatives for the 1983 Article IV Consultation*, 24 October 1983, in NA, T 439/142, *International Monetary Fund, People's Republic of China*.

25 Ann Lane, 'Foreign and Defence Policy', in Anthony Seldon and Kevin Hickson (eds.), *New Labour, Old Labour: The Blair, Wilson and Callaghan Governments, 1974–1979* (London and New York, NY: Routledge, 2004), 164.

26 Kissinger, *World Order: Reflections on the Character of Nations and the Course of History* (London: Penguin Books, 2015), 227.

27 Marcus Vinicius De Freitas, *Policy Paper 19/05: Reform and Opening-Up: Chinese Lessons to the World* (Rabat: Policy Center for the New South, 2019), 15–16.

28 Chen Jian, *From Mao to Deng: China's Changing Relations with the United States*, Cold War International History Project, Working Paper 92 (Washington, DC: Woodrow Wilson International Center for Scholars, 2019), 2.

29 Chen, *Mao's China and the Cold War* (London and Chapel Hill, NC: University of North Carolina Press, 2001), 278.

30 Jonathan Fenby, *The Penguin History of Modern China: The Fall and Rise of a Great Power, 1850 to the Present* (London: Penguin Books, 2019), 558.

31 Martin Jacques, *When China Rules the World: The End of the Western World and the Birth of a New Global Order* (London: Penguin Books, 2012), 177–178, 199.

32 Deng Ziliang and Zheng Yongnian, 'China Reshapes the World Economy', in Wang Gungwu and Zheng Yongnian (eds.), *China and the New International Order* (Abingdon and New York, NY: Routledge, 2008), 139–142.

33 Avery Goldstein, *Rising to the Challenge: China's Grand Strategy and International Security* (Stanford, CA: Stanford University Press, 2005), 76.

1 The Nixon Legacy

1.1 Ford and Kissinger's Last Year

By reading archival documentation, the first thing surfacing is the common sense of containment towards the Soviet Union. During the Autumn 1975 trip to China, we can see how Kissinger highlighted the necessity to prevent Moscow from achieving hegemony in Asia as well as in Europe.[1] As far as South East Asia was concerned, Deng Xiaoping, more than Mao, continued to cope with the differences with the Euro-Asian communist power, probably to keep the Americans aware of the problem.[2] Actually, he thought that the Soviets would soon increase influence in Vietnam and Laos by pushing a collective security system in Asia.[3] The problem during these talks was that the leadership of both countries was rather weakened. On one hand, President Ford relied heavily on his secretary of state to run foreign policy issues. Kissinger, to tell the truth, was committed to normalisation, as we can easily realise not only from his memoirs, but especially by reading what he proposed and observed whenever he met Chinese officers. However, says Warren I. Cohen, the point was that Ford needed the support of the Republican Party's conservative wing to win the presidency in 1976. On the other hand, the foreign policy debate in the Far Eastern capital could no longer be separated from the question of succession. The radicals did not pursue a policy of rapprochement with the Soviet Union, but they opined that Zhou and Deng were exaggerating the Soviet threat to justify their unnecessary overtures to the United States.[4] To confirm such comments, of paramount importance are the remarks made by the diplomats of the Ford administration. For example, we can quote Richard Solomon, member of the National Security Council from 1971 to 1976, who said that Ford and Kissinger viewed normalisation as an obligation to complete during what remained of the presidential term. However, the message coming from the White House political staff was that conservative Republicans would not support Jerry Ford in pursuing this task. Donald Anderson, political officer at the liaison office in Beijing, states that Kissinger saw the opening to China as part of a global strategic move, with an inclination to accommodate the Chinese, rather than having a show-down, and then debating over details.[5]

DOI: 10.4324/9781003390138-2

As regarded trading issues, we may quote the words of Herbert Horowitz, director of the Department of State Office of Research, East Asia, from 1975 to 1978, who reminds that in those times what government officers learned was mostly what American businessmen would tell them. Instead Charles W. Freeman, Jr., deputy director, Taiwan Affairs, from 1975 to 1978, asserts that the process of opening trade relations was going rather smoothly, though in the Chinese society there were practically no commercial code and legal system to enforce contracts.[6]

Going back to Kissinger's remarks, his comment is that Mao wanted to highlight at least three questions: (a) China was prepared to stand alone, as in the previous decades against both the United States and the Soviet Union; (b) the principles of permanent revolution were always valid; (c) the opening to America did not imply the end of ideology in foreign policy.[7] To be honest, Mao observed that he expected nothing great to take place in Sino-American relations during the 1976 presidential election campaign and its aftermath.[8] As a matter of fact, election issues were paralysing Washington's China policy, so that Kissinger had been obliged to tell his collaborators that the question of normalisation was impossible until after the new Administration would take office. Ford's reluctance to break ties with Taiwan and recognise the People's Republic was undermining moderates like Deng Xiaoping, who argued that closer relations with the West and Japan would bring China important commercial and security gains.[9] Kissinger himself writes that although Chinese leaders could have no interest in showing a cooling of relations with Washington, ideological prejudices could prevail if they reached the conclusion that the administration was becoming irrelevant to Beijing due to domestic travails.[10]

In the meantime, it is important to remind that Kissinger saw military and technology fields as a way to promote relations with China. One of the first intelligence reports on this issue suggested that military ties with Beijing, and the consequent import of Western technology, could help strengthen the position of those who favoured stronger links with the West. In a few words, the Ford administration was prepared to purchase Chinese oil and sell what was called "equipment of special nature", thus suggesting that Beijing could use its oil sources to buy American military technology. To show that Washington really meant business, a few weeks after Mao's death the White House approved the sale of the first American computers to China, supposed to work on oil exploration and seismological studies, but actually useful for military applications as well. Hence, Washington was choosing a posture supplying the Dragon the necessary technology to be also used for military purposes.[11] In order to protect himself from domestic criticism, Kissinger had briefed state department officers to try to stop British and French intentions to transfer military technology to China, but he had at the same time told the British to ignore American attempts to block the sales. The state secretary chose to acquiesce to British bypassing of COCOM (the Coordinating Committee of NATO nations plus Japan supervising export of strategic commodities to communist countries), thus avoiding tensions with the Atlantic ally and also using London to suggest stronger NATO ties with China.[12] CIA studies seem to confirm this attitude. In fact, within Chinese leadership acquisition of foreign technology was thought to be permissible in the short term in order to reduce the need for future imports, though it was always necessary to avoid the risk of being exploited or contaminated by foreigners. Several factors were regarded to have caused the Chinese to purchase military technology from abroad.[13] First of all, the usefulness to copy Soviet technology was coming to an end. Moreover, the Chinese were experiencing serious difficulties to develop their own sophisticated weapons system. Finally, Western technology had generally become more available, not only because political restrictions were being gradually eased, but it was also due to Western nations competing with one another.[14]

Meanwhile, Deng had commissioned major studies in the areas of industry and science. Among the recommendations which later surfaced outside the country was a passage in a September 1975 secret document, stating that in order to import more advanced technologies from abroad, it was necessary to increase exports and in particular raise the proportion of industrial and mineral products among export commodities. Moreover, with the aim of accelerating the exploitation of coal and petroleum, long-term contracts with foreign countries had to be signed to have complete sets of modern equipment supplied in exchange of raw materials.[15] As a consequence of this, when discussing cooperation in petroleum development with an American delegation in October 1975, the old leader stated that China had to import advanced technology and sophisticated equipment from the United States, without excluding imports for the exploration and exploitation of oil.[16] Nevertheless, as Robert Ross reminds, during the Ford administration Beijing had a decreasing interest in seeking immediate improvement in relations with the United States. Despite the perceived Soviet threat, in fact, growing tensions between the two superpowers were welcomed in the Far Eastern country. In addition, China was winning new friends among non-communist governments, though it was not certainly possible to let the relationship with Washington deteriorate too much.[17] In the meantime, according to David Goodman, Deng and his supporters stressed the importance of providing workers and peasants with material incentives to encourage them to produce more, rather than relying on ideology. In particular, the People's Republic was supposed to export raw materials, as well as manufactured chemical products, in order to import advanced technology and raise the productivity of labour.[18]

In order to realise how important China had become to US foreign policy, the head of the State Department used to publicly stress crucial relations with Asia, since in that area the interests of all major powers intersected. Exaggerating the outcome of the president's trip to China, he said that American strength was basic to any stable balance of power in the Pacific region. Moreover, the process of normalisation was regarded as indispensable, for America's relations with one quarter of mankind were inevitably of essential importance to the world. Finally, economic cooperation within the Pacific Basin was something necessarily to pursue.[19] At the same time, US intelligence carried on monitoring the People's Republic in view of the succession of an ill and ageing Mao. It does not seem that the Americans were worried too much about possible deterioration of relations with Beijing, which always had the desire to project its influence globally but was thought to enjoy a limited capability to compete with the superpowers in doing so. Actually, the Asian country could not compete even with larger European powers in providing advanced-technology material aid to lower developed countries. In a word, China was essentially a regional, not a global power, still estimated to be confined to a secondary role. Hence, the report's conclusion was that the realistic course to follow was always to continue to use American influence with the aim of deterring the Soviets from attacking or encircling China. Paramount importance was given to Japan, seen as the key element in Beijing's anti-Soviet strategy in the Far East. The situation in former Indochina, instead, was thought to be the weak point in the Sino-Soviet competition, for it was considered as extremely difficult for the Chinese to prevent Vietnam and Laos from leaning towards Moscow.[20] As a matter of fact, pivotal to stress is that as early as 1975 Deng had already realised that the Cold War was by then pointless as an ordering principle for East Asia, thus starting to work for international collaboration.[21] Such a thesis is also confirmed by Shu Guang Zhang, according to whom Deng had already come to the conclusion that the categories of capitalist or socialist were no longer correct to identify enemies and friends. On the contrary, national interests and economic development were to replace ideology as a basis of foreign policy.[22]

Very recent studies show how the Nixon and Ford administrations managed to get close to China and take the initiative in the US-USSR-PRC (People's Republic of China) triangle without provoking the Soviets to retreat from détente, while at the same time the Sino-Soviet rivalry harmed Moscow's capacity to wage a global battle with the United States. As leader of the Western world, the United States inspired or encouraged Western allies to open to China, being also pleased to see other partners even take advantage of such interactions to serve US purposes. In short, the United States was trying to become close to China without excessively provoking the Soviets or Chinese military, thus a limited engagement towards technology transfers had to be adopted.[23]

1.2 The Modernisation Project and the British Posture

The report that Zhou Enlai had delivered in January 1975 at the Fourth National People's Congress was his legacy and the foundation of the programme of modernisation which Deng was going to implement. In order to convince the radicals, Zhou had reminded Mao's statements on the need of a technical revolution and borrowing know-how from foreign countries. Learning from abroad, therefore, was not something negative, as it was possible to assimilate positive experiences and avoid what was regarded as counterproductive.[24] As far as economic pragmatism is concerned, interesting to notice is Jan S. Prybyla's comment, stating that Deng followed two basic principles: (a) the only purpose of an economic system was producing increasing quantities and qualities of goods that people were willing to pay for; (b) only a state led by a hard Communist party could pursue such a policy in the conditions of a developing country.[25] The basic features of the new economic programme had already been drafted at the 1974 State Planning Commission, stating that the whole party should give serious thought to the country's overall interest, not only by making revolution, but above all by promoting production.[26] In May 1975, he had stressed the necessity to rely on three important directives from the Leader: "On questions of theory [...], we must struggle against external revisionism and not permit domestic revisionism; we must calm down and unite; we must develop the economy".[27] On what concerned industrial strategy, Deng was able to unfold a series of development targets, such as: (a) modernising agricultural expansion; (b) importing new technology and equipment; (c) developing export trade to accumulate foreign currency and purchase what was necessary; (d) building up scientific research; (e) stressing organisational efficiency in work accountability.[28] Finally, David Bachman reminds how wholeheartedly Deng supported quick economic progress also to serve his own political goals by moving the agenda away from the primacy of class struggle.[29]

As concerned the ideological clash within the Chinese Communist Party, the US Senate Majority Leader, Mike Mansfield, highlighted the confrontation between "ideological perfectionism" and "technocratic activism". The former was said to put great stress on the full implementation of Mao's doctrine towards the final achievement of the dictatorship of the proletariat. The latter, instead, pursued the development of China into a fullest modern state by following a more pragmatic pattern. To be more specific, in his report to the president the senator saw the following American interests in regard to China: (a) in the following decade, Beijing had to be peacefully inclined towards the Anglo-Saxon power; (b) a stable international structure in the Western Pacific area made unnecessary for the United States to massively deploy military forces to keep security; (c) cultural and commercial exchanges between the two countries were to improve more and more.[30] In addition, in a conversation with the Majority Leader, Vice Premier Li Hsien-nien underlined the necessity for China to balance the budget in order not to make too much money circulate and thus keep prices stable, while Mansfield and his colleagues stressed the importance of China's oil reserves as a way to increase international trade with friendly countries.[31]

As for Chinese economic issues, we must not forget that Barry Naughton is quite disapproving about Deng's strategy in the mid-1970s, stating that the plan to accelerate economic growth was deeply flawed. According to his studies, the Ten-Year-Plan for development of the economy from 1976 to 1985 was unrealistic and inconsistent, still reflecting concentration on the heavy industrial sectors that had been top priority under the Maoist strategy.[32] Just to be more explicit, due to the decimation of the planning apparatus during the Cultural Revolution years, planners were not able to manage absorption of new technologies and massive resource flows. As a matter of fact, the so-called leap outward collapsed for two main reasons. Investment plans kept being raised, thus a lot of Chinese agencies scrambled to sign contracts with foreign suppliers. Moreover, China's effort to expand oil production and export ran into unexpected problems, such as depletion and scarce discovery of new oil fields.[33] Curiously enough, American analyses suggested instead that China's policy seemed to be based on a well established programme, giving priority to agriculture, inserting commerce ahead of heavy industry and calling for the establishment of a sound market.[34] The fact that China was adjacent to the East Asian economic region eased technology transfer and the expansion of international markets. Hence, the potential of international trade in the reform process was enhanced by China trading primarily with market economies even before reform. As a matter of fact, Naughton reminds us that eighty-six per cent of China's foreign trade in 1978 took place predominantly towards market economies, with Hong Kong playing a major role as a middleman. Such orientation provided Beijing with some opportunities to learn about world markets.[35] What is more, as concerns East Asia, we must not forget that while in 1970 most leaders of the area still perceived China as their main security threat, at the end of the decade the Dragon was by then becoming a sort of ally.[36]

An important source to understand how trade had become essential in a world whose North-South connections were igniting what a few years afterwards was known as globalisation are the reports of the Trilateral Commission, a non-governmental think-tank forum that brings together leaders from the worlds of business, government, academia, press and media. The Trilateral Commission was formed in 1973 by private citizens of Japan, Western Europe and North America to foster closer cooperation among these core industrialised areas. As an evidence of this, in 1977 the Commission published a report on the collaboration with communist countries in managing global problems. As far as energy was concerned, immediate advantages for Trilateral countries were thought to be feasible and desirable in order to invest in Soviet or Chinese energy production and secure increased imports. The question of leadership in China was therefore becoming of paramount importance to decide the future pattern of Western-oriented collaboration, with the hope also to secure the cooperation of Japanese and North American corporations in exploiting oil fields, especially offshore ones.[37]

As far as the United Kingdom was concerned, Tom Buchanan has written an interesting overview on the British Left's assessment of the People's Republic. In particular, he stresses that Mao's death gave British Maoists the opportunity to express their enthusiasm about the one they called the greatest leader the international socialist movement had ever produced.[38] The most remarkable responses were on the left of the Labour Party. For example, Tony Benn wrote in his diary that Mao was going to be regarded as one of the greatest, if not the greatest figures of the century, towering above other leaders for his philosophical contribution and military genius.[39] On the other hand, the government's interests were focused on science and technology, with of course the aim to promote trade. As a secondary objective, Downing Street sought generally to bind China closer to Britain and Western Europe. A pivotal issue to develop for the British was the field of aeronautics. In addition to importing a substantial number of Spey engines, Beijing also wanted to acquire the necessary technology to build up its own production line. From the British point of view, this was also another step towards giving the Chinese access to sophisticated defence technology, as well as a way to grant Britain's leading position in the Chinese market of aeronautical technology. Beijing, instead, wanted to import technology to produce a highly sophisticated product based on Western licences, though policy makers in London felt unable to meet Chinese wishes for a comprehensive technology partnership.[40] The chance for Britain to benefit from China's new course was so good, that on 12 October 1977 *The Times* published a special report on the Asian country praising Yu Chiu-Li, the so-called genius of China's petroleum industry and by then also a key economic planner in the new executive. The timing was also of paramount importance, as British exports to China were falling by about forty per cent, while imports from the Asian counterpart had increased by about the same amount. Despite this, the outlook for the following year was quite optimistic, said officials of the Sino-British Trade Council, and even the Bank of China was supposed to probably get into the commercial borrowing business. What is important to highlight in this article is the remark that in the long run China's capacity to purchase would be bound to its export power, thus making trading connections indissoluble.[41] Concentration on economic development and the rejection of outbursts of revolutionary struggles made the British public opinion and analysts think that the new leadership might shift away from Sino-centric tendencies and become more cooperative worldwide.[42] Finally, the People's Liberation Army was making no secret of the desire to modernise equipment with new aircraft, missiles and tanks enabling the Army to meet the enemy on the border and counter attack across the line. As a matter of fact, the International Institute for Strategic Studies stated that Chinese weapons were mainly fifteen to twenty years out of date, while military technology was something like fifteen years behind that of the USSR and the West. The overwhelming impression was that everything depended on how much money China was willing and able to spend, and on how far the West was available to help.[43] Nicola Casarini assumes that Chinese leaders hoped the European Community to have a higher profile in world affairs, in order for both playing a more active role in containing the Soviet Union and at the same time contributing to the PRC's own economic and technological modernisation. By supporting NATO, China hoped to get access to European defence suppliers and North Atlantic Alliance bases.[44]

In a word, Cold War tensions moulded China's view of the EEC in the 1970s and into the 1980s through the prism of bulwark against Soviet hegemonism.[45] On grounds of this, the other pivotal issue in Sino-Western relations, that is containment of the Soviet Union, was defined by Kissinger as a question of expansionism on a geo-political scale, rather than a question limited to one region. According to the American leading diplomat, the Soviets were facing powerful countries in the West, potentially powerful countries in the East and confusion and weakness in the Middle East. The secretary of state did not deny that China was an ideological opponent. However, it was always a country that in strategic terms the United States globally cooperated with. Despite the stalemate in bilateral relations, Kissinger compared the importance of China with that of Western Europe as a factor on the world scene.[46] Nevertheless, despite China's desire to line up Western Europe against the Soviet Union, Michael Yahuda says that China and Europe were geopolitically too distant from each other to manage to exercise significant strategic influence on their respective parts of the world.[47] As far as the Chinese attitude is concerned, interesting to underline is what Zhang Zuqian wrote as Senior Researcher at the Shanghai Institute for East Asian Studies. According to him, both China and the European Economic Community were under the threat posed by the Soviet Union.[48] Consequently, they had security and strategic motivations to establish diplomatic relations, rather than commercial ones. Apart from this, Beijing pursued an independent foreign policy after breaking away from the Soviet Union, hoping to see Europe play a more independent role from the two superpowers. At the same time, the EEC wished China to move closer to the West strategically and politically.[49] To even better realise such a rivalry, we may quote the speech delivered in March 1975 by the director of the Chinese Communist Party Central Committee International Liaison Department, Geng Biao, who affirmed that revisionism was the main danger to the international communist movement. Regarded as the head of revisionism willing to expand its power everywhere, the Soviet Union was accused of being the main enemy. In the international communist movement, therefore, the first thing was to concentrate on striking Soviet revisionists.[50] As a consequence of that, it was important to strengthen the willingness of the Chinese to cooperate with the West and aim at an exchange of political and military information, though Beijing was always suspicious about possible collusion or a general understanding between the Atlantic Alliance and the Soviet Union.[51] It is easy to realise that such a reference to China and developing countries slotted in the Sino-Soviet rivalry in the Third World, as Beijing blamed Moscow of charging high interest rates and imposing aid recipients to purchase its products and pay back loans with raw materials and low-priced goods. Moreover, the Chinese also denounced the Soviets to take advantage of their aid policy to intervene in the domestic affairs of their clients. The Asian communist power also argued that the notions of "limited sovereignty", "socialist big family" and "export of revolution" were incompatible with proletarian internationalism.[52] In light of all this, just a few days after Jimmy Carter's inauguration day at the White House, the Central Intelligence Agency issued a report expecting modernisation of agriculture to be given continued priority. Apart from that, a more rapid and balanced growth in industry was supposed to begin, especially in the field of a more expansive foreign trade policy. Finally, modernisation of China's national defence forces was believed to continue.[53]

1.3 Carter at the White House

On his first meeting with Ambassador Huang Chen, in charge of China's Liaison Office at Washington, DC, the newly elected Democratic president agreed that the basis of Sino-American relations would be the Shanghai Communiqué issued five years previously. Interesting to notice, the document provided both a mutual commitment to oppose hegemony in the Asia-Pacific region – a clear reference to the Soviet common enemy – and an agreement on trade as a mutual benefit.[54] Apart from the Taiwan issue as pivotal point of Sino-American bilateral relations, Huang Chen was very clear about the Soviet Union, stating that the Russians had wild ambitions, seeking advantage everywhere, while the United States had only vested interests to protect. The fact that in his first conversation with the new president the ambassador highlighted the Soviet question, even more than the problem of the sovereignty over Taipei, gives the idea of how Beijing felt the danger of isolation surfacing from the policy of détente, which instead the Chinese interpreted as the Kremlin's attempt to set up a smokescreen to hide the objective to disintegrate Western Europe.[55] In his diary, Jimmy Carter looks impressed by the Chinese diplomat's antagonist attitude whenever he spoke about the Soviet Union, contradicting any suggestion that Soviet leaders might be sincere in wanting to preserve peace and control atomic weapons. As far as the Indo-Pacific region was concerned, Huang urged the president to maintain a strong American presence in the Western Pacific.[56] To tell the truth, according to the available documentation we are allowed to say that improving relations with the People's Republic was also profitable for military and national security reasons. By reading the papers, it is also evident how the National Security Adviser, Zbigniew Brzezinki, favoured a closer relationship with Beijing. According to the Department of Defence, in fact, the new course inaugurated by the former administration had substantially reduced the danger of conflict in North-East Asia. Moreover, improved US-PRC relations and the tension between the USSR and China were not regarded as unconnected. In view of this assessment, Secretary Brown thought that the most important factor for the following decade was that the Washington-Beijing relationship would be a major influence on Washington-Moscow relations. Therefore, collaboration with China was supposed to foster greater global balance to the American national security position.[57]

In light of American studies, the connection with the Atlantic superpower was primarily important to China as a deterrent to a major Soviet attack. In particular, Mao's successors were said to be concerned about the declining US role in NATO, should Washington deal with a hostile China in the Far East. Instead, intelligence assessments stated that the Chinese saw the Atlantic Alliance as a symbol of the American intention to intervene in Europe if necessary, thus posing a serious threat to the Russians on the Western front in case of a major Soviet attack to China.[58] In order to show that containment towards the Soviet Union and trade followed a common pattern, suffice it to quote a treasury memorandum dating back to March 1977. In a few words, the Americans complained that for the first time since 1971 the trade balance with the PRC had registered a negative balance of $66.5 million in 1976. This was thought to be due to several reasons, such as Beijing's will to hold down imports because of a tight foreign exchange situation. Moreover, relatively good harvests had caused a decreased dependence on foreign sources of agricultural commodities. Finally, lack of oil exports growth had added hard currency difficulties. With regard to trade with the United States, it appeared to Secretary Blumenthal that the Chinese would not seriously augment their imports until normalisation of bilateral political relations. As a matter of fact, the People's Republic was favouring other sources of supply, when available, in purchasing commodities from the West. What the federal government could do, therefore, was encouraging US-PRC trade and economic cooperation by supporting the American business community.[59] According to the first analyses of the new Administration, advantages of moving ahead with a serious effort to establish formal diplomatic relations with the PRC certainly involved the benefit of a continuing Sino-Soviet rivalry. In substance, placing the relations with Beijing on the best possible footing was thought to help deal most effectively with any changes in the Sino-Russian leg of the triangular relationship. In addition, there was the regional factor involving a significant easing of confrontation in Asia. Tellingly, failure to move ahead with normalisation was likely to generate pressures from highly vocal elements of the press, academia and the business world. The pivotal question was that Washington enjoyed a closer relationship with each communist superpower than either had with the other. Secretary Vance believed that this fragile equilibrium was to be maintained, thus normalisation was the best way to move forward the relations with Beijing. However, it was important for the Chinese to accept that the White House perceived relations with Beijing to be framed in a wider international context.[60] With respect to economic development and military strength, instead, the secretary objected that China was no major strategic issue. Any assistance provided to the Chinese, says Cyrus Vance in his memoirs, would have not changed Beijing's overall military potential. Despite this, due to Soviet excessive fears Sino-American security cooperation was regarded to have serious repercussions on the relations with Moscow, as well as with Tokyo and other Asian allies.[61] Such particular issue is debated by Raymond L. Garthoff, who reminds that ever since 1973 some elements at the Department of Defence and in the political opposition to détente had become intrigued with the idea of building the Chinese military capability as a way to complicate and burden Soviet military planning. Once he had left office, in an article in October 1976 Secretary Schlesinger urged an American quasi alliance with China. The previous year Michael Pillsbury, Rand Corporation analyst, had first discussed the idea of arms sales and military security relationships with the People's Republic in a "Foreign Policy" article. Analysts at the Department of Defence were very interested in the subject and undertook a number of internal studies on possible military ties with China, though professional military planners were much less inclined to establish such an essential relationship with a communist foe whom the United States was supposed to arm and militarily cooperate with.[62]

As regards Jimmy Carter's attitude towards communist China, Brian Hilton has quite a dissenting position from mainstream scholarship. As a matter of fact, he reminds that historians examining the Administration's China policy have mainly focused on those subordinates most experienced in foreign affairs, namely the national security adviser and the secretary of state. In particular, references to Brzezinski monopolising access to the president have reinforced the view that Carter lacked foreign policy perspective. Hilton's thesis, instead, is that the former governor of Georgia's foreign policy began taking shape as early as 1973 when he was asked to join the Trilateral Commission. By the time he did it, Carter had already decided to run for president, thus he took the opportunity to prepare for the task of guiding both the country and the world into an era of enhanced international cooperation.[63] During his first months in office, President Carter thought that too quick an opening to China would probably stop the dialogue with the USSR over the control of armaments, as well as other delicate Congress debates such as those dealing with the Panama Canal Treaty. Both these initiatives, in fact, were opposed by the same conservative forces trying to block any change in relations with Taiwan.[64]

A watershed in China policy was certainly Presidential Review Memorandum/NSC 24, through which the president charged the Policy Review Committee to undertake a three-part review towards the People's Republic concerning: (a) an analysis of broad options towards Beijing; (b) an assessment of the possible ways to withdraw troops from Taiwan; (c) an overview of the transfer of defence-related technologies to the PRC.[65] Regardless of the ways to pursue such a commitment, President Carter was adamantly clear on the Asian Giant during his address at the University of Notre Dame Athletic and Convocation Center on 22 May 1977: "We see the American and Chinese relationship as a central element of our global policy and China as a key force for global peace [...] And we hope to find a formula which can bridge some of the difficulties that still separate us".[66]

Tellingly, speaking about the strategic importance of the relation with China, a month after this speech the defence secretary stated that at least the opening to China reduced the chances of Sino-Soviet détente, as the Chinese were able to tie down a significant portion of Soviet military effort. Finally, the national security adviser noted that it was of paramount importance to understand how to deepen the strategic relationship and expand the areas of tacit cooperation, thus engaging the PRC in wider global questions.[67] In summary, from the declassified documentation what surfaces is that the defence establishment aimed at seeing the Chinese remain a counterweight to the Soviets and hoped the Administration would do everything possible to promote such a task. As a matter of fact, according to Secretary Brown normalisation of US-PRC relations would also make sure that the Chinese did not move towards a more pro-Soviet stance. In short, since the Soviets had twenty per cent of their military forces along the Chinese border, it was always better to avoid these troops to be moved back to Europe.[68] On grounds of all that, according to Dr. Brzezinski there were three main elements affecting the relationship with China: (a) global strategic elements, including the Soviet Union; (b) normalisation; (c) trade and technology transfer.[69] Particularly interesting is the national security adviser's position on the question of oil supplies. Actually, though he did not likely view China as an alternative supplier, he certainly hoped to advance strategic ties with Beijing, which was also worried about Soviet threats to oil supplies to Western Europe and Japan. Furthermore, the Democratic administration was shaping its global strategy when Deng Xiaoping was back to power in 1977, after having been ousted the previous year, a man who shared Brzezinski's antagonism towards Soviet activities in the Third World.[70]

As far as this first evaluation of Carter's policy on China is concerned, interesting to remind is the difference between the President's main collaborators. Secretary Vance, in fact, writes that in terms of economic development and military strength China was no major strategic power. The Soviets had an excessive fear of the Chinese, thus any form of cooperation between the Asian communist country and the Anglo-Saxon power was expected to have serious repercussions on Soviet-American relations. Therefore, the head of the State Department thought that a US-PRC security relationship implied substantial risks for the relations with Moscow and other Asian allies like Japan. In short, China's role in the world was to be seen as a way in the long run to increase global order, not simply as a useful counterweight to the Kremlin.[71] As regards Brzezinski's memoirs, instead, he wrote that a more active policy towards China would probably help keep a balanced relation with the Soviets. Carter, in fact, had declared that the worsening rapport with Moscow was the main cause of concern. Therefore, if the Russians were worried a little more about Sino-American relations, said the president, maybe Washington would feel a little relieved. Brzezinski himself states that within the administration he was rather isolated in mid-1977, as he came out for a commitment to normalisation while most White House officers felt that it was better not to move too quickly.[72] Ironically enough, Republicans opposing the administration were quite eager to pursue further ties with Communist China. At the same time, Lu Sun reminds how a few years previously Premier Zhou Enlai had predicted that by developing trading relations with the United States the doors of other countries allied with Washington would be open, thus making the new China market competitive.[73]

What we may assess quite easily is that, by reading Chinese records and leadership's speeches, it had become almost impossible for the Americans not to take advantage of Beijing as a lever against the Soviets, especially in the Indo-Pacific area which had been a vital US interest since the Open Door policy of the early twentieth century. As an evidence of this, while ideologically the successors of Mao continued to portray both superpowers as the source of a new world war, Soviet social-imperialism in particular was supposed to be the greater danger. Soviet revisionists, stated Hua Guofeng on 12 August 1977 during the political report addressed to the XI National Congress of the Communist Party, were working to push their global offensive strategy with the purpose to pocket all Europe, Asia and Africa. Equally promising for West-China relations was the intention to build an independent and fairly comprehensive industrial and economic system within the following three years.[74] A very good article on China's economic policy was published by Frederick C. Teiwes and Warren Sun in *The China Journal*. The two scholars argue that several factors help explain such a determined drive for higher targets in 1977–1978. For example, the month before Hua's speech the State Planning Commission had reported that there had been a huge increase in industrial production in the first half of the year. Given these circumstances, importing advanced technology became central to opening up to the international economy. In actual fact, in July 1977 the SPC had presented an import plan setting a target of $6.5 billion by 1985. Deng Xiaoping himself proposed to increase the target, suggesting that ten billion were possible on the basis of exports of oil, coal and products from light industry. Hua praised Deng's view, and the target was subsequently raised to fifteen billion in November.[75] Meanwhile, CIA estimates on China's economic prospects for 1977 were rather mixed, as a year of recovery and readjustment was expected. The new leadership was acknowledged to give economic issues high priority, with agriculture at the top, but more resources were supposed to be oriented to raise the level of technology in industry. This required heavy investment and imports of equipment, along with management reforms and incentives to encourage efficiency.[76] Moreover, China was thought to also look more closely at national defence modernisation, after considerable debate over the past several months, with defence costs believed to be around eight-ten per cent of the GDP. In light of this, Beijing was supposed to hold growth of military spending in check while allowing selective improvements in military equipment. By virtue of all that, and due to the fact that the Asian communist country had an economy approximately one tenth of the American one, the military threat coming from the Chinese was regarded as very low.[77]

1.4 Vance's Trip to China: An Assessment

The secretary of state flew to Beijing in late August 1977 with a clear commitment to proceed on the path to establish full diplomatic relations, recognising the communist government as the sole legal representative of China. In principle, said Vance, the administration was ready to begin the process, but the head of US diplomacy was trying to link the Taipei legacy to international issues by tying Beijing to the network of interests the Americans pursued in the Far East. Playing a major world role for the United States depended on the credibility of the Atlantic Alliance's connection with such nations as Japan and NATO allies. To sustain both public support for normalisation and the credibility of American commitments abroad, it was necessary not to be placed in the position of appearing to jeopardise stability.[78] Once Foreign Minister Huang gave the Chinese point of view on the world situation, it must not have been by chance that he started with US-Soviet relations. Moscow was therefore accused of making a feint in the East while actually attacking in the West. To be honest, the Chinese analysis was that the USSR was trying to maintain strategic supremacy over the Atlantic competitor and thus breaking the balance. Huang's assessment of the Kremlin was very harsh and his words seemed to be inspired by Kennan's Long Telegram when he said that the Soviet objective of seeking world hegemony was determined by the nature of social imperialism. While on bilateral relations the Chinese statesman simply stated that the longer the Americans delayed in severing all relations with Taiwan, the heavier the debt to the Chinese people, by reading the transcripts of the conversation we realise how the Sino-Soviet rivalry was on top of the agenda for Beijing. The foreign minister's reflections on this question, in fact, were not only much longer than Vance's comments on the Soviet Union, but also his attitude looked much more resolute when he asserted that Soviet ambitions for aggression and expansion had become bigger.[79]

On this particular question, Robert G. Sutter reminds us that in the late 1970s China's international priorities were actually less focused on bilateral relations with the United States and more concerned on dealing with Soviet intimidation and threat. Especially after the collapse of South Vietnam, Chinese officials showed considerable alarm at the turn of events around Beijing's periphery, where stronger efforts were being made by the Soviet Union to use military power and foreign relations to put pressure on the People's Republic. As a consequence of this, the sense of isolation and encirclement made Chinese leaders worry about relying on United States and other governments about what was depicted as a united front against expanding Soviet power and influence.[80] On the other hand, the other Asia expert, Michael Yahuda, writes that the Soviet Union had some permanent weaknesses in the area that tended to undermine attempts to play a significant role. Moscow lacked a history of engagement in the Indo-Pacific region, missing also economic capabilities to make a significant difference to Asian economies. Therefore, the USSR did not manage to compete with China for establishing better institutionalised relations with Japan, which instead Beijing sought to gain as a support to break what Deng Xiaoping saw as Moscow's chain of encirclement.[81] As concerned the other leg of the relationship with China, despite Deng's insistence on Beijing's determination to liberate Taiwan, the importance of trade was never called into doubt. As an evidence of this, the secretary of state said the administration would always encourage the National Council for US-China Trade as a positive force in respect to relations between the two nations.[82] On the Chinese side, the other organisation involved in the promotion of trade was the China Council for the Promotion of International Trade.[83] By working together, carried on Vance, they could be effective in developing mutually beneficial marketing techniques and a general awareness of existing trade opportunities.[84]

Tellingly, the possibility to involve Chinese companies and state enterprises in security, economic and technological business was becoming the best way to enhance Sino-American relations in a period of uncertainty due to the decision not to establish a full diplomatic relationship for the following months.[85] Such an attitude is not surprising, since the United States had never relied so heavily on government-led initiatives to exert influence in Asia. On the contrary, as Robert Sutter affirms, Washington had developed an extensive network of non-government ties, such as the extensive web of personal connections following the Executive's decision in 1965 to end discrimination against Asians in US immigration policy. This step implied the influx of many millions entering the mainstream while sustaining strong links with their motherland.[86] Moreover, it is important to notice the meeting that the National Committee on United States China Relations (NCUSCR)[87] had on 23 October 1977 with Deng Xiaoping. Once having spoken about the Soviet Union, and having said how lack of normalisation penalised business, Deng shifted to practical issues and reminded the efforts his government was making to mechanise agriculture and export more oil products in order to introduce technology from abroad.[88] In short, Chinese leaders were focused on maintaining a stable international environment supporting the economic modernisation programme. This objective required to avoid a hostile relationship with the United States.[89] As concerned Chinese policy of self-sufficiency, according to the CIA this was due to several reasons, such as being a large continental country with vast domestic resources, as well as minimising dependence on imports. In light of that, China was using a good portion of the limited foreign exchange supplies to try to solve food problems, since imports of grain and agriculture-related industrial plants had recently made up around twenty-five per cent of Beijing's total imports.[90]

In his diary, Jimmy Carter does not seem surprised or disappointed with the Chinese firm stance on their questions of principle. Despite the setback in normalisation, the president looked quite optimistic about indirect means to send signals on the American willingness to proceed, thus taking advantage of Beijing top leaders' eagerness to discuss such matters as commercial trade and possible future access to United States technology.[91] Such a statement was corroborated by American intelligence assessments according to which the personal involvement of Deng in military modernisation programmes underlined the importance attached to this commitment. In short, the CIA forecast that if Beijing managed to adopt a more flexible stance on foreign indebtedness, it could significantly improve military capability. Moreover, ties with European producers were supposed to be forged, thus strengthening China's defence capabilities against the Soviets.[92] Vance himself admits it was not the right time to work on an issue as controversial as the one dealing with normalisation with China, and he was determined to stick on the projected course and not going any faster.[93] Meanwhile, Brzezinski acknowledges that Vance's mission re-established the dialogue with Beijing, though in an atmosphere of mutual disappointment. Moreover, he claims that the administration had never sought a merely tactical relationship with the Chinese. In other words, the national security adviser seems to blame American columnists to place any US movement in the larger Russian context, so much so that the Soviet Foreign Minister, Gromyko, told Jimmy Carter in September 1977 that it would be a serious mistake to play any sort of dirty game with China against the interests of the Kremlin.[94] Apart from that, Carter was being obliged to toughen his stance on China to win Republican support at the Senate to ratify the treaty gradually transferring control of the Panama Canal to the Republic of Panama.[95]

However it was, access to Western defence technology was expected to be a way not only to improve bilateral relations with the People's Republic, but also to keep Beijing as a check on Soviet power. Nevertheless, while China was willing to increase imports of military-related items in the future, it was unlikely for the communist government to risk dependence upon major purchases from the West. From this point of view, the Carter administration was aware that the liberalisation of this kind of trade would provide a potential benefit for the US stake in that area. In addition, even a modest American initiative with limited commercial gains was able to emphasise to the Soviet Union the potential of improved relations with the PRC. As far as the embargo to nations threatening US security was concerned, China as a communist country could be an exception in terms of sales of industrial and scientific items with civil as well as military applications. The point was that there was evidence indicating Chinese interest in defence-related imports from the West. Once again, it seems the Department of State tended to hold back the initiatives of the other branches of the administration, assessing that even modest moves would run the risk of hardening Moscow's positions on important bilateral issues. Instead, both the Central Intelligence Agency and most Department of Defence thought that the Kremlin would react less strongly, provided the United States did not attempt to improve Chinese strategic capabilities.[96] As far as the modernisation of the People's Liberation

Army was concerned, Michael Yahuda was one of the first to analyse the issue in the early 1980s, stating that this implied immense problems, since the costs of importing advanced weapons sufficient to develop a credible deterrent force against either of the two superpowers would be so high to undermine sustained economic growth.[97] In actual fact, the relationship between economic and military modernisation was becoming one of the most difficult problems in resource allocation within the post-Mao leadership, and the new flexibility in foreign policy would be most noticeable in the areas of trade and technology transfer.[98] More recently, Yahuda said that the Chinese were giving evidence of an independent diplomatic stance, as demonstrated by the shift from alliance with the Soviet Union to revolutionary isolationism and then to an alignment with the United States. Finally, the Sino-Soviet confrontation was no longer confined to the ideological realm, but was on the way to become more readily apparent. Consequently, the significance of China for all the countries in the region made political, security and economic consequences both immediate and far reaching.[99]

The importance of the Far Eastern country from a global trade point of view was also shown by the visit of the minister of foreign trade to the United Kingdom in late 1977. Actually, serious expectations were being built up in business and banking circles about increased trade with Beijing, which seemed to be determined to make up the lost time of the previous years and attach great importance to the European Community, seen as an economically and politically strong organisation able to become the best bulwark against the USSR and members of the Warsaw Pact. In particular, an article published in the *People's Daily* stressed the need to import the necessary Western technology and promising to set up a growing market for the United Kingdom, especially as providers of aerospace and mining.[100] According to Mao's Three Worlds Theory, as reminds Song Xinning, along with the growth of their economic capacities, West European countries realised that they had to keep the power of European integration in their own hands. However, facing the military threat from the Soviet Union, Western Europe had to keep the military alliance with the United States. In spite of that, the establishment of the common market indicated that Western Europe had become an increasingly autonomous actor in the capitalist world against Soviet and American hegemony.[101]

Notes

1 *Memorandum of Conversation*, Beijing, 20 October 1975, 10:00–11:40 a.m., Secret, Sensitive, in FRUS 1969–1976, Vol. XVIII, Doc. 121, 753–764.
2 To tell the truth, such an affirmation seems to be contradicted by what the German Federal Chancellor reported on his talks with the Great Helmsman in October-November 1975. Schmidt said that Mao looked emphatic that there would be war with the Soviet Union. On that circumstance, Deng was completely aligned to his leader, since he said that peace or détente would not be durable. *Karl-Günther von Hase to Harold Wilson, Notes of Talks of*

Chancellor Schmidt with Chairman Mao Tse-tung and Vice-Premier Teng Hsiao-ping, 30 January 1976, in NA, PREM 16/890, *The Visit of the Federal German Chancellor, Herr Schmidt, to China in October/November 1975*, Confidential.

3 *Memorandum of Conversation*, Beijing, 3 December 1975, 9:25–11:55 a.m., Secret, Sensitive, in FRUS 1969–1976, Vol. XVIII, Doc. 136, 876–892.

4 Warren I. Cohen, *America's Response to China: A History of Sino-American Relations* (New York, NY: Columbia University Press, 2010), 220–221.

5 Nancy Bernkopf Tucker (ed.), *China Confidential: American Diplomats and Sino-American Relations, 1945–1996* (New York, NY: Columbia University Press, 2001), 303–306.

6 *Ibidem*, 308–309.

7 Kissinger, *On China*, 311.

8 *Memorandum of Conversation*, Beijing, 2 December 1975, 4:10–6:00 p.m., Secret, Nodis, in FRUS 1969–1976, Vol. XVIII, Doc. 134, 856–867.

9 Michael Schaller, *The United States and China: Into the Twenty-First Century* (New York, NY: Oxford University Press, 2002), 187.

10 Kissinger, *Years of Renewal: The Concluding Volume of His Memoirs* (London: Weidenfeld & Nicolson, 1999), 886.

11 James Mann, *About Face: A History of America's Curious Relationship with China, from Nixon to Clinton* (New York, NY: Alfred A. Knopf, 1999), 73–76.

12 Robert S. Ross, *Negotiating Cooperation: The United States and China 1969–1989* (Stanford, CA: Stanford University Press, 1995), 89.

13 In January 1973, the Chinese leadership had approved the import of a $4.3 billion complete set of equipment from Western countries, *Ibidem*, 73.

14 *National Intelligence Estimate: PRC Defense Policy and Armed Forces*, 11 November 1976, NIE 13–76, Secret, https://www.cia.gov/readingroom/docs/DOC_0001097855.pdf, accessed 8 August 2021.

15 Kenneth Lieberthal, James Tong and Sai-cheung Yeung, *Central Documents and Politburo Politics in China* (Ann Arbor, MI: University of Michigan Press, 1978), 128.

16 Kenneth Lieberthal and Michel Oksenberg, *Policy Making in China: Leaders, Structures, and Processes* (Princeton, NJ: Princeton University Press, 1988), 201.

17 Ross, *Negotiating Cooperation*, 72.

18 David S.G. Goodman, *Deng Xiaoping and the Chinese Revolution: A Political Biography* (London and New York, NY: Routledge, 1994), 82.

19 'Statement by Secretary Kissinger: The Future and US Foreign Policy, Submitted to the Senate Committee on Foreign Relations on March 16 during Hearings on Foreign Policy Choices for the 1970's and 1980's', in Department of State Bulletin, 75/1920, 12 April 1976, 481–493.

20 *Paper Prepared in the Central Intelligence Agency: The Foreign Policies of China's Successor Leadership*, June 1976, PR 76 10053, Secret, Noforn, in FRUS 1969–1976, Vol. XVIII, Doc. 148, 931–935.

21 Lorenz M. Lüthi, *Cold Wars: Asia, the Middle East, Europe* (Cambridge and New York, NY: Cambridge University Press, 2020), 536–537.

22 Shu Guang Zhang, *Beijing's Economic Statecraft during the Cold War, 1949–1991* (Washington, DC and Baltimore, MD: Woodrow Wilson Center Press and Johns Hopkins University Press, 2014), 263.

23 Lei Liu, 'China's Large-Scale Importation of Western Technology and the US Response, 1972–1976', Diplomatic History, 45/4, 2021, 818–820.

24 Chou En-lai, 'Report on the Work of the Government (Delivered on January 13, 1975, at the First Session of the Fourth National People's Congress of the People's Republic of China)', *Peking Review*, 18/4, 1975, 21–25.

25 Jan S. Prybyla, 'Is China a Model of Economic Success?', in Hafeez Malik (ed.), *The Roles of the United States, Russia, and China in the New World Order* (New York, NY: St. Martin's Press, 1997), 301.

26 Deng Xiaoping, 'Speech at a Meeting of Secretaries in Charge of Industrial Affairs from the Party Committees of Provinces, Municipalities and Autonomous Regions: The Whole Party Should Take the Overall Interest into Account and Push the Economy forward', 5 March 1975, in *The Selected Works of Deng Xiaoping*, Vol. II, 1975–1982, https://dengxiaopingworks.wordpress.com/2013/02/25/the-whole-party-should-take-the-overall-interest-into-account-and-push-the-economy-forward/, accessed 11 August 2021.

27 Alexander V. Pantsov and Steven I. Levine, *Deng Xiaoping: A Revolutionary Life* (New York, NY: Oxford University Press, 2015), 289.

28 David Wen-wei Chang, *China under Deng Xiaoping: Political and Economic Reform* (New York, NY: Palgrave Macmillan, 1991), 27–28.

29 David Bachman, 'Differing Visions of China's Post-Mao Economy: The Ideas of Chen Yun, Deng Xiaoping, and Zhao Ziyang', *Asian Survey*, 26/3, 1986, 303–304.

30 Senator Mike Mansfield, *Report to the President on a Third Mission to the People's Republic of China: China after Mao*, 1976, in Jimmy Carter Presidential Library (thereafter JCPL), Atlanta, GA, Office of Staff Secretary, Series: 1976 Campaign Transition File, Confidential File, 11/76-1/77, Container 1, Confidential, https://www.jimmycarterlibrary.gov/digital_library/sso/148838/1/SSO_148838_001_09.pdf, accessed 11 August 2021.

31 *Meeting with Vice Premier Li Hsien-Nien*, 9 October 1976, 3:50 p.m., Confidential, in *Ibidem*.

32 Barry Naughton, 'Deng Xiaoping: The Economist', *The China Quarterly*, Special Issue: *Deng Xiaoping: An Assessment*, 34/135/3, 1993, 499.

33 Naughton, *The Chinese Economy: Adaption and Growth* (London and Cambridge, MS: The MIT Press, 2018), 88.

34 *Telegram 070917Z from AmConsul Hong Kong to SecState WashDC 3323, People's Republic of China-Economic Review 1*, 7 January 1977, 1977HON GK00283, Limited Official Use, in National Archives and Records Administration (thereafter NARA), College Park, MD, Record Group (thereafter RG) 59, Central Foreign Policy Files (thereafter CFPF) 1973–1979, Electronic Telegrams, https://aad.archives.gov/aad/createpdf?rid=4228&dt=2532&dl=1629, accessed 13 August 2021.

35 Naughton, *Growing out of the Plan: Chinese Economic Reform, 1978–1993* (Cambridge: Cambridge University Press, 1996), 54.

36 Odd Arne Westad, 'China and the Long 1970s as a Field of Research', in Roberts and Westad (eds.), *China, Hong Kong*, 330.

37 Chichiro Hosoya, Henry Owen and Andrew Shonfield, *Triangle Paper 13: Collaboration with Communist Countries in Managing Global Problems: An Examination of the Options* (New York, NY, Tokyo and Paris: The Trilateral Commission, 1977), 20–22, http://trilateral.org//download/doc/collaboration_communist_countries_managing_global_problems.pdf, accessed 13 August 2021.

38 Tom Buchanan, *East Wind: China and the British Left, 1925–1976* (Oxford: Oxford University Press, 2012), 210.

39 Tony Benn, *Against the Tide: Diaries 1973–76* (London: Hutchinson, 1989), 609.

40 Martin Albers, *Britain, France, West Germany and the People's Republic of China, 1969–1982: The European Dimension of China's Great Transition* (London: Palgrave Macmillan, 2016), 130–132.

41 'New Course of Trade Should Benefit Britain', The Times, 12 October 1977.

42 Richard Harris, 'Soviet Union Remains Chief Bogy', *Ibidem.*

43 Henry Stanhope, 'An Awakened Giant Seeks to Build its Strength', *Ibidem.*

44 Nicola Casarini, *Remaking Global Order: The Evolution of Europe-China Relations and its Implications for East Asia and the United States* (Oxford: Oxford University Press, 2009), 26.

45 Robert Ash, 'Europe's Commercial Relations with China', in David Shambaugh, Eberhard Sandschneider and Zhou Hong (eds.), *China-Europe Relations: Perceptions, Policies and Prospects* (Abingdon and New York, NY, 2008), 190.

46 *Memorandum of Conversation*, New York City, 8 October 1976, 8:30–11:30 p.m., Secret, Nodis, in FRUS 1969–1976, Vol. XVIII, Doc. 157, 961–978.

47 Michael Yahuda, 'The Sino-European Encounter: Historical Influences on Contemporary Relations', in Shambaugh, Sandschneider and Zhou (eds.), *China-Europe Relations*, 25

48 Such a sharp assessment of Moscow, portrayed as a ferocious socialist imperialist, provoked of course a furious protest at the Kremlin, which claimed that the anti-Soviet hysteria was designed to undermine the process of détente in Europe and divide socialist countries all over the world. Ronald C. Keith, *Deng Xiaoping and China's Foreign Policy* (Abingdon and New York, NY: Routledge, 2018), 101.

49 Zhang Zuqian, 'China's Commercial Relations with Europe', in Shambaugh, Sandschneider and Zhou (eds.), *China-Europe Relations*, 231.

50 'Speech by Comrade Geng Biao of the CCP CC International Liaison Department at the Symposium on National Tourism Work', 6 March 1975, in Zhou Yi (ed.), *Less Revolution, More Realpolitik: China's Foreign Policy in the Early and Middle 1970s*, Cold War International History Project Working Paper 93, (Washington, DC: Woodrow Wilson International Center for Scholars, 2020), 27.

51 *Cable from Ambassador Wickert to the Foreign Office: Benefits of Relationship with China for the Alliance*, 29 November 1976, 114–17096/76 Strictly Confidential, https://digitalarchive.wilsoncenter.org/document/119987, accessed on 13 August 2021.

52 Michael Ng-Quinn, 'International Systemic Constraints on Chinese Foreign Policy', in Samuel S. Kim (ed.), *China and the World: Chinese Foreign Policy in the Post-Mao Era* (London and Boulder, CO: West View Press, 1984), 98.

53 *Intelligence Report Prepared in the Office of Economic Research, Central Intelligence Agency: China: Economic Situation Facing the New Leadership*, February 1977, ER 77–10049, Secret, in Adam M. Howard (gen. ed.) and David P. Nickles (ed.), FRUS 1977–1980, Vol. XIII, *China* (Washington, DC: United States Government Printing Office, 2013), Doc. 4, 17–18.

54 *Joint Statement Following Discussions with Leaders of the People's Republic of China*, 27 February 1972, in Edward C. Keefer (gen. ed.) and Steven E. Phillips (ed.), FRUS 1969–1972, Vol. XVII, China 1969–1972, (Washington, DC: United States Government Printing Office, 2006), Doc. 203, 812–816.

55 *Memorandum of Conversation*, Washington, DC, 8 February 1977, 10 a.m., in JCPL, National Security Affairs, Staff Material, Far East, Oksenberg Subject File, Box 55, Policy Process: 10/76-4/77, Top Secret, Sensitive.

56 Jimmy Carter, *Keeping Faith: Memoirs of a President* (Toronto, Sidney, London and New York, NY: Bantam Books, 1982), 190.

57 *Department of Defense Inputs on US-PRC Relations*, Washington, DC, 14 February 1977, in JCPL, National Security Affairs, Brzezinski Material, Country File, Box 8, China (People's Republic of): 1–2/77, Secret, Eyes Only.

58 *Intelligence Memorandum Prepared in the Central Intelligence Agency: The Value of the United States to China's National Security*, Washington, DC, March 1977, RP 77–10038, Secret, in FRUS 1977–1980, Vol. XIII, Doc. 14, 45–48.

59 *US-P.R.C. Trade Relations*, Washington, DC, 12 March 1977, in JCPL, National Security Affairs, Brzezinski Material, Country File, Box 8, China (People's Republic of): 3–6/77, Confidential.

60 *Memorandum from Secretary of State to the President: Normalization of Relations with the People's Republic of China*, Washington, DC, 15 April 1977, in JCPL, National Security Affairs, Staff Material, Far East, Oksenberg Subject File, Box 42, Meetings, 4–5/77, Secret, Nodis.

61 Cyrus Vance, *Hard Choices: Critical Years in American Foreign Policy* (New York, NY: Simon and Schuster, 1983), 78.

62 Raymond L. Garthoff, *Détente and Confrontation: American-Soviet Relations from Nixon to Reagan* (Washington, DC: Brookings Institution, 1985), 695–696.

63 Brian Hilton, 'Maximum Flexibility for Peaceful Change: Jimmy Carter, Taiwan, and the Recognition of the People's Republic of China', Diplomatic History, 33/4, 2009, 596.

64 Enrico Fardella, 'The Sino-American Normalization: A Reassessment', *Ibidem*, 550.

65 *Presidential Review Memorandum/NSC 24*, Washington, DC, 5 April 1977, in JCPL, National Security Affairs, Staff Material, Office, Institutional File, Box 26, INT Documents: 1500s–1800s: 2–4/77, Secret.

66 Jimmy Carter, *Address at Commencement Exercises at the University of Notre Dame*, 22 May 1977, https://www.presidency.ucsb.edu/node/243018, accessed 18 August 2021.

67 *Options toward the People's Republic of China and Taiwan Troop Drawdown*, Washington, DC, 27 June 1977, 3–4:30 p.m., in JCPL, National Security Affairs, Staff Material, Far East, Oksenberg Subject File, Box 47, Policy Review Committee 6/27/77 on PRM 24: 6–7/77, Top Secret, Eyes Only.

68 *Normalization of US-PRC Relations*, Washington, DC, 13 July 1977, in JCPL, National Security Affairs, Staff Material, Far East, Oksenberg Subject File, Box 43, Meetings: 6–7/77, Secret, Exdis.

69 *China Policy*, Washington, DC, 30 July 1977, 9:30–11:15 a.m., in JCPL, National Security Affairs, Staff Material, Far East, Oksenberg Subject File, Box 47, Presidential 7/30/77 on Cyrus Vance Trip to China: 4–8/77, Top Secret, Sensitive.

70 Minami, 'Oil for the Lamps of America?', 974–975.

71 Vance, *Hard Choices*, 78–79.

72 Zbigniew Brzezinski, *Power and Principle: Memoirs of the National Security Adviser 1977–1981* (New York, NY: Farrar Straus Giroux, 1983), 200.

73 Lu Sun, 'Deng Plays the "China Card": Deng Xiaoping's Visit to the United States and its Implications for China's New Long March to Modernization', in Priscilla Roberts (ed.), *Chinese Economic Statecraft from 1978 to 1989: The First Decade of Deng Xiaoping's Reforms* (Singapore: Palgrave Macmillan, 2022), 69.

74 Hua Kuo-feng, 'Political Report to the 11th National Congress of the Communist Party of China (Delivered on August 12 and Adopted on August 18, 1977)', Peking Review, 20/35, 1977, 23–57.

75 Frederick C. Teiwes and Warren Sun, 'China's New Economic Policy under Hua Guofeng: Party Consensus and Party Myths', *The China Journal*, 33/66, 2011, 10–11.

76 *Allocations of Resources in the Soviet Union and China, 1977: Hearings before the Subcommittee on Priorities and Economy in Government of the Joint Economic Committee, Summary of Statements and Excerpts from Oral Testimony*, Congress of the United States, Ninety-Fifth Congress, First Session, Part One, Executive Sessions, 23 June 1977 (Washington, DC: US

Government Printing Office, 1977), https://www.jec.senate.gov/reports/95th Congress/Allocation of Resources in the Soviet Union and China 1977 Part I (848).pdf, accessed 22 November 2021.

77 *Statement of Adm. Stansfield Turner, Director, Central Intelligence Agency, Accompanied by Sayre Stevens, Deputy Director for Intelligence, Robert E. Hepworth, Congressional Support Staff; Douglas Diamond, Office of Economic Research; Robert Field, Office of Economic Research; Donald Burton, Office of Strategic Research; George L. Cary, Legislative Counsel; and Bernard McMahon, Executive Assistant to the Director*, in *Allocations of Resources in the Soviet Union and China, 1977: Hearings before the Subcommittee on Priorities and Economy in Government of the Joint Economic Committee*, Congress of the United States, Ninety-Fifth Congress, First Session, Part Three, 23 and 30 June (Executive Sessions), and 6 July 1977 (Washington, DC: US Government Printing Office, 1977), https://www.jec.senate.gov/reports/95th%20Congress/Allocation of Resources in the Soviet Union and China 1977 (876).pdf, accessed 22 November 2021.

78 *Memorandum of Conversation*, Beijing, 23 August 1977, 9:30–11:50 a.m., in JCPL, National Security Affairs, Staff Material, Far East, Oksenberg Subject File, Box 56, Policy Process: 8/22–31/77, Secret, Nodis.

79 *Memorandum of Conversation*, Beijing, 24 August 1977, 9:30 a.m.–12:20 p.m., in JCPL, National Security Affairs, Staff Material, Far East, Oksenberg Subject File, Box 56, Policy Process: 8/22-31/77, Secret, Nodis.

80 Robert G. Sutter, *US-Chinese Relations: Perilous Past, Pragmatic Present* (Plymouth and Lanham, MD: Rowman & Littlefield Publishers, 2013), 77.

81 Michael Yahuda, *The International Politics of the Asia-Pacific, Fourth and Revised Edition* (Abingdon and New York, NY: Routledge, 2019), 45.

82 The National Council for United States-China Trade (NCUSCT) was formed in 1973 to promote and facilitate trade between the United States and the People's Republic. Following the spirit of the Shanghai Communiqué, the National Council became the facilitator of trade for the United States.

83 The China Council for the Promotion of International Trade was founded in 1952, developing business and exchanges with foreign countries.

84 *Memorandum of Conversation*, Beijing, 25 August 1977, 9:30–10:10 a.m., in JCPL, National Security Affairs, Staff Material, Far East, Oksenberg Subject File, Box 56, Policy Process: 1-4/78, Secret, Nodis.

85 *China Policy in the Doldrums: Analysis and Measures for Minimizing Risks of Erosion in the Relationship*, Washington, 23 September 1977, in JCPL, National Security Affairs, Staff Material, Far East, Oksenberg Subject File, Box 56, Policy Process: 9-12/77, Top Secret, Sensitive, Exclusively Eyes Only.

86 Robert G. Sutter, 'The United States in Asia: Challenged but Durable Leadership', in David Shambaugh and Michael Yahuda (eds.), *International Relations of Asia* (Plymouth: Rowman & Littlefield Publishers, Inc., 2008), 95.

87 Founded in 1966, the National Committee has been the leading American organisation dedicated to promoting mutual trust and collaboration between the United States and China. Its membership consists of private citizens, corporations and professional firms sharing the belief that productive US-China relations require ongoing face-to-face contact and forthright exchange of ideas.

88 *Telegram 250329Z from USLO Peking to SecState WashDC Priority 8993: Transcript of October 23 NCUSCR Board Meeting with Teng Hsiao-Ping*, 25 October 1977, 1977PEKING02447, Confidential, in NARA, RG 59, CFPF 1973–1979, Electronic Telegrams, https://aad.archives.gov/aad/createpdf?rid=248303&dt=2532&dl=1629, accessed 25 August 2021.

89 Phillip C. Saunders, 'China's Role in Asia', in Shambaugh and Yahuda (eds.), *International Relations of Asia*, 128.
90 *Memorandum for the Secretary of Agriculture: China's Grain Imports and Agricultural Policy*, 23 December 1977, https://ia800809.us.archive.org/7/items/ CIA-RDP80M00165A001700080001-8/CIA-RDP80M00165A001700080001-8_ text.pdf, accessed 8 August 2021.
91 Carter, *Keeping Faith*, 192.
92 *PRC: Military Contacts and Modernisation of the PLA*, Washington, DC, 31 October 1977, in JCPL, National Security Affairs, Staff Material, Far East, Oksenberg Subject File, Box 24, Arms Sales: 4-11/78, Secret, Noforn, Nontract, Orcon.
93 Vance, *Hard Choices*, 79–83.
94 Brzezinski, *Power and Principle*, 201–202.
95 Schaller, *The United States and China*, 188.
96 *Paper Prepared in Response to Section III of Presidential Review Memorandum 24*, undated, in JCPL, National Security Affairs, Staff Material, Far East, Oksenberg Subject File, Box 56, Policy Process: 9-12/77, Secret.
97 Yahuda, *Towards the End of Isolationism: China's Foreign Policy after Mao* (Salisbury: Macmillan Press Ltd., 1983), 161.
98 *Policy Issues in the Post-Mao Leadership*, RP 77-10328, December 1977, in JCPL, National Security Affairs, Staff Material, Far East, Oksenberg Subject File, Box 28, Brzezinski 5/78 Trip to China: 2-12/77, Secret.
99 Yahuda, *The International Politics of the Asia-Pacific, Second and Revised Edition* (London and New York, NY: Routledge Curzon, 2005), 56–60.
100 *British Embassy Peking - Her Majesty's Ambassador at Peking to the Secretary of State for Foreign and Commonwealth Affairs: Visit of the Chinese Minister of Foreign Trade*, 4 November 1977, in NA, PREM 16/1533, Confidential.
101 Song Xinning, 'China's View of European Integration and Enlargement', in Shambaugh, Sandschneider and Zhou (eds.), *China-Europe Relations*, 175.

2 The Road to the Third Plenum

2.1 Arms Negotiations

From Beijing's perspective, Europe potentially mattered as a source of high-tech imports, a market for consumer goods, and as a stabilising force in world politics. It was obvious for China to acquire hardware and technology to modernise the economy, and Europe could provide something mostly similar in quality to the US and Japanese competition. In short, cooperation with Western Europe was one of many essential conditions for the success of the Chinese reform programme, also because the People's Republic of China (PRC) needed a friendly and peaceful international environment to concentrate on domestic development.[1] On 10 March 1978, the Resolution on the Report on the Work of the Government was published in the *Peking Review*. The document stressed the need to develop the modernisation programme within the following years. Apart from questions of agriculture, the plan called for the growth of light industry to produce first-rate, attractive and reasonably priced goods. In addition, new sources of raw materials were to be explored in order to favour a big increase in foreign trade, raising the amount of industrial and mineral products to export. As far as trading relations were concerned, it was necessary to conscientiously study advanced science and technology of all countries and turn them to Chinese account. On foreign policy, the strictest assessment was always the one towards the Soviet Union, regarded as a late-comer among imperialist powers relying only on military strength to carry out expansion. On the other hand, China was ready to develop relations with Western European countries in several fields, with the hope to see a united and powerful Europe. Finally, despite the difference in terms of social system and ideology, with the United States there were a few points in common.[2] At the same time, on 5 March the National People's Congress approved the new Constitution of the Republic, stating that the Liberation Army was the pillar of the dictatorship of the proletariat.[3] If this was not enough, on 24 March Hua Guofeng delivered a speech at the National Science Conference whose main point stated that, while upholding independence and self-reliance, and though opposing the so-called "comprador philosophy" holding that anything foreign was good, the Chinese were not supposed to indiscriminately refuse to learn

DOI: 10.4324/9781003390138-3

from foreign countries.[4] In the meantime, the Trilateral Commission interpreted the new course as a sharp break with the Maoist thought of uninterrupted revolution. As regarded Sino-Soviet relations, there was every reason to believe China's emancipation from Soviet tutelage as irreversible. Granting Beijing favourable conditions in economic relations was considered as absolutely in the political interest of the West. The situation was different as far as arms supplies or advanced military technology were concerned, though the Commission thought equipment serving specific defensive purposes was always possible to sell.[5] These particular questions were pivotal to China because the Dragon's view of its own international role had also begun to change in the military realm. Succinctly, international trade played a key role not only in increasing Chinese influence around the world, but also in financing military build-up.[6]

In light of all this, the British government did not miss that China was seeking a closer relationship with the Soviet Union's other adversaries in the West. According to both the British Foreign Office and Department of Defence, this was due to Sino-Soviet tensions as well as American domestic political constraints on the Taiwan issue. As a matter of fact, all this left Japan and Western Europe as main sources of equipment and technology for China. By reading records, it seems Beijing had two main targets to pursue this particular issue. In fact, while strategically the Far Eastern giant viewed increased trade as a means to strengthen Western Europe against the Soviets and at the same time weakening détente, from an economic point of view technology transfer could play an important role to speed up modernisation, which implied the United Kingdom to be a paramount supplier in the civil and defence fields. Whitehall was very attentive to the new Chinese leadership. In the two previous years, in fact, the United Kingdom had ranked tenth among China's non-communist trading partners, while Beijing was London's fifty-fifth most important market. This meant that from that moment onwards it was likely to have a steady increase in the number of orders placed in the West by tripling foreign trade over the following twenty years. It was difficult for China to become one of Britain's major trading partners, but an expanding market was probable, particularly in aircraft and mining industries, as well as in electronics and oil technology. As far as defence sales were concerned, it was already accepted in all Western countries to allow the sale of advanced civil technology and equipment to the Russians. The question was whether military equipment sales had to be less restrictive towards China than to the Soviet Union. Almost certainly, specified the memorandum, a stronger China was supposed to be a more effective balance to Soviet attempts to expand influence in the world, apart from benefiting British industry and employment. One of the reasons why this issue was seriously debated was that China was not regarded as a historically expansionist power and there was no concern about territorial expansion, though on the long term it was almost inevitable for such a large country with an ideology alien to most neighbours and to the West as a whole not to be seen as a growing threat. However, on balance strategic arguments favoured some controlled sales of military equipment to China.[7] Such a topic had become so important that a debate was held at the House of Lords on 22 March 1978. Lord Peart, speaking on behalf of the government, stated that there was no possible doubt that if China's defences were bolstered up by the West, NATO and the whole of the Western world would have a much stronger hand to play in the game of détente. Interesting to notice is that the question of COCOM possible objections was by-passed through remarks that China had practically been an ally of the United States since Nixon's visit in 1972. As far as Russian protests were concerned, the British Peer said that it was about time for the Russian Bear to be baited by the English Bulldog. In substance, although the ongoing reference to self-reliance, China was now more willing than in earlier years to look abroad for some of the technology and equipment necessary to achieve ambitious economic targets. Therefore, the United Kingdom was naturally keen to expand commercial relations in this new climate. Obviously, competition among allies was expected to be fierce while Beijing had already initialled a trade agreement with the European Economic Community. In a few words, Downing Street's attitude was well-known: any formal approach from the Chinese government for the sale of a particular item of equipment was to be considered on its merits.[8]

Economy expert Barry Naughton reminds that elders like Deng Xiaoping, being part of the founding revolutionary generation instrumental in the creation of the command-economy system, enjoyed enormous credibility legitimising the introduction of market reforms. It was always assumed that the process of economic development would drive market transition forward and guarantee its eventual success. In a few words, after the Cultural Revolution, Chinese reformers wanted to rehabilitate the economy and avoid further disruptions in order to ward off collapse.[9] Moreover, Martin Jacques states that Deng's project involved not only economic revolution, but also silent political transformation of the state replacing the universalistic and ideological model of Maoism with something much closer to the pragmatic and developmental system of East Asian countries. At the dawn of the globalisation age it was no longer possible for China and the so-called Asian Tigers to grow within a wall of tariffs and barriers until their industries were ready to compete in the international market. In spite of that, the final objective was never westernisation, but rather the need to restore party legitimacy after the disaster of the Cultural Revolution.[10] What is more, Deng argued that the East-West military confrontation was linked to North-South economic relations. He therefore claimed that the North required markets and the South needed advanced technology. The old leader further developed a view of China's special role in this regard, stating that the stronger Beijing grew, the better the chances for preserving world peace.[11] Actually, Chinese leaders were learning that there had been dramatic economic development in Western Europe, so the way in which those countries regulated their economy did not resemble the kind of capitalism the Chinese had learned about from the Soviet Union.[12]

Nevertheless, the British did not intend to completely break off their relationship with the Soviets. On the contrary, the attempt to appease Moscow and try to pursue a steady pattern of détente was evident when British officers said that the UK and the USSR shared an interest in a stable China, which was trying to restore order and get rid of radical influences. Finally, any decision to sell arms to the Chinese bore the risk to be taken in a very negative way by the Soviets,[13] who certainly regarded the military factor as the most important part of the modernisation project. The Russians were so obsessed with the China danger that in Hua's words they did not see any real focus on the economy. Instead, everything was directed to turn Beijing into a military power. Since no one was really threatening the Asian country, Moscow believed that its rivals were interested in acquiring offensive capability. Consequently, such a fever of militarism was supposed to be a matter of concern for all other countries, especially the ones located in South East Asia, which was said to be the natural object of Chinese expansionist policies.[14] On the other hand, the British Foreign Office promoted arms sales to China as long as this matched London's strategic interests. Succinctly, the Chinese had to be encouraged to look upon Britain as supplier in the field of aerospace. In particular, Harrier aircraft contracts could undoubtedly increase the prospects for further sales of other kinds of goods. Unlike Kremlin officers, London did not believe the sale of Harrier aeroplanes could undermine Moscow's overwhelming military superiority over Beijing, especially because the Harrier had no strategic offensive capability. As a matter of fact, Britain's concern was not Moscow-oriented, but it was rather focused on encouraging the modernisation process of the potentially endless market of China, thus linking that country to the West and at the same time strengthening its defensive stance towards the Soviet Union. Nevertheless, the Foreign Office was not so optimistic about the attitude of the Carter administration, supposed to be concerned about not irritating the Russians during complex détente negotiations.[15] In any case, there was considerable interest at the British Parliament in the possibility of arms sales to China, with particular emphasis on commercial and industrial benefits.[16] Similar studies were being developed in the United States, such as the CIA research paper reminding that Chinese trading policies were supposed to be oriented towards the West more and more. Even with improvement in political relations with Moscow and Eastern European countries, trade with communist partners was assessed to remain at only twenty per cent of China's total commercial exchanges.[17]

Such statements and comments were well founded if we consider that Sung Chin-Kuang, assistant foreign minister, said that the modernisation of China's defence system was a current priority and therefore the PRC had planned to purchase equipment and know-how from Britain and other Western European countries.[18] Actually, as Lorenz Lüthi reminds, we must not forget that the Sino-American rapprochement and possible arms deliveries to the PRC were also a serious cause of concern for regional powers like India, even after Deng's call on all Asian nations to improve relations. Nevertheless, in January 1978, Indian companies invited a Chinese trade delegation and the following month, while visiting Nepal, Deng expressed his hope to improve Sino-Indian relations.[19] On the other hand, Jonathan Fenby is rather negative about Hua's attitude, for he states that the premier was adopting some Dengist phraseology on modernisation. In addition, his Ten-Year Plan was focused on heavy industry, as almost forty per cent of the national budget was allocated to capital investment. Unfortunately, this is Fenby's strict assessment, Deng was mocking Mao in seeking to do everything at the same time, thus creating chaos on a massive scale, with investment spending sending the budget deficit to a record 15.5 per cent and wage increases fuelling inflation.[20] Meanwhile, the serious intentions of both parties were shown by the conversations taking place at the highest levels between Chairman Hua Guofeng and the chief of Defence Staff, during which the Chinese leader tried to persuade his British counterpart about the dangerousness of the Soviet threat against Western Europe. By reading through the lines, what we may assume is that the communist government in all circumstances stressed the importance of a united Europe as a bulwark opposing Soviet expansionism. The ideology of appeasement, as détente negotiations were called by the Chinese, was to be prevented to pursue instead a strategy of sabotage of Soviet positions on the international chessboard.[21]

2.2 Brzezinski's Trip to the Far East: The Breakthrough

In November 1977, the Head of the PRC Liaison Mission had invited Zbigniew Brzezinski to China. Brzezinski himself admits the invitation gave him the necessary opening to push more energetically towards normalisation, as the National Security Adviser seemed to share Chinese concerns about Moscow's geopolitical stance in the Middle East and around the Arabian Peninsula.[22] Meanwhile, Deng had spoken about the importance to pursue a pragmatist policy by seeking truth from facts in order to achieve the four modernisations by the end of the century.[23] Enrico Fardella helps us better understand how the Chinese made up their mind about the necessity and the benefit of a closer cooperation with the West. In a few words, the Asians seemed to be comforted by what they saw as a new sense of solidity in Washington's policy regarding Moscow. Most probably, the report that Huang Chen had presented on his return to Beijing had described the complex relations that linked American internal policy and normalisation. Moreover, through the nomination at the beginning of 1978 of Xu Xiangqian as Minister of Defence, Deng Xiaoping took over control of the Army. One of the first to realise that Deng was moving towards market values was Brzezinski, who shared his enthusiasm with Carter in a memorandum stating that after twenty years in search for a distinctive path to modernity, the regime appeared to be joining the rest of the world.[24] Kissinger himself underlines that Deng had understood that China could not maintain the leading historic role played for centuries unless becoming internationally engaged and economically modern. The former secretary of state also says that a balance of power is always necessary between China and the United States, but this must be mitigated by agreements on laws and norms and strengthened through cooperation.[25] Apart from that, in 1978 Soviet policies towards China looked seriously threatening to Beijing. In military relations, Moscow was deploying a lot of modern weaponry along the border with the PRC, even SS 20 intermediate-range ballistic missiles. As far as the Indochina region was concerned, the Kremlin was by then supporting Vietnam's anti-China posture, such as confiscating personal savings of ethnic Chinese who had started to cross the border into South China.[26]

To tell the truth, Vance thought the USSR was a conservative power whose advances in the Third World reflected opportunism and a reaction to American initiatives, rather than a plan for world domination. Improving relations with China was desirable but secondary, and certainly this could not be allowed to imperil détente. On the contrary, Brzezinski was persuaded that the USSR was in a phase of geopolitical self-assertion. Therefore, if the United States did not want Moscow to continue to grow bolder and threaten American leadership, détente had to be made more balanced, thus Washington had to react to Soviet and Cuban advances in the Horn of Africa and elsewhere by playing the Chinese card on a military level as well.[27] By virtue of that, on 27 February 1978 Brzezinski submitted a memorandum to President Carter claiming the importance for the United States to maintain a better relationship with both China and the USSR than either of them had with each other.[28] As Brzezinski confirms in his memoirs, the Department of Defence worked with him to persuade the president about the necessity of a closer relationship with the Chinese. In a memorandum to the president dated 11 March, in fact, Harold Brown warned Carter on Soviet adventurism displayed in the Horn of Africa and the consequent measures to implement as a retaliation. In light of this, it was certainly not by accident that the defence secretary suggested to respond by initiating talks with the PRC on questions of common interest, such as how to work together in the Horn and make efforts to frustrate Kremlin adventurism. Another pivotal nuance to notice in this document is the attitude to freeze normalisation talks while waiting to deal with the Taiwan issue and a consequent agreement on that. In the meantime, the best way to make progress with China was working on the common anti-Soviet posture.[29]

The National Security Council worked in concert with the Department of Defence claiming that US global strategy was deficient insofar as the Russians were allowed to define the regions of the world where the Americans had to compete for influence. Consequently, the response to give was not to be confined to Africa, though it seemed the communist superpower had chosen that continent as principal locus of competition for the foreseeable future. The NSC believed the most effective strategic rejoinder could be moulded through adjustments in Asian policies, especially on China. Tellingly, the report added that, since the Soviets were seeking to extend their influence to the South, the Atlantic power was supposed to remind them of their vulnerabilities in the East. Hence, a strengthened China connection, including formal diplomatic relations, expanding trade, and fuller strategic consultations, was the most effective card to play. Moreover, such a response to Soviet African adventure was supposed to meet domestic conservative reservations and also force the Kremlin to cooperate in other areas and strengthen China's commitment to a moderate policy in Asia. Finally, the time was ripe also because the National Party Congress in China had confirmed a moderate leadership interested in developing relations with the United States while accelerating internal industrial development.[30] A few weeks later, the president authorised Brzezinski to address the question of normalisation, as well as engaging the Chinese in a strategic review of the world situation. Emphatically, the most important interest China and the United States had in common was the opposition to global or regional hegemony by any single power:

> I could not help but think of the strange coincidence that the Sino-American relationship was being forged in the course of a single decade by two US officials who were of immigrant birth and who approached this task with relatively little knowledge of or special sentiment for China, but with larger strategic concerns in mind.[31]

To confirm this framework, once he had met Foreign Minister Huang Hua, Brzezinski asserted that the United States and China shared certain common, fundamental interests and had similar long-term strategic concerns. The most important of these, as it was easy to realise, was the stance on global and regional hegemony, provided the relations between the two countries got fully normalised. Probably we may say that the most important thing the national security adviser said on that circumstance, to clarify how important China had become to the United States as a counterweight to the Soviet rivalry, was that the People's Republic played a central role in the maintenance of the global equilibrium in a pluralistic world, thus acknowledging that the communist bloc was no longer Soviet-dominated. Brzezinski could not have been more explicit when he said that the two countries, despite the difference of system and life style, should cooperate again in the face of the common threat of the emergence of the Soviet Union as a global power. Such was the determination to woo the new leadership of China, that the first part of the conversation between the two statesmen was completely focused on the USSR. Interestingly enough, among the many allegations the Carter administration addressed to Moscow, such as gaining political preponderance in Western Europe, radicalising the Middle East, reaching and penetrating the Indian Ocean, there was also the one referring to the project to encircle China. Through words like these, the administration aimed at tickling Chinese ambitions and Western orientation by showing that the Atlantic power could by then offer something that no-one else was able to. As an evidence of that, Brzezinski said the White House pursued not only wider cooperation with key allies, but also wanted to broaden this collaboration to include countries regarded as newly regional influential, thus responding to changes of the last fifteen-twenty years in the global distribution of power.[32]

The national security adviser led the section of the administration seeking quick progress in normalising US-China relations and in subsequent steps advancing that collaboration as a means to counter Soviet power and expansion. Chinese officials, on the other hand, were in the lead among international advocates in warning the United States to avoid the dangers of appeasing the Soviets.[33] As a consequence of that, Huang Hua confirmed that China and the United States shared common ground, especially on working together to cope with the Russian Bear. As a matter of fact, maintenance of stability in South Asia was in the interests of deterring Soviet infiltration and expansion in the region. This was supposed to be proved by the pro-Soviet coup in Afghanistan, through which Russian influence in the region had pushed forward several hundred kilometres farther, making Pakistan particularly concerned. Inciting Washington's worst fears, the Chinese said that, if the Soviet Union succeeded in Afghanistan, it was expected to push further till breaking into the Indian Ocean. Another serious problem of hegemony was the one dealing with Indochina, where the PRC interpreted the ambition of Vietnam to establish primacy in the region as the root of the conflict against Cambodia. To finish the job, the Chinese politician stimulated the Carter administration's concern about the Japanese international position, by saying that the Soviets had adopted a policy of pressure towards the Rising Sun to serve their interests of expansion in the Pacific.[34] The conversation with Deng also dealt with commercial issues, and the old leader stated that on scientific and technological expansions, as well as economic relations, the Chinese government would give priority to the countries having diplomatic relations with Beijing. Brzezinski assured trade restrictions to communist countries were a legacy of the past, thus recognising that China was no longer closely associated to Moscow.[35] With respect to Japan, Brzezinski told Hua Guofeng that close friendship between Japan and China was complementary to the one between the United States and Tokyo. Once again the American statesman stressed the usefulness of the friendship with the People's Republic as a central part of Washington's foreign policy within the attempt to shape a truly cooperative world, organised on the basis of independent states with new political and social relationships.[36]

In the same days, the Soviets clearly feared further rapprochement between China and the West, thus blaming Beijing of militarism and hegemonism, specifying that the new leadership was implementing the most negative aspects of the Maoist foreign policy, and therefore being the most ardent supporter of a stronger NATO alliance. In particular, Moscow accused the PRC of pursuing a racist nationalist policy aiming at separating

Afro-Asian countries from the socialist bloc.[37] As far as military modernisation was concerned, the Soviets did not like at all the Chinese to acquire modern electronic equipment, which could only help them pursue armed provocations to destabilise other nations.[38] From the British point of view, instead, arms trade with the Asian country was welcomed, as the United Kingdom had recently decided to increase the defence budget as a reaction to the concern of the Soviet build-up,[39] something Beijing favoured as an appreciation of the dangers confronting Western Europe.[40] In the meantime, American Intelligence was monitoring the situation in South-East Asia, where the Sino-Vietnamese quarrel over the treatment of the ethnic Chinese population of Vietnam and Hanoi's ties with Moscow threatened to provoke a chain reaction over the competition for influence in Indochina. In particular, Cambodia was pivotal since it was the focus of their rivalry for regional influence. Bitterness was so deep that the situation could deteriorate further, especially if Hanoi felt necessary to allow a Soviet military presence in Vietnam, thus jeopardising the new balance of power developed since the withdrawal of the Americans and the unification of the country. What seemed to be encouraging from the US point of view, however, was that the deterioration of Sino-Vietnamese relations would probably prompt Hanoi to seek better relations with the North Atlantic power as alternative source of economic assistance.[41]

Michel Oksenberg's assessment of the trip was very positive, as he stated that Brzezinski had established the basis for a long-term rewarding relationship with the Chinese. What mainly struck him was the strong convergence of views about the Soviet Union as major source of instability. Nevertheless, Oksenberg was not too optimistic about the potentialities of the Sino-American relationship, for altering the Chinese world view was likely to prove only marginally effective. The areas of overlapping interests were in Europe and the Third World, since none of the two parties had an adequate strategy for preventing Soviet meddling.[42] As a matter of fact, the first thing the national security adviser wrote in his report to the president was that the Chinese were somewhat reassured by American willingness to compete with the Soviet Union. Beijing looked particularly concerned about the situation in Indochina, specifically referring to it as a Soviet-backed design to establish hegemony. In that case, China was doomed to face adversaries both in the South and in the North. As far as commercial relations were concerned, both Hua and Deng were said to be ready for expanded economic and cultural contacts with the United States.[43] On the contrary, Cyrus Vance was disturbed by his colleague's public provocative remarks on Soviet international commitments, while the secretary of state was seeking Russian cooperation in the Horn of Africa, apart from possible repercussions on arms limitations negotiations.[44] On this particular issue, Breck Walker says that Brzezinski's achievements overshadowed Vance's equally significant contributions to the normalisation process. The secretary had always thought that formal rapprochement with China was a vital foreign policy objective; therefore, as direct negotiations began to unfold in 1978, Vance was an active participant who had come to the conclusion that the pursuit of normalisation could actually benefit the SALT II Treaty. However, he was very concerned that any effort to threaten the Soviets through the China card was likely to backfire and result in a more aggressive and uncooperative USSR.[45]

2.3 Accelerating Negotiations

Brzezinski's visit to China had given a push to the negotiations between the two governments. The Chinese were by then eager to cooperate and get access to Western technology and loans. As an evidence of this, the foreign minister told Vance in New York that he was sure the relationship between the two countries could further expand, provided normalisation of relations. In addition, Huang encouraged the Americans to assist Pakistan in facing the threatening situation in Afghanistan following the pro-Soviet coup.[46] Rosemary Foot observes that progress steadily occurred once several topics were in place. First of all, Deng Xiaoping was concerned about the USSR in the context of deepening relations with Vietnam. Moreover, he thought China desperately needed the United States as a major factor to develop and modernise the economy. Finally, on the American side there was President Carter who had decided to put less faith in the policy of détente.[47] Actually, the Chinese were eager to accelerate commercial relations when they said they welcomed energy, scientific and technological delegations to visit China and start talking about business.[48] Concerning energy issues, we have to keep in mind that the CIA had predicted that Chinese oil production would peak. Therefore, several analysts suggested to promote offshore output. Such a remedy of course benefited American corporations, for they had expertise, technology and world market knowledge to help out China. At the same time, by relying on US enterprises the Asian country could become dependent on Western technology, thus allowing multinationals to influence Chinese oil supplies. Moreover, by choosing the offshore option China would probably take a decade before making any important difference in the energy picture, thus being obliged to be oriented towards the United States for a long time to come.[49] Further indication of Chinese interest in US oil technology came in May 1978, when Beijing invited four American oil companies – Pennzoil, Exxon, Union Oil and Phillips Petroleum – to discuss joint exploration and development of offshore resources. Beijing urged to invest in offshore oil on generous terms by stressing competition with European and Japanese firms. Few understood this strategic context better than Henry "Scoop" Jackson, the chairman of the Senate Energy Committee. In February 1978, Jackson paid his second visit to China, where he boldly said that it was in American interest to help the Far Eastern country develop its own oil industry. Moreover, Jackson and Deng agreed upon most strategic issues, including a stronger NATO and US bases in Japan and the Philippines. In his report to the Senate, Jackson urged the Department of Energy to take the initiative to deepen cooperation between the United States and the Chinese government,[50] while in an article in the *New*

York Times he had asserted that a stronger China would be "an asset" for the United States to maintain the strategic balance against the Soviet Union. Through wise diplomacy, therefore, the United States had the opportunity to influence Chinese receptivity to foreign technology and the degree to which Beijing was supposed to enter world energy markets.[51] Last but not least, we must not forget that Deng was still threatened at home and obsessed abroad by Soviet hegemonism, once a pro-Soviet regime had seized power in Afghanistan and pro-China Cambodia was under attack by pro-Soviet Vietnam. Hence, the old leader had decided to make the job a little easier to the American administration by giving implicit assurance that the PRC would not liberate Taiwan by force. As a matter of fact, the danger perceived from Moscow was more stressful than the Taipei question.[52]

Parallel to normalisation issues, business negotiations carried on with the British as well. The ambassador at Beijing, in fact, remarked that trade of all kinds would be a pivotal part of Sino-British bilateral relations in the following years, especially as far as oil and coal were concerned, as well as aircraft, since at the moment the level of transactions was still very low in comparison with the needs and capacities of both countries.[53] Moreover, science and technology was another field on which Whitehall wanted to cooperate with China to strengthen general relations.[54] Such a confidence was also due to the prediction that the Russian reaction to defence sales to China would be limited by what Moscow perceived as its own interest to do business with London.[55] The Americans as well claimed their Asian character by reminding entrance into a new era in the Asia-Pacific region bearing prosperity and stability. Communist countries were accused to be economically weak and by then also bitterly divided. From the standpoint of security, it was fair to say that the United States, China and Japan shared an interest in maintaining that stability which had paved the way to strategic, economic and political opportunities throughout Asia. As a consequence of that, the assistant secretary of state for East Asian and Pacific Affairs, Holbrooke, used a language the Chinese must have appreciated a lot when he claimed that the Carter administration was seeking to maintain the current equilibrium and not allowing any single power to achieve a preponderance of influence or military superiority in the area. Moreover, economic relations had become the single most important emerging element of US relationship with Asia. As an outcome of the political stability in capitalistic economy countries, in fact, there was a huge regional market supposed to be increasingly hungry for American quality products and attractive to US capital. To achieve such a task, the White House had to work in order to insure that the competition caused by an Open Door policy be conducted according to accepted international trade rules.[56] As an evidence of how serious the Chinese were on finding new markets, in Spring 1978 Deng had asked Vice Premier Gu Mu, in charge of foreign trade and the economy, to visit Western Europe and learn as much as possible. On his return, Gu delivered a report explaining that European development since the end of the

second world conflict had mostly relied on advanced technology transforming productivity. On grounds of this, first of all China was thirty years
behind at least. Secondly, due to economic stagnation European countries
were looking for new outlets for their capitals and goods. Hence, they
seemed anxious to collaborate with the PRC. Thirdly, Beijing had no time to
waste to work with them and accept practices such as joint ventures and
foreign direct investment. Deng seemed persuaded and instructed Gu to
speed up negotiations with Western companies.[57]

The regime was definitely distancing itself from the Great Helmsman, thus
showing increasing pragmatism and the modesty to learn from others.
Despite the Communist Party's grip, such a breakthrough was extremely
hopeful for the West, like all British and American analyses remarked.
Industrialists and suppliers of modern technology were being invited, and
offshore oil explorations were being planned with Americans, as well as
British and Japanese enterprises. Succinctly, the course pursued by the
Chinese government supporting a strong and united Europe and a healthy
Atlantic Alliance was regarded as the best way to ensure Asian and world
stability,[58] keeping however in mind that Britain was only one of the many
countries willing to develop commercial relations with China. Hence,
London wished the West to act in concert as much as possible, avoiding to
raise the political temperature which might trigger off Soviet reactions,
though it was also true that the Chinese considered the attitude towards
arms sales as an indication of how serious the relationship with the Dragon
had become.[59] Chinese leaders, in fact, did not miss any chance to remark
how much they needed up-to-date science and technology to transform step
by step all the sectors of the national economy. Since a big leap in production
was expected, this was supposed to invariably require a corresponding
widening of the area of exchange. Foreign trade had to be increased with the
purpose to assimilate as far as possible everything good from other countries.
The aim behind this policy was to adopt as quickly as possible the most
advanced techniques and methods to increase output and strengthen self-
reliance. Apart from commodities production, China was required to open
up new commerce and service trades and accumulate more funds, thus
achieving better financial and bank work, as well as finance and trade
management.[60] In a nutshell, Deng and his main collaborators had started to
realise that the ideological world of the Cold War should no longer work as
a guideline of China's foreign policy orientation. Instead, national interests
were supposed to be the intrinsic determinant of the decision making process, with economic development and technological advance as China's
pivotal topic.[61] Such a frenzy debate showed that the communist leadership
of China was on the move to get emancipated from collectivistic economy
with the aim of carving out a paramount role on the global scenario.
Accepting an Open Door policy and getting acquainted with the capitalistic
world of finance was plausibly a way to put pressure on the American
administration to normalise bilateral relations. Just to give evidence about

that, in Summer 1978 the PRC State Council convened to debate basic issues, and during one of those talks Yu Guangyuan, vice minister of the State Commission for Science and Technology, said that there were very good systems in capitalist countries. In addition Li Xiannian, Hua's chief economic adviser, said that the international scenario was by then favourable to China, supposed to exploit the opportunity to use foreign advanced technology, equipment and capital to accelerate modernisation. Soon afterwards, the National Planning Conference recommended that the PRC abandon closed-door policy and instead begin entering the international market.[62]

Such an attitude was not obviously welcomed in Moscow, whose press stated that the heirs of Mao Zedong were by then ready to join an international front against the Soviet Union and other socialist countries to put an end to the process of détente and negotiations on arms limitation.[63] Chinese rulers were also accused of seeking to gain access to NATO military arsenal by advertising their animosity towards the USSR everywhere and having acquired a chauvinistic attitude on Vietnam.[64] As far as this particular kind of allegation was concerned, the theme of Chinese nationalism, or variations like social chauvinism, or great-Han chauvinism, were by then shaping the Soviet conception of China, accused of working to build a threatening militarist state, removing class struggle as the main factor of domestic policy and accelerating the rehabilitation of rightist and reactionary elements.[65] By virtue of that, on 30 August 1978 the Central Committee of the Communist Party of the Soviet Union issued a paper evaluating Sino-American normalisation. Obviously, the Soviets believed that Beijing pursued a global strategic alliance with the United States. As for the Carter administration, the Politburo blamed the White House of playing the Chinese card to secure the interests of American imperialism in Africa, Asia and the Middle East. In addition, the trade agreement between the PRC and the European Economic Community was supposed to offer opportunity of access to military equipment and strategic material from NATO. In light of that, on the eve of resuming peace and friendship treaty negotiations between China and Japan, both the Chinese and the Americans were said to have exerted pressure on the Japanese to agree to an anti-hegemonial stance against Vietnam and the Soviet Union.[66]

This irritability could be easily explained, since in those days, precisely on 12 August, the PRC and Japan had signed a Treaty of Peace and Friendship igniting the competition between the two communist powers in South-East Asia. Tellingly, Tokyo had by then begun to enjoy a higher international profile, thus coming under pressure to take a more active role in regional issues. Japan's reluctance to do so was also due to the opposition of other powers, especially China and Korea, for a long time after the war deeply suspicious of Tokyo's motives.[67] Hence, the treaty was regarded as a serious blow to Soviet ambitions in Asia, for the Russians had been trying to bring Japan into their own orbit by associating the Empire of the Rising Sun more closely through the opening up of Siberia to Japanese need of raw materials.

On the other hand, the Chinese had been able to persuade their Eastern neighbour that it had much more to gain from access to Western-oriented Chinese markets and the setting up of a more stable political relationship.[68] What worried the Soviets most was the inclusion of a clause through which the PRC and Japan affirmed the common opposition to attempts by any other power to establish hegemony in that region. By insisting on that clause, the Chinese had proved their determination to attract the Japanese towards their own camp against Moscow. On the other hand, it seemed there was no opposition from the other side of the Pacific Ocean to the rapprochement between the two Asian countries, thus in a way ensuring American protection and not leaving Japan at the mercy of two communist giants. Finally, while Sino-Japanese economic cooperation was certainly to be improved and talks had already been announced to this purpose, China was expected to become less and less isolationist and pave the way to fuller collaboration with the West.[69] Interesting to notice, the Americans did not deny that Beijing was led by a nationalist approach, but Michel Oksenberg used the expression "confident nationalism" to describe PRC policies in those years. Tellingly, the confidence of Chinese leaders was based on their belief in strengthening the economy through a market-oriented system and the opening up to the West while keeping national independence. Due to this confidence, extreme nationalist tendencies could also be held back in order not to have such a massive impact on foreign policy.[70]

To tell the truth, the Russians were not so wrong to suspect that communist China was setting up an anti-Soviet stronghold wherever possible. As a matter of fact, this was the same comment the Americans were making. China was by then engaged in attempting to build a durable, world-wide anti-Soviet consensus, said Michel Oksenberg in a memorandum to the national security adviser. Moreover, the denunciation of the Sino-Soviet Treaty stipulated between Stalin and Mao was of course welcomed by the Americans, who claimed that such a move put an end to all hopes of resurrecting amity between the two countries. Instead, China was thought to have definitely embarked on a strategy to modernise its own system by turning to the West. On balance, the tilt towards the West was regarded as a favourable watershed. By playing the China card carefully, it was finally possible for Washington to exclude Soviet power from footholds in East Asia and prevent it from expanding in Southeast Asia.[71] By reading Chinese editorials, we may say that Beijing was making every effort to portray the Kremlin's global strategy as expansionist and dangerous in several areas. The Russians were also blamed of instigating Vietnamese anti-China campaigns, trying to use Vietnam as a Cuban-style proxy in the Asia-Pacific region.[72] Of course the Sino-Soviet dispute was object of study by Western powers, especially once the Soviets had become extremely critical about the possibility of arms sales to China. Since the West was going to be benefited from Chinese political stability and closer trading relations with capitalistic countries, the Sino-Soviet dispute was useful to limit Moscow's freedom of action. Beijing could never be regarded as a reliable partner from an ideological point of view, but China was on the path of modern industrialisation and this task was going to be pursued with or without Western help. Therefore, British interests lay in taking advantage of this process and build up ties with the PRC in all civil and defence fields.[73]

2.4 Huang Hua's Visit to the United Kingdom

On 16 September 1978, Deng delivered an important speech on the principle of "Seeking Truth from Facts", stating that the famous doctrine known as the "Two Whatevers", according to which whatever documents the Great Helmsman had read and endorsed and whatever he had done and said must always determine Chinese actions, was certainly not the right way to hold high the banner of Mao. Instead, Comrade Mao himself had written the four-word motto "Seek truth from facts" in order to integrate the universal truth of Marxism-Leninism with the concrete practice of the Chinese Revolution.[74] This was the first time that the long-march veteran had criticised the old theory outside the inner circle of the Party, thus proving pivotal change in the national political mood.[75] Essentially, Deng observed the importance to always proceed from current reality when handling questions of principle and policy. For example, although the historic leader thought about expanding economic and technical exchanges with other countries and even absorbing foreign capital and undertaking joint ventures, the necessary conditions were not present, due to the embargo imposed on China. After several years of effort, therefore, the Chinese leadership had managed to secure international conditions enabling Beijing to make use of capital from foreign countries and of their advanced technology and experience in business management. Hence, holding high the banner of Mao Zedong Thought meant proceeding from present realities and make full use of all favourable conditions to achieve the task.[76] Propositions on practice as the sole criterion of truth were actually justified, not merely by the argument that it had worked in the past, but by the fact that it was in conformity with Mao's words. Essentially, it was necessary to debate in this way in order to have the greatest possible chance of winning the argument. Moreover, Deng and his main collaborators tried to demonstrate their legitimacy as heirs and disciples of Mao, though the ideological framework was no longer necessarily decisive in all respects.[77] In conclusion, the time had come for China to develop technology in order to catch up with the developed countries, let alone surpass them. The world's advanced scientific and technological achievements had to be acquired as starting points for the country's development. Hence, Deng was speaking like a private company manager when he stated that qualified managerial staff and workers should enjoy better treatment in order to encourage people to advance, while those who were unqualified were supposed to be designated as supernumerary personnel.[78]

The Chinese offensive was also carried out at the United Nations, where on 28 September Foreign Minister Huang Hua delivered a speech at the plenary meeting of the 33rd Session of the General Assembly. Apparently, the Chinese representative criticised both superpowers for intensifying the struggle for world hegemony. However, everybody realised that the real target of his philippic was the Soviet Union, openly accused of pursuing unbridled acts of aggression and expansion. On grounds of this, said Huang Hua, the countries of the so-called Second World were obliged to pay ever greater attention to the defence of their national independence. Thus, Beijing welcomed Western European countries' harmonisation of their mutual relations and strengthening of their economic, political and military alliance. As far as China's foreign policy was concerned, the goal set by the new leadership was turning the Asian giant into a prosperous socialist society with modernised agriculture, industry, national defence and science and technology by the end of the century. In light of this, relations with other nations were to be established on the basis of mutual respect for territorial integrity and non-interference in each other's internal affairs.[79] Through words like these, the Foreign Minister was quite explicitly saying that China was ready to deal with anybody, provided certain principles were respected. The chance was by then to be exploited in order to accelerate trade and political negotiations. The Chinese domestic debate had not been missed by American intelligence analyses, which appreciated Deng's efforts to assess what role Maoist theory should play in the solution of China's problems. In practice, the point was then how much and by whom Mao's ideological legacy was to be revised to take into account the needs of modernisation.[80]

A few days after the UN speech, Huang confirmed this approach during a conversation with the US State Secretary, warning that some new features in Soviet strategy had emerged, such as deploying a large number of troops and military equipment in Europe with the aim of controlling strategic areas and sea lanes to the continent. Therefore, the Chinese regime regarded the in-itiatives in Angola and Zaire and the wars in Somalia and Ethiopia, as well as the military coups in Afghanistan and South Yemen, as part of the overall plan to push for strategic superiority. The situation in Indochina was thought to be of the same nature, with the Soviets resorting more and more to the use of mercenaries to carry out direct intervention to insure safe-guarding of the areas of paramount importance.[81] Indochina was of par-ticular concern to American Intelligence, as testified by a memorandum released the following month and stating that China considered an inde-pendent Kampuchea as an essential buffer against the expansion of Vietnamese, and by extension Soviet, influence in the area. Tellingly, the USSR was regarded as the most likely to benefit, at least over the short term, trying to establish a sphere of influence on China's Southern boundary. Moscow, in fact, was the major source of aid to Vietnam, and hoped to eventually obtain access to military facilities.[82] As far as this was concerned, it seemed the Chinese did not mind if Washington normalised the relations with Vietnam, also because it was regarded as inevitable. Nevertheless, the ideal option for Beijing leadership was to let the Vietnamese stew in their

Soviet juice, forcing Hanoi into near-total reliance on the USSR and then trust that frictions between the two partners would develop over the years, after which China would again attempt to build influence in Vietnam.[83]

Meanwhile, Deng Xiaoping met representatives of foreign powers reminding that the PRC had been sending many people abroad to get familiar with the outside world. As a starting point, therefore, advanced technology and equipment from the rest of the world had to be introduced, with the aim of expanding domestic productive forces and improve people's living standards.[84] Such was the boost to market overture that a series of editorials and articles were being published in the *Beijing Review*, reminding how Mao himself had praised the capitalistic production system employing fewer people with greater efficiency.[85] International and domestic conditions were thought to be favourable for accelerating the pace towards modernisation under the firm leadership of the Central Committee of the Communist Party. China claimed to be rich in natural resources and on the regional scenario the Soviet Union, though still aggressive, had become isolated and increasingly exposed to criticism. Most countries in the world – this was the turning point persuading the leadership to doubtless carry on – wanted China to grow strong and rich, thus the time had come to introduce advanced techniques and equipment, utilise foreign funds and organisational expertise. In short, independence did not mean isolationism and self-reliance did not imply blindly excluding everything foreign.[86]

On approaching the visit of the Chinese foreign minister, Downing Street knew that defence was one of the main priority areas of modernisation for Beijing, thus Rolls Royce had already been authorised to negotiate a contract on marine propulsion units.[87] As it was easily understandable, trade was one of the main points of discussion, if we bear in mind that the previous year British exports to China had amounted to £62 million, while imports from the Far East country had increased up to £104 million. Although overall trade was rather small, China was always an important market for specific British sectors, such as aerospace and mining machinery.[88] After a series of major Chinese delegations to the UK and British commissions' journey to China, there were signs that a new expanding stage was beginning.[89] As an evidence of that, the Chinese had indicated their preliminary interest in a number of items such as tanks, lasers, small arms and optical equipment. Moreover, there were rumours that Beijing was willing to purchase something like forty Harriers aircraft, while seeking production rights to manufacture under licence in China itself. This request was rather embarrassing for Whitehall, since it could involve the transfer of sensitive and advanced technology.[90] Agriculture was another pivotal issue to discuss, so that Huang Hua told Prime Minister Callaghan that China still relied primarily on manual labour, thus mechanisation was a priority. On the other hand, the fact that only three and a half per cent of the British workforce was employed on the land made the UK agricultural machine industry quite efficient and export-minded.[91] On this particular question, Beijing resumed imports from the United States, thus having payment problems due to a trade of almost five hundred million dollars with the United States. To sustain commercial expansion, the PRC decided to apply for various forms of foreign loans, and Deng went even further by accepting the concept of joint venture.[92] Raw materials, of course, were another crucial commodity, as David Owen stated that, due to instability in Southern Africa, the United Kingdom was not so well provided when it came to raw materials other than energy. Hence, Huang said this was something worth exploration, for if China should increase imports to the United Kingdom, exports to Britain had also to be augmented in order to establish stable relations.[93]

Friendly relations with the PRC had by then become a basic pillar of British international relations, therefore Foreign Secretary Owen certainly matched the Chinese attitude by saying that for a few years by then he had become more worried by the ongoing Soviet military expansion in relation to domestic economy. Consequently, though encouraging the two superpowers to pursue sensible arrangements on disarmament, Whitehall did not accept détente as a one-way street where the Soviets got their costless way.[94] To tackle Soviet aggressive stance, Huang considered that three roads were to be followed: (a) strengthening defensive capability; (b) supporting all forces struggling against Soviet expansionism; (c) opposing the policy of appeasement towards the Soviet Union. By virtue of that, China welcomed the British decision to increase military expenditure and hoped to see a united and strong Europe cooperating with a strong and prosperous China. As far as technical assistance to the USSR was concerned, the point was that Western European countries relied on market forces tending to operate rather erratically, which was something exploited by Moscow. However it was, London was not ready to withdraw technology from the Soviet Union, as this was regarded more hurting for the United Kingdom, due to competitors taking advantage. The Chinese attitude was easy to adopt, said the Secretary, but the government of Beijing did not have bankers and industrialists making pressure to trade with any possible country.[95] Nevertheless, the British Labour government had decided to positively respond to Chinese overtures, as there were clear trade opportunities in helping the Dragon fulfil its ambitions, which in the long run would provide gains for all Western countries. Obviously, defence sales were always to be supplied to the PRC, though certainly not relating to offensive weapons and on condition to affect efforts to build up a constructive relation with the USSR as well.[96]

Such was the will to deal with the Far Eastern power on a regular basis, that the British organised a conference divided into three sessions covering political, economic and military relations with the People's Republic up to 1985. China was certainly abandoning its aloofness from the rest of the world, but it was not yet possible to assess whether the leadership was going to indefinitely follow the way to modernisation paved by Deng Xiaoping. This statement is relevant to understand how Western leaders backed Deng's control over reforms. Radicalism in China had not disappeared, but an excellent way to encourage the new leadership not to sacrifice trading profitable relations with the West was the positive response to Beijing's wishes, especially bearing in mind that the Sino-Soviet dispute led the Dragon to welcome a strong grouping of countries feeling threatened by the Soviets.[97] An end of this controversy was thought to widen Soviet military options, at the same time removing obstacles to Russian influence in developing countries. Similarly, a possible relaxation of tension between the two communist powers was said to permit China a free hand to exploit opportunities in the Third World. No China card against the USSR was claimed by Downing Street, but the Soviet reaction was probably going to depend on the way Sino-British relations were publicly presented and on how far London was ready to act in concert with Western allies.[98] For specific domestic reasons, neither the Japanese nor the Germans were available to sell arms to the Chinese. Since the Americans were not ready yet, braked by concerns about Taiwan security, Beijing was expected to look particularly at London and Paris to acquire modern weapons, a potential business worth hundreds of millions of pounds. Three categories of weapons had been listed in which the PRC was interested, that is offensive, defensive and grey areas. Within such a frame, Harrier aircraft was rather a difficult item to sell, for the Russians had already warned that they would react quite sharply. Therefore, such an issue needed further discussion before taking any decision,[99] but the Chinese had also referred to advanced fighter aircraft, armed helicopters, air to air and air to ground missiles.[100]

The importance of the treaty signed with Japan was marked by the historic visit that Deng Xiaoping paid to Tokyo, addressing local and foreign correspondents at a press conference on 25 October, when he stressed once again the common threat of hegemonism, against which it had been the first time for an explicit anti-hegemony clause to be included in an international treaty. Such a stance was necessary to keep the peaceful environment China needed to pursue modernisation and an omni-directional foreign policy seeking friendship and trade with all countries.[101] Through this statement, we may realise that Deng was certainly pointing an enemy towards whom a containment circle was to be set up, but at the same time the door was not locked to at least a stable relation with the USSR, thus freezing tensions and all reasons to harm order in the Asia-Pacific region. In the late 1970s, Japan was not only one of China's closest neighbours, but also a highly developed economy from which the PRC was trying to easily transfer modern technology. The former arch-enemy was to become, if not a political ally, certainly an economic partner in China's drive for modernisation.[102] Deng's visit to Singapore was even more important, as it was not his practice to visit a country until Beijing had established full diplomatic relations. Uppermost in his mind was perhaps the trade with the former British colony. Second, the Soviet Union had already established diplomatic relations with Singapore in 1968 and a number of joint Soviet-Singaporean companies had been set up. Furthermore, Russian naval expansion and presence in the waters around

Singapore must have alarmed China. Therefore, the former British colony could not be ignored.[103] The importance of such a visit is confirmed by what Singapore's Prime Minister, Lee Kuan Yew, stated a few months afterwards, when he warned that the Chinese were not yet strong enough to counterbalance the Soviets. In order to achieve the necessary balance of power for the West and its allies to choose their own partners, the People's Republic needed something like fifteen to twenty years. Nonetheless, even if China was still a weak country on an international scale, Lee reminded that its leaders sought success, though he was not sure whether they realised what kind of global consequence the transformation of China could bear.[104]

At the same time, the People's Republic was looking at the United Kingdom to offer facilities for increasing exports, but was always ready to purchase from several sectors, such as power generating units, coal mining equipment, offshore oil prospecting and technology for the exploitation and extraction of rare earths. As far as Harrier aircraft was concerned, a model suitable to use along the Russian border with temperatures well below zero, Vice-Premier Wang Chen admitted that Beijing wished to buy the improved version, as well as its manufacturing licence.[105] This was a matter of great concern to Number 10, as the government had authorised British Aerospace to discuss the supply of Harriers with the Chinese, while the executive was going to discuss political aspects of the issue with their allies. Nevertheless, the United Kingdom did not have any intention to become only a military supplier to China.[106] As an evidence of this, London claimed to be delighted to assist the Asian country on how to make best use of economic resources, especially in the field of extraction, refining and petrochemical processing, since British Petroleum was already interested in this cooperation.[107] As far as Sino-UK relations are concerned, an important voice to hear is also that of Ma Zhengang, who served as director general in the Department of North American and Oceanian Affairs at the Chinese Ministry of Foreign Affairs, before being appointed ambassador to the United Kingdom in 1997. As a matter of fact, on addressing a conference on Sino-European relations he reminded how representative of Sino-British relations the military exchanges between the two sides were. In fact, in April 1978 Neil Cameron, the British Chief of Defence Staff, led a delegation to China. During his visit to the People's Liberation Army 6th Tank Division, Marshal Cameron said that Britain and China had a common enemy in Moscow and, if necessary, the two armies should join forces to challenge the Soviet tank force. Apart from negotiations on Harrier jets, there was also an agreement that Britain would help China remodel the J-7 fighter jet, the most advanced fighter plane the PRC had at the time.[108]

2.5 The Third Plenum of the Eleventh Central Committee

In order to thoroughly understand such a pivotal passage in the history of modern China, as well as highlighting the path towards an ongoing trading relation with the West, we cannot avoid quoting Ezra Vogel's work. Vogel reminds how Deng's trip to the Northeast of China in September 1978 helped activate dramatic changes. The old leader himself recalled that there had been three occasions during which he had lit a spark for reform and opening: (a) in November 1977 he had met PLA officials and civilians to liven up Guangdong economy; (b) in February 1978 he had discussed rural and urban reforms with Zhao Ziyang in Sichuan; (c) during his trip to the Northeast, he finally championed a daring departure from Maoism than Hua Guofeng's. Deng emphatically said that the Chinese system was basically taken from the Soviet Union, thus it was backward and bureaucratically superficial. The best thing to do, therefore, was growing faster than capitalist countries to show the superiority of the Chinese system.[109] On 10 November 1978, Hua Guofeng inaugurated the Central Work Conference of the Communist Party of China, leading the following month to the historic Third Plenum of the 11th Central Committee, with a speech announcing the three topics to debate, that is agriculture as the foundation of national economy,[110] economic development and the guidelines to follow. In short, he agreed that the international situation demanded to seize the moment to accelerate the pace of socialist modernisation, with several Third World countries hoping that China could quickly establish itself as a socialist modern power, while capitalists in Europe, Japan and North America were ready to strengthen their links and conduct more business with Beijing. On the one hand, said the premier, this tendency reflected the fact that the West was bogged down in an economic crisis and needed the Chinese market. On the other hand, a strong China was a way for European countries to contain Soviet hegemony. For the Asian State this raised the issue of absorbing foreign technology and capital in order to catch up with the world's advancements.[111] These words were followed by deeds, as we can read in a memorandum the secretary of energy addressed to President Carter after his trip to China, during which American technical teams had carried out extensive discussions on questions of coal, renewable energy, oil and gas, nuclear physics and magnetic fusion. The Chinese used these meetings to present a large number of energy projects with potentially lucrative commercial opportunities for US industry which the Department of Energy aimed at exploiting to ensure an effective and responsible follow-up.[112]

As far as the British were concerned, on 12 December at the House of Commons the minister of state for defence, John Gilbert, reported that the Harrier issue was closely connected with the deepening of the relationship with the People's Republic over a whole range of areas, but any defence sales were going to be part of a wider trade relationship. Whitehall was naturally well aware that China's modernisation programme included defence, and it was clearly prepared to help the Chinese, taking into account the usual political, strategic and international obligations.[113] A few days previously, a long debate had taken place at the House of Lords, on the occasion of which it had been underlined there was no other country in the world with such a trading potential. The British government, said Lord Goronwy-Roberts, welcomed Beijing's willingness to play a greater part in the world community and was ready to cooperate across a wide spectrum of activities. As regarded modernisation, the PRC's interest in Western Europe had been highlighted in the last couple of years, so that China's formerly reserved attitude towards foreign credit and joint ventures had been considerably eased.[114] While debates were being held at the Parliament, government ministers and officers met Chinese delegations to talk about business, such as Beijing's proposal of non-ferrous and raw materials supplies in exchange of help in exploration, mining and processing procedures.[115]

A historic breakthrough took place on 13 December, when Deng Xiaoping delivered his speech at the closing session of the Central Working Conference which made preparations for the Third Plenum that immediately followed. Actually, this speech served as the keynote address for the Third Plenary Session. In order to look forward and achieve modernisation, said Deng, it was essential to overcome the evils of bureaucracy and learn to manage the economy by economic means, studying from those who already did it. A pivotal passage was the one announcing Special Economic Zones, for the Chinese leader said that, pending the introduction of a unified national programme of modern management, it was possible to begin with a particular region or a given trade, and then spread the methods gradually to others. In economic policy, some regions and enterprises, as well as workers, had to be allowed to earn more and enjoy more benefits sooner than others, in order for that to be an impressive example to other people and regions.[116] Deng was disillusioned with Maoist revolutionary strategy emphasising politics at the expense of the economy. Therefore, to give a boost to the economy leaders had to reduce political interference, decentralise leadership to basic levels, adopt and differentiate responsibility, beside giving material incentives.[117] As far as decentralisation was concerned, Deng's remarks at the Central Work Conference were important both for what he did not say as for what he said. For example, he never mentioned the role of the market in reforming the economy. Instead, he preferred to emphasise decentralisation, but he failed to use phrases such as "running the economy according to economic laws".[118] Hua Guofeng's speech on the same day seemed to stress his anxiety about frictions within the party, as he claimed stability and unity to accelerate the pace of socialist modernisation. Under the new circumstances and given the new mission ahead, he quoted, it was extremely important to strengthen party unity and raise leadership standards, supposed to march to a single tune to be able to lead people to fight and build.[119] During Third Plenum days, Deng held four talks with the chief of the American Liaison Office in China, Leonard Woodcock, setting up the details of the communiqué establishing official diplomatic relations, and therefore playing a decisive role to move forward within the process of normalisation. With the culmination of diplomatic negotiations with the United States, the relationship entered a new stage, resulting in the development of political, technological, scientific and even military exchanges and cooperation.[120] A month afterwards, Vance and Brzezinski had a briefing with the press, highlighting the reasons why the administration had decided to move on the path of normalisation. A stable equilibrium among the United States, Japan, China and the Soviet Union was necessary to grant peace in the Indo-Pacific area, where the Anglo-Saxon power wanted to always play an active role. In consequence of that, the rapidly expanding relations with China required the kind of structure that diplomatic relations were able to provide. Therefore, Washington felt in a far better position to encourage Beijing's role as a constructive member of the world community. As it was easy to expect, economic benefits were supposed to flow, including American participation as a regular supplier of agricultural commodities to China, resumption of shipping, banking and other normal economic relations. The Carter administration admitted that the process of normalisation was only a recognition of the reality of East Asia and the increasing role China could play in world affairs. Washington considered its Asian counterpart as a key force for global peace simply by being what it was, that is an independent and strong nation remaining basically self-reliant. The United States had great economic and security interests around the rim of Asia. To protect such interests, almost nothing was better than a constructive involvement with China and the consequent favourable balance of power in the Far East.[121]

The Chinese government agreed that normalisation with the United States and the signing of the treaty with Japan were conducive to peace and stability in the Asia-Pacific region, though not implying the formation of any axis or alliance. However, Chairman Hua never forgot to stress that the new situation was also favourable to the struggle of all peoples against hegemonism.[122] By virtue of this, it was certainly not by chance that in the same days an editorial in the *Beijing Review* highlighted that the Vietnamese authorities believed that their country had become the first military power in Southeast Asia due to powerful armed forces and sophisticated weapons. Hanoi was being accused to not only want to rig up an Indochina federation playing the role of the boss, but also to arrogantly try to lord it over the whole of Southeast Asia. Such ambition of regional hegemonism had won the support of the Soviet Union, blamed of aiming at world domination through political subversion and armed invasion. In a few words, the Soviet Union was accused to have provided weapons, money and advisers to assist Vietnam in its aggression against Kampuchea, as well as trying to compel other Warsaw Pact countries to act likewise.[123] These statements leave no doubt on how the Chinese interpreted their relationship with the United States and Japan. Despite friendly words in general, Beijing's foreign policy target was always Moscow with its proxies in the Indo-Pacific area. In the meantime, on 22 December the 11th Central Committee of the Communist Party, summoned in its third plenary session, approved Deng's line both along the economic path and as far as the international posture was concerned. Expanding economic cooperation with capitalist countries on terms of equality and mutual benefit was by then pivotal to transform the system and methods of economic management, with agriculture to develop as fast as possible as the foundation of national economy.[124] Finally, a few words are important to understand the debate taking place within the Chinese leadership in those days. Zhao Ziyang's reflections are maybe what gives the idea about the watershed the People's Republic was living. Zhao said that he was enormously enthusiastic about Deng's reform programme, but he had reservations over emphasis on speed. What worried him the most was the danger that overemphasis on pace could give priority on high targets and speed at the expense of efficiency. Instead, he set relatively modest production targets with a higher level of economic efficiency.[125]

Notes

1 Albers, *Britain, France, West Germany*, 173–175.
2 'Resolution on the Report on the Work of the Government (Adopted on March 5, 1978)', *Peking Review*, 21/10, 1977, 8–40.
3 Yeh Chien-Ying, 'Report on the Revision of the Constitution (Delivered on March 1, 1978, at the First Session of the Fifth National People's Congress of the People's Republic of China)', Peking Review, 21/11, 1978, 15–28.
4 Hua Kuo-feng, 'Raise the Scientific and Cultural Level of the Entire Chinese Nation (Speech at the National Science Conference on March 24, 1978)', *Peking Review*, 21/13, 1978, 6–14.
5 Jeremy R. Azrael, Richard Löwenthal and Tohru Nakagawa, *Triangle Papers 15: An Overview of East-West Relations* (New York, NY, Tokyo and Paris: The Trilateral Commission, 1978), 12–15, 57–58, http://trilateral.org//download/doc/overview_east_west_relations.pdf, accessed 31 August 2021.
6 Sutter, *Chinese Foreign Relations Power and Policy since the Cold War*, Third Edition (Plymouth and Lanham, MD: Rowman & Littlefield Publishers, Inc., 2012), 77.
7 *Joint Memorandum by the Secretaries of State for Foreign and Commonwealth Affairs and Defence: Defence Sales to China*, 16 March 1978, SC 2/78, in NA, FCO 49/782, *Planning Paper on China*, Confidential.
8 House of Lords Debate, *China: Arms Export Policy*, 22 March 1978, https://hansard.parliament.uk/lords/1978-03-22/debates/fee4ebfb-f38d-45b2-a96d-800260387c3b/ChinaArmsExportPolicy, accessed 31 August 2021.
9 Naughton, *The Chinese Economy: Adaption and Growth*, 98–99.
10 Jacques, *When China Rules the World*, 177–180.
11 Yahuda, 'Deng Xiaoping: The Statesman', *The China Quarterly*, 34/135/3, 1993, 562.
12 Julian B. Gewirtz, *Unlikely Partners: Chinese Reformers, Western Economists, and the Making of Global China* (London and Cambridge, MA: Harvard University Press, 2017), 36.
13 *Meeting in the Far Eastern Department, MFA, Moscow, with Mr M.S. Kapitsa*, 11 April 1978, 3:00 p.m., in NA, FCO 28/3460, *Sino-Soviet Relations*, Confidential.
14 *Note of a Discussion with the Institute of the Far East, Moscow*, 12 April 1978, in NA, FCO 28/3460, Confidential.
15 Cabinet Defence and Oversea Policy (Official) Committee, Sub Committee on Strategic Exports, *Memorandum by the Foreign and Commonwealth Office:*

Sale of Harrier Aircraft to China, 17 April 1978, DOPO (SE) (78)4, in NA, FCO 28/3460, Confidential.

16 Visit of CDS to China, *Defence Sales: Steering Brief*, 20 April 1978, in NA, FCO 49/783, *Planning Paper on China*, Confidential.

17 *China: Foreign Trade Policy in the 1970s – A Research Paper*, August 1978, Secret, ER 78–10455, https://ia600808.us.archive.org/31/items/CIA-RDP80T00702A000 200060012-0/CIA-RDP80T00702A000200060012-0.pdf, accessed 10 December 2021.

18 *Record of a Meeting between Mr Sung Chin-Kuang, Assistant Foreign Minister of the People's Republic of China and Mr Hugh Cortazzi, Deputy Under Secretary of State at the Foreign and Commonwealth Office, at a Luncheon Held at the Residence of the British Ambassador in Peking*, 28 April 1978, in NA, FCO 21/1610, *UK-China Political Relations*, Confidential, UK Eyes A.

19 Lüthi, *Cold Wars*, 527–528.

20 Fenby, *The Penguin History of Modern China*, 536–537.

21 *Record of a Meeting in the Great Hall of the People between Chairman Hua Kuo-Feng and the Chief of the Defence Staff*, 30 April 1978, in NA, FCO 21/1610, Confidential.

22 Brzezinski, *Power and Principle*, 200–204.

23 Deng Xiaoping, 'Mao Zedong Thought Must Be correctly Understood as an Integral Whole', 21 July 1977, in *The Selected Works of Deng Xiaoping*, Vol. II, https://dengxiaopingworks.wordpress.com/2013/02/25/mao-zedong-thought-must-be-correctly-understood-as-an-integral-whole/, accessed 10 September 2021.

24 Fardella, *The Sino-American Normalization*, 555–557.

25 Kissinger, *World Order*, 227–231.

26 Ross, *Negotiating Cooperation*, 125–126.

27 Justin Vaïsse, *Zbigniew Brzezinski: America's Grand Strategist* (London and Cambridge, MA: Harvard University Press, 2018), 279–280.

28 *Trip to the Far East*, Washington, DC, 27 February 1978, in JCPL, National Security Affairs, Staff Material, Office, Outside the System File, Box 46, China: Brzezinski, May, 1978, Trip: 11/77-5/17/78, Top Secret.

29 *Memorandum from Secretary of Defense Brown to President Carter: Consultations with the PRC as a Response to Soviet Actions in the Horn of Africa*, Washington, DC, 11 March 1978, Secret, in FRUS 1977–1980, Vol. XIII, Doc. 83, 300–302.

30 *A Proposal for Asian Policy Adjustments*, Washington, DC, undated, in JCPL, National Security Affairs, Staff Material, Far East, Oksenberg Subject File, Box 43, Meetings: 1–3/78, Secret, Sensitive, Eyes Only.

31 Brzezinski, *Power and Principle*, 207–209.

32 *Summary of Dr. Brzezinski's Meeting with Foreign Minister Huang Hua*, Beijing, 20 May 1978, 3:30–6:40 p.m., in JCPL, National Security Affairs, Staff Material, Office, Outside the System File, Box 46, China: Brzezinski, May, 1978, Trip: 5/25/78-6/78, Top Secret, Sensitive.

33 Sutter, *US-Chinese Relations*, 78.

34 *Summary of Dr. Brzezinski's Meeting with Foreign Minister Huang Hua*, Beijing, 21 May 1978, 9:52 a.m.–1:20 p.m., in JCPL, National Security Affairs, Staff Material, Far East, Oksenberg Subject File, Box 56, Policy Process: 5/16-31/78, Top Secret, Sensitive.

35 *Meeting with Vice Premier Teng Hsiao P'ing*, Beijing, 21 May, 1978, 4:05–6:30 p.m., in JCPL, National Security Affairs, Staff Material, Office, Outside the System File, Box 46, China: Brzezinski, May, 1978, Trip: 5/28/78-6/78, Top Secret, Sensitive, Eyes Only.

36 *Summary of Dr. Brzezinski's Meeting with Chairman Hua Kuo-feng*, Beijing, 22 May 1978, 5:05–7:25 p.m., in JCPL, National Security Affairs, Staff Material, Office, Outside the System File, Box 46, China: Brzezinski, May, 1978, Trip: 5/18-24/78, Top Secret, Sensitive.

37 N. Sergeyev and V. Midtsev, Izvestia Article, *China and Developing Countries*, 20 May 1978, as Reported in British Embassy Moscow, *Soviet Comment on China*, 24 May 1978, 020/301/1, in NA, FCO 28/3460.

38 T. Alexandrev, Pravda Article, *Peking's Policy: Threat to Peace*, 13 June 1978, as reported in British Embassy Moscow, *Soviet Comment on China*, 19 June 1978, 020/301/1, in NA, FCO 28/3460.

39 *Record of a Meeting between the Foreign and Commonwealth Secretary and the Chinese Foreign Minister at the UN at 3:30 PM*, 1 June 1978, in NA, PREM 16/1534, *The Visit to the United Kingdom by Mr Huang Hua, the Chinese Foreign Minister*, Confidential.

40 *Record of a Meeting between HMA and He Ulanfu, Vice-Chairman of the NPC Standing Committee Following Presentation of Credentials in Peking*, 15 June 1978, 10 a.m., in NA, FCO21/1611, *UK-Sino Political Relations*, Restricted.

41 *Intelligence Assessment Prepared in the National Foreign Assessment Center, Central Intelligence Agency: The Peking-Hanoi-Phnom Penh Triangle Key Judgments*, Washington, DC, June 1978, RP 78-10267C, Secret, in FRUS 1977–1980, Vol. XIII, Doc. 125, 507–508.

42 *Appraisal of the China Trip*, Washington, DC, 25 May 1978, in JCPL, National Security Affairs, Staff Material, Far East, Oksenberg Subject File, Box 56, Policy Process: 5/16-31/78, Secret, Sensitive.

43 *Report on My China Visit (May 20–23)*, Washington, DC, 25 May 1978, in JCPL, National Security Affairs, Staff Material, Office, Outside the System File, Box 46, China: Brzezinski, May, 1978, Trip: 5/25/78-6/78, Top Secret, Sensitive.

44 Vance, *Hard Choices*, 116.

45 Breck Walker, 'Friends, but not Allies: Cyrus Vance and the Normalization of Relations with China', *Diplomatic History*, 33/4, 2009, 593.

46 *Secretary's Meeting with PRC Foreign Minister Huang*, New York, 2 June 1978, 10:55–11:55 p.m., in JCPL, National Security Affairs, Staff Material, Far East, Oksenberg Subject File, Box 56, Policy Process: 6-9/78, Secret, Nodis.

47 Rosemary Foot, 'Prizes Won, Opportunities Lost: The US Normalization of Relations with China, 1972–1979', in William C. Kirby, Robert S. Ross and Gong Li (eds.), *Normalization of US-China Relations: An International History* (London and Cambridge, MA: Harvard University Asia Center, 2005), 97.

48 *Summary of Dr. Brzezinski's Meeting with Ambassador Han Hsu*, Washington, DC, 19 June 1978, 11:30 a.m.-Noon, in JCPL, National Security Affairs, Staff Material, Far East, Oksenberg Subject File, Box 56, Policy Process: 6-9/78, Secret.

49 Bruce Cumings, 'The Political Economy of China's Turn outward', in Kim (ed.), *China and the World*, 242–243.

50 Minami, *Oil for the Lamps of America?*, 976–980.

51 Henry M. Jackson, 'The Geopolitics of China's Oil', *The New York Times*, 25 March 1978, https://www.nytimes.com/1978/03/25/archives/the-geopolitics-of-chinas-oil.html, accessed 11 September 2021.

52 Cohen, *America's Response to China*, 222.

53 *Record of a Meeting between HMA and Mr Sung Chih-Kuang, Assistant Minister of Foreign Affairs, at the Ministry of Foreign Affairs*, 23 June 1978, in NA, FCO 21/1611, Confidential.

54 *Record of a Conversation between the Minister of Foreign Affairs of the People's Republic of China and HMA Held in the Ministry of Foreign Affairs,* 28 June 1978, 11 a.m., in NA, FCO 21/1611, Restricted.

55 *EAJ Ferguson to Sir Curtis Keeble: Sino/Soviet Relations,* 30 June 1978, in NA, FCO 49/783, Personal and Confidential.

56 *Address by the Assistant Secretary of State for East Asian and Pacific Affairs (Holbrooke): Changing Perspectives of US Policy in East Asia,* Honolulu, 16 June 1978, in FRUS 1977–1980, Vol. I, Doc. 88, 418–428.

57 Shu Guang Zhang and Hua Zheng, 'Toward Technological Statecraft: Revisiting Beijing's Economic Statecraft in the 1980s', in Roberts (ed.), *Chinese Economic Statecraft,* 106–107.

58 *Peking Revisited,* British Embassy Peking, 7 August 1978, in NA, FCO 21/1611, Confidential.

59 *David Owen to the Prime Minister, Sino-British Relations,* 30 August 1978, PM/78/83, in NA, FCO 21/1611, Confidential.

60 'Vice-Chairman Li Hsien-nien on Finance and Trade', *Peking Review,* 21/30, 1978, 15–22.

61 Shu Guang Zhang and Hua Zheng, 'Toward Technological Statecraft', 93.

62 Li Jie, 'China's Domestic Politics and the Normalization of Sino-US Relations, 1969–1979', in Kirby, Ross and Gong (eds.), *Normalization of US-China Relations,* 81.

63 I. Alexandrov, *Pravda Article: In the Militarist Hysteria,* 5 August 1978, as Reported in British Embassy Moscow, *Further Soviet Attacks on China,* 9 August 1978, 020/301/1, in NA, FCO 28/3460, Restricted.

64 *KBA Scott to Mr Hibbert, Sino/Soviet Relations,* 1 September 1978, in NA, FCO 28/3460, Confidential.

65 Chi Su, 'China and the Soviet Union: Principled, Salutary, and Tempered Management of Conflict', in Kim (ed.), *China and the World,* 142–143.

66 *Evaluation by the Central Committee of the Communist Party of the Soviet Union of the Normalization of US-Chinese Relations,* 30 August 1978, https://digitalarchive.wilsoncenter.org/document/114809, accessed 9 September 2021.

67 Michael Dillon, *Contemporary China: An Introduction* (Abingdon and New York, NY: Routledge, 2009), 221.

68 As far as the territorial dispute about the Senkaku/Diaoyu Islands, Deng had adopted the strategy to prevent the sovereignty dispute from blocking the development of China-Japan relations. Mike M. Mochizuki, 'China-Japan Relations: Downward Spiral or a New Equilibrium?', in Shambaugh (ed.), *Power Shift: China and Asia's New Dynamics* (London, Berkeley and Los Angeles, CA: University of California Press, 2005), 145.

69 *The Triangular Relationship between China, Japan and the Soviet Union,* 29 August 1978, ISD/198, in NA, FCO 28/3460, NATO Confidential.

70 Tianbiao Zhu, 'Nationalism and Chinese Foreign Policy', *China Review,* 1/1, 2001, 17.

71 *Chinese Foreign Policy: Leaning to One Side Again-This Time our Side,* Washington, DC, 21 August 1978, in JCPL, National Security Council, NSC Institutional Files (H-Files), Box 42, PRM–24 [1], Top Secret, Codeword.

72 *JWB Richards to RE Allen: China's View of Soviet Global Strategy,* 25 September 1978, in NA, FCO 28/3461, Sino-Soviet Relations, Restricted.

73 *The Sino-Soviet Dispute,* 29 September 1978, in NA, FCO 28/3461, Confidential.

74 Deng had already criticised the 'Two Whatevers' theory the previous year, saying that it was absurd to mechanically apply what Mao had stated about a particular question to another question, or what he had affirmed under particular circumstances to other circumstances. The great leader himself had

repeatedly said that some of his own statements were wrong. Deng, 'The "Two Whatevers" Do not Accord with Marxism', 24 May 1977, in *The Selected Works of Deng Xiaoping*, Vol. II, https://dengxiaopingworks.wordpress.com/2013/02/25/the-two-whatevers-do-not-accord-with-marxism/, accessed 10 September 2021.

75 Richard Evans, *Deng Xiaoping and the Making of Modern China* (London: Penguin Books, 1995), 229.

76 Deng, 'Hold High the Banner of Mao Zedong Thought and Adhere to the Principle of Seeking Truth from Facts', 16 September 1978, in *The Selected Works of Deng Xiaoping*, Vol. II, https://dengxiaopingworks.wordpress.com/2013/02/25/hold-high-the-banner-of-mao-zedong-thought-and-adhere-to-the-principle-of-seeking-truth-from-facts/, accessed 10 September 2021.

77 Stuart R. Schram, 'Economics in Command? Ideology and Policy since the Third Plenum, 1978–84', *The China Quarterly*, 99/3, 1984, 419–420.

78 Deng, 'Update Enterprises with Advanced Technology and Managerial Expertise', 18 September 1978, in *The Selected Works of Deng Xiaoping*, Vol. II, https://dengxiaopingworks.wordpress.com/2013/02/25/update-enterprises-with-advanced-technology-and-managerial-expertise/, accessed 10 September 2021.

79 Huang Hua, 'The International Situation and China's Foreign Policies: Speech by Huang Hua, Chinese Foreign Minister and Chairman of the Chinese Delegation to the U.N. General Assembly', 28 September 1978, *Peking Review*, 21/40, 1978, 12–17, 35.

80 *Collective Leadership and Policymaking in Post-Mao China: Key Judgments*, RP 78-10392, Washington, DC, October 1978, in JCPL, National Security Affairs, Staff Material, Far East, Oksenberg Subject File, Box 49, Mondale 8/79 China Trip: Briefing Material: 3/78-8/79, Secret.

81 *Summary of Secretary Vance's Meeting with Foreign Minister Huang Hua*, New York, 3 October 1978, 6:55–11:55 p.m., in JCPL, National Security Affairs, Staff Material, Office, Outside the System File, Box 51, Chron: 10/1-7/78, Top Secret, Sensitive, Eyes Only, Alpha.

82 *Interagency Intelligence Memorandum: Sino-Soviet Cooperation in Indochina*, Washington, DC, 14 November 1978, NI IIM 78-10024, Secret, in FRUS 1977–1980, Vol. XIII, Doc. 152, 590–592.

83 *Chinese Attitude towards US-Vietnamese Relations*, Washington, DC, 21 November 1978, in JCPL, National Security Affairs, Staff Material, Far East, Oksenberg Subject File, Box 57, Policy Process: 10-11/78, Secret.

84 Deng, 'Carry out the Policy of Opening to the Outside World and Learn Advanced Science and Technology from other Countries', 10 October 1978, in *The Selected Works of Deng Xiaoping*, Vol. II, https://dengxiaopingworks.wordpress.com/2013/02/25/carry-out-the-policy-of-opening-to-the-outside-world-and-learn-advanced-science-and-technology-from-other-countries/, accessed 12 September 2021.

85 During the Mao Era, multinationals were viewed as a means of capitalist exploitation of poor countries and were debarred from conducting business in China. By contrast, Deng Xiaoping emphasised the positive role of inward flows of capital as an important catalyst of development. Ash, 'Europe's Commercial Relations with China', 194.

86 Lo Fu-wen, 'Can China Quicken Its Pace of Socialist Construction?', *Peking Review*, 21/45, 1978, 12–15.

87 *Visit of the Chinese Foreign Minister 10–14 October 1978, Brief No. 10: Bilateral Relations: Points to Make*, undated, in NA, PREM 16/1534, Confidential.

88 A few years later, Deng stressed that China should take advantage of economic difficulties in West European countries to import more technology. China provided a huge market, hence it was a matter of strategic importance to develop

cooperation or do business with all those countries wishing Beijing to develop. Zhang, *China's Commercial Relations with Europe*, 235–236.

89 *Visit of the Chinese Foreign Minister 10–14 October 1978, Brief No. 13: UK/ China Trade*, undated, in NA, PREM 16/1534, Confidential.

90 *Visit of the Chinese Foreign Minister 10–14 October 1978, Brief No. 14: Defence Sales to China*, undated, in NA, PREM 16/1534, Confidential.

91 *Record of the Prime Minister's Discussion with the Foreign Minister of the People's Republic of China, Mr. Huang Hua, at 10 Downing Street between 1630 and 1720*, 11 October 1978, in NA, PREM 16/1534, Confidential.

92 Min Song, 'A Dissonance in Mao's Revolution: Chinese Agricultural Imports from the United States, 1972–1978', *Diplomatic History*, 38/2, 2014, 428–429.

93 *Note of Meeting in Ashdown House on 11 October at 2.45 pm*, 13 October 1978, in NA, FCO 21/1616, *Visit of the Chinese Foreign Minister*, Confidential.

94 *Record of a Meeting between the Secretary of State for Foreign and Commonwealth Affairs and the Chinese Minister of Foreign Affairs, Held at the Foreign and Commonwealth Office on Wednesday, 11 October 1978, at 10.45 AM*, 18 October 1978, in NA, FCO 28/3461, Confidential.

95 *Record of a Meeting between the Secretary of State for Foreign and Commonwealth Affairs and the Chinese Minister of Foreign Affairs, Held at the Foreign and Commonwealth Office on Thursday, 12 October 1978, at 15.00 PM*, 18 October 1978, in NA, FCO 28/3461, Confidential.

96 *Prime Minister's Visit to Bonn 18–19 October 1978: Brief by Foreign and Commonwealth Office: Points to Make*, 12 October 1978, PMVM (78) 10, in NA, FCO 21/1611, Confidential.

97 *Chatham House Main Study Group on British Foreign Policy to 1985: On Playing the China Card*, 20 October 1978, in NA, FCO 21/1611, Confidential, Restricted.

98 *Cabinet Defence and Oversea Policy Committee, Memorandum by the Secretary of State for Foreign and Commonwealth Affairs, Annex A: The Sino-Soviet Dispute: Implications for the West*, 25 October 1978, in NA, FCO 49/ 783, Confidential.

99 *Cabinet Defence and Oversea Policy Committee, Memorandum by the Secretary of State for Foreign and Commonwealth Affairs: Sino/British Relations: Defence Sales*, 25 October 1978, DOJ (78) 20, in NA, FCO 49/783, Confidential.

100 *Cabinet Defence and Oversea Policy Committee, Memorandum by the Secretary of State for Foreign and Commonwealth Affairs, Annex B: Defence Sales to China*, 25 October 1978, DOJ (78) 20, in NA, FCO 49/783, Confidential.

101 'Vice-Premier Teng at Tokyo Press Conference: New Upsurge in Friendly Relations between China and Japan', *Peking Review*, 21/44, 1978, 14–17.

102 Dillon, *Deng Xiaoping*, 231–234.

103 Lee Lai To, 'Deng Xiaoping's ASEAN Tour: A Perspective on Sino-Southeast Asian Relations', *Contemporary Southeast Asia*, 3/1, 1981, 69–70.

104 Kissinger, *Leadership: sei lezioni di strategia globale* (Milano: Mondadori Libri S.p.A., 2022), 399.

105 *Note of a Meeting between the Secretary of State for Trade and Vice-Premier Wang Chen on 8 November 1978 at 10.30 AM*, 10 November 1978, in NA, PREM 16/1949, *Possible Visit to the UK by Chinese Vice-Premier Wang Chen*, Confidential.

106 *Record of Prime Minister's Discussion with Vice-Premier Wang Chen at 10 Downing Street between 16.15 and 17.25*, 16 November 1978, in NA, PREM 16/1949, Confidential.

107 *Note of a Meeting between the Secretary of State for Energy and Wang Chen, Vice-Premier of the People's Republic of China, Held in Room 1239, Thames House South on 8 November 1978*, 14 November 1978, in NA, T 370/1501, *Nationalised Industries Trade Agreements with China*, Confidential.

108 Enrico Fardella, Christian F. Ostermann and Charles Kraus (eds.), *Sino-European Relations during the Cold War and the Rise of a Multipolar World: A Critical Oral History*, Panel II, *The Sino-American Engagement and China's Relations with Western Europe*, Session II (Washington, DC: Woodrow Wilson International Center for Scholars, 2015), 117.

109 Ezra F. Vogel, *Deng Xiaoping and the Transformation of China* (London and Cambridge, MA: The Belknap Press of Harvard University Press, 2011), 227–228.

110 At the second plenary session Ji Dengkui, member of the Political Bureau and Vice Premier of the State Council, emphasised the question of low agriculture output, the overwhelming pressure of a growing population and the necessity to import grain due to insufficient domestic supply. China had to import ten million tons of grain for the following year, while the amount of money given in loans to agriculture was supposed to double. Yu Guangyuan, *Deng Xiaoping Shakes the World: An Eyewitness Account of China's Party Work Conference and the Third Plenum* (Manchester: Eastbridge Books, 2017), 39–41.

111 *Hua Guofeng's Speech at the Opening Session of the CCP Central Work Conference*, 10 November 1978, History and Public Policy Program Digital Archive, Hubei Provincial Archives SZ1-4-791, https://digitalarchive.wilsoncenter.org/document/121688.pdf?v=d4d2d74e67b8fca3c471886b19386eaf, accessed 16 September 2021.

112 *Report on Technical Discussions on Energy Cooperation with China*, Washington, DC, 27 November 1978, in JCPL, National Security Affairs, Brzezinski Material, Country File, Box 8, China (People's Republic of): 9-11/78, Confidential.

113 *House of Commons Debate: Harrier Aircraft (Sale To China)*, 12 December 1978, https://hansard.parliament.uk/Commons/1978-12-12/debates/3496f6a9-1549-45ed-93ef-bbba48b42b19/HarrierAircraft(SaleToChina), accessed 17 September 2021.

114 *House of Lords Debate: China-Relations with the United Kingdom*, 6 December 1978, https://hansard.parliament.uk/Lords/1978-12-06/debates/80b00412-8251-46c3-9305-9d7ef91b64f8/ChinaRelationsWithTheUnitedKingdom, acccsscd 17 September 2021.

115 *Note of a Meeting Held on Tuesday 12 December 1978*, 14 December 1978, in NA, PREM 16/1949, Confidential.

116 Deng, 'Emancipate the Mind, Seek Truth from Facts and Unite as One in Looking to the Future, 13 December 1978', in *The Selected Works of Deng Xiaoping*, Vol. II, https://dengxiaopingworks.wordpress.com/2013/02/25/emancipate-the-mind-seek-truth-from-facts-and-unite-as-one-in-looking-to-the-future/, accessed 17 September 2021.

117 His-Sheng Ch'i, *Politics of Disillusionment. The Chinese Communist Party under Deng Xiaoping, 1978–1989* (London and Armonk, NY: M.E. Sharpe, Inc., 1991), 15–16.

118 Bachman, *Differing Visions of China's Post-Mao Economy*, 305–306.

119 *Hua Guofeng's Speech at the Closing Session of the CCP Central Work Conference*, 13 December 1978, History and Public Policy Program Digital Archive, Hubei Provincial Archives SZ1-4-791, https://digitalarchive.wilsoncenter.org/document/121690.pdf?v=5597447f39898cc07e3423843d51ef3, accessed 17 September 2021.

120 Gong Li, 'The Difficult Path to Diplomatic Relations: China's US Policy, 1972–1978', in Kirby, Ross and Gong (eds.), *Normalization of US-China Relations*, 141–145.
121 'East Asia: US Role in Its Stability', in Department of State Bulletin, 79/2023, February 1979, 14–21.
122 'Chairman Hua Gives Press Conference', *Peking Review*, 21/51, 1978, 9–11.
123 'Soviet and Vietnamese Hegemonists' True Colours', *Peking Review*, 21/51, 1978, 16–19.
124 'Communiqué of the Third Plenary Session of the 11th Central Committee of the Communist Party of China, Adopted on December 22, 1978', *Peking Review*, 21/52, 1978, 7–16.
125 Bao Pu, Renee Chiang and Adi Ignatius (eds.), *Prisoner of the State: The Secret Journal of Zhao Ziyang* (New York, NY: Simon & Schuster, 2009), 92.

3 The Policy of Adjustment

3.1 Deng Xiaoping's Visit to the United States

Henry Kissinger's assessment of Third Plenum conclusions is that the break with Maoist orthodoxy revealed the reformer's dilemma, that is most revolutions occur in opposition to what is perceived as abuse of power. However, the more existing obligations are dismantled, the more force is necessary to re-create a sense of obligation. Deng Xiaoping was seeking to preserve one-party rule not because he enjoyed power so much, rather, because he believed the alternative was anarchy.[1] While Deng was delivering his address at the Central Work Conference, the British Embassy to the Chinese capital issued a report describing the present juncture as the most hopeful moment for many decades, though it was important not to forget that China was still a communist state lumbered with Mao's legacy. The Asian nation was assessed to be well placed to at last approach learning from advanced Western states and overcome economic backwardness. Deng was expected to become increasingly dominant, and this is what was needed for modernisation to go ahead at full speed and thus adopt economic policies which in China were quite unorthodox. Nevertheless, it was impossible for anyone, including Deng, to completely deny the legacy of Mao, as this was supposed to leave a void greater than the one left in the USSR after the denunciation of Stalin.[2] At the beginning of 1979, Deng distanced himself from a faulty economic plan with which he was closely associated, and embraced economic ideas with which he had no past association. Not a long time afterwards, he was able to promote Zhao Ziyang as Premier, placing an effective administrator in the key economic policy-making role.[3] In a country where eighty per cent of the population still worked in the countryside, the economy was always vulnerable, especially because in 1978 there had been only marginal improvement. As far as agricultural reforms were concerned, communes were dissolved and farmer families received land under the so-called household responsibility system, providing them with a kind of long-term lease allowing to work the land on their own, while obliging them to sell a part of their harvest to the state at fixed prices. This reform freed dynamic forces and brought about growth and diversification in agricultural production.[4] Modernisation suggested an

DOI: 10.4324/9781003390138-4

export bonanza of Middle East proportions, thus causing worries about the Chinese capacity to absorb and finance imports on such a large scale. What seemed to be happening was that central authorities were going to formulate an ideal package to then downsize to a manageable level. A Science and Technology Agreement had been signed between the United Kingdom and the People's Republic of China (PRC), and British exports in 1978 were likely to increase by almost one-third compared with the previous year. The balanced relationship the British government was thinking about was not going to forbid the supply of military equipment.[5] As a matter of fact, the defence supply issue was very serious and delicate to deal with, but Britain could not ignore that the perceived Soviet military threat had been the basic stimulus for the PRC to talk and seek normalisation. Hence, the rapprochement with Washington alleviated China's concerns on the external security environment, especially military pressure from Northern borders. In a word, Beijing started playing an indispensable role in American security policy,[6] which certainly encouraged arms supplies, even though not offensive ones.

Meanwhile, in early January Deng met a US Congress delegation to discuss the effort to give China the Most Favoured Nation tariff treatment, which the Chinese vice premier said it was a pivotal condition to augment import of advanced technology from the United States, as the removal of those restrictions was also supposed to improve Beijing's ability to pay for imported goods. Deng said that first of all China needed oil fields, as well as oil and water power. On agriculture, instead, what was more urgent was the necessity to increase the output per acre.[7] On the other hand, stability in Asia and along the Pacific area was a major US objective, whose achievement depended on the establishment of full diplomatic relations with the PRC. As far as economic relations were concerned, the secretary of state mentioned that the United States expected regular supplies of agriculture commodities to the Asian country and the resumption of shipping, air and banking activities.[8] Nevertheless, the British Foreign Office noticed that the PRC's public line on the inevitability of war had changed a bit, for the communiqué adopted by the Third Plenum only stated that the grave danger of war still existed, thus acquiring a less anxious stance on the international chessboard.[9] Actually, the issue of Most Favoured Nation and export credits was essential to the kind of relation the Americans were seeking with China. However, said Secretary Vance, extending MFN to Beijing and not doing so for the Soviet Union was thought to involve the administration in a sort of "China tilt". MFN status, on the other hand, was also reminded by Secretary Blumenthal, according to whom regular economic relations were impossible to establish without ExIm Bank financing.[10]

Such words were aligned with Deng Xiaoping's statements to American journalists. In short, several forms of cooperation were expected with the United States, as well as Western Europe and Japan, including bank loans and compensatory trade.[11] China and the United States were said to have many points in common on political questions and on issues of global strategy, such as combating hegemonism and defending world peace. Moreover, Beijing needed a peaceful international environment to better learn from countries more advanced in science and technology.[12] To tell the truth, before departing for Washington Deng proposed China, Japan and the United States to further develop the relationship, therefore getting united to place curbs on the Bear. As a matter of fact, a Chinese leader had never so openly suggested a strong strategic association with the Americans, thus starkly depicting China's pro-NATO alignment against the Soviets.[13] On the other hand, the Soviets argued that it was difficult to believe that the United States was forging a proper anti-Soviet alliance with Beijing, but still China was about to be used as a useful means to put pressure on Moscow. In addition, Western weapons sales could stimulate an arms race in Asia, as the successors of Mao knew very well that agreements with the Americans would quickly open the door to Western European markets.[14] As far as Washington was concerned, the Izvestia said the deal with the PRC would strengthen its positions in the region. What Russian papers really criticised, however, was American big businesses' intention to squeeze everything they could from the Chinese modernisation process. North American capitalism, in fact, was said to have expressed dissatisfaction about being excluded from such a huge market.[15] By reading American statements, instead, we realise how the administration wanted to keep stability by avoiding to fan on fire. Balance among Japan, China, the USSR and the United States had to be guaranteed through the necessary flexibility. Therefore, good relations with both communist powers were important to keep the Indo-Pacific area as stable and quiet as possible.[16]

What was objective, we can read in a memorandum for the president just before Deng's visit to the United States, was that for the first time in the post-war era the Atlantic superpower had better relations with Japan, China and India than any of those states had with the Soviet Union, thus enjoying a good outlook on stability for the region and protection of American political and economic interests. In that context, while Brezhnev had delayed SALT agreement and his visit to Washington with the purpose to discourage a "China tilt" in US policy, Deng's interests were to postpone the conclusion of SALT and to limit détente mood to heighten Soviet-American tension and therefore increasing China's tactical value to the United States. Although the Carter administration aimed at improving relations with both Beijing and Moscow, the two capitals did not have to be equated, as it was only the Soviet Union threatening the US militarily and encouraging war by proxies. The Chinese counterstrategy was to foster a line of containment against Soviet expansionism stretching from Japan through China, Pakistan, Iran and Turkey to NATO, all backed by the United States. In a nutshell, the American long-term objective was to include China in the international framework of key nations. A world ordered through a Soviet-American condominium was not possible due to dispersal of power, but national security could be partly attained by cultivating good relations with newly emerging countries, none of which was more important than China. However, in order to encourage the

Chinese to commit themselves to a more binding relationship with the United States, they had to be confident that Washington had an adequate strategy for countering Soviet efforts to establish a position of global prominence. In short, the Americans shared the view that the Soviet Union was the major threat to a "world of diversity".[17]

On the other hand, in opposition to Washington's use of the "China card", the Soviets tickled Chinese nationalism, pointing out that for American plans the Asian nation was just an object, not a subject, of international relations. Instead, Moscow was proposing to set some key principles to base the relations with China on.[18] In particular, what Brezhnev accused the Americans of was that attempts were being made to encourage with an economic bait, as well as with deliveries of modern weapons, those who had declared their hostility to détente and disarmament.[19] According to Secretary Vance, Deng's central direction aimed at putting pressure for the most vigorous resistance to the expansion of Soviet power. Deng's final objective, we may read in a memorandum for President Carter, dealt with maximising American hostility to the Vietnamese by portraying them as Soviet surrogates. On the contrary, Vance highlighted that rapidly ex-panding relations with China were important to Washington to draw Beijing further into involvement with the community of primarily non-Communist nations. As far as this was concerned, important to notice is how the sec-retary thought the White House had to involve also Hua in such a process, in order not to rely only on Deng Xiaoping.[20] From the British point of view, London had the necessity to have a close relationship with China in a wider context involving other countries of immediate importance, but there was no alternative to treating Beijing as a world power, since it was a permanent member of the United Nations Security Council, with about one-quarter of the world population and traditions and resources making it formidable despite economic and demographic problems. In short, the internalisation of China's policies was an interest Britain shared with the West as a whole. In the trade field in particular, such a stance offered room for substantial contacts and there was no reason why the United Kingdom should give up the chance to compete with European partners and the United States.[21] However, rapid industrialisation was thought to impose a heavy burden of foreign borrowing and London had to be determined to secure orders which China could not obtain from the United States, or other countries like Japan and the Federal Republic of Germany.[22]

The Chinese leader had his first meeting with President Carter on 29 January, and, as it was easy to predict, he immediately promoted anti-Soviet policy by warning that Moscow was seeking to get bases in key countries such as Afghanistan, Iran, Vietnam. In a few words, the Soviet Union was accused of attempting to build positions of strength in the East and in the West linked by the sea. Consequently, Deng thought it was effective for Western Europe, China, Japan and the United States to unite in order to deal with that threat. Under such a premise, the Chinese government was not recommending the establishment of a formal alliance, but it was of paramount importance to coordinate activities and adopt necessary measures.[23] Carter agreed that it would be a mistake to form an alliance against the Soviet Union, but it was also true that there were many areas of the world where it was possible to act in concert, since the USSR was getting increasingly isolated from formal allies and friends.[24] To tell the truth, it seems Dr. Brzezinski fanned on fire when he said there was some indication that the Soviets had increased their ground forces near the Chinese frontier,[25] but what concerned Deng the most was the situation in Vietnam, which he said had become totally Soviet-controlled, and whose plan to establish an Indochinese Federation under Vietnamese control was regarded as more threatening than the Americans could think. Obviously, the Kremlin was supposed to make use of Vietnam to harass China, thus Beijing had no choice but disrupt Soviet strategic dispositions by punishing the Vietnamese over a short period of time. As a matter of fact, the president neither encouraged, nor tried to dissuade China from taking any particular initiative, so that Carter said *à la* Pontius Pilate that he did not even need to know what punishment Beijing had in mind.[26] He simply warned that it could result in escalation of violence and a change in the world posture to partial support for Vietnam.[27] Probably, the most important meeting took place on 31 January between Deng and US economic ministers. First of all, solving the agriculture output problem was pivotal to carry out modernisation, thus Secretary Blumenthal stated that an agreement in the area of science and technology would be signed in those same days. Such a deal was therefore supposed to lead to commercial activities.[28] To tell the truth, there were some Americans sceptical about the outlook for the People's Republic to learn from the democratic tradition of American life. Rather, Deng was accused of being interested in the United States only as a source of technology and trading opportunities to help his own country build a modern future.[29] On this particular question, Lu Sun's remarks are that Deng deliberately emphasised the economic factor of Sino-American relations in order to bypass ideological differences and postpone the Taiwan issue. As an outcome of that, bilateral trade relations between the two nations deepened, thus producing breakthrough on a broad range of subjects.[30]

As far as the British were concerned, the Embassy in Washington clearly stressed the threat of Soviet hegemonism to international peace as Deng's main foreign policy issue, for Chinese media wrote that friendly ties across the Pacific Ocean would change the pattern of international relations,[31] of course without ignoring the importance the Americans gave to trading relations, as it was shown by the agreements signed and the old leader's tour of key factories of US industry, such as Ford Motor Company outside Atlanta, Lyndon Johnson Space Center at Houston, and Boeing plant in Seattle. In order to understand the Chinese perception of Soviet threats, suffice it to quote the attention paid to the Straits of Malacca, which gave the idea of encirclement against Beijing's sea routes. In summary, China's foreign trade was expected to increase by ten-twenty per cent each year, while the most immediate benefit in the US administration's view was probably the Chinese policy to treat the United States as a residual supplier, purchasing Uncle Sam's goods only when similar products were not available in countries with which earlier trading relations had been established.[32] Furthermore, projects under discussion included off-shore oil machinery, mining procedures, steel plants, hydroelectric facilities, transport equipment and agriculture programmes. As a matter of fact, the outlook of a market formed of a quarter of the world population was thought to be blinding American business to the low Chinese per capita income.[33] To tell the truth, Whitehall was not really worried about possible Soviet reactions to the British behaviour, as China was not expected to become a real danger to the Russians for the following twenty or thirty years. In any case, it was important to London that Moscow should not win a victory over the Chinese, as this could alter the balance between the West and the communist world.[34]

Maybe Western powers did not seek to play a Chinese card against the Soviet Union, but certainly a sharp balance of power between the two main socialist nations was something positive for Atlantic interests. Those words were likely referring to the Economic Cooperation Agreement signed in February between Britain and the PRC, so much so that Vice Premier Wang Zhen had to point out that it was necessary to slow down the trade flow coming from the United Kingdom in order to let China absorb it quickly. The crux of the question was that Beijing wanted to develop imports in step with exports, being ready to accept foreign loans but keeping the chance to repay them when they became due. At the moment, Chinese exports were mainly focused on agricultural products, raw materials and textiles. As regarded minerals, Chinese technology was rather obsolete, thus it was necessary to increase output through the assistance of British companies.[35] Hence, Sino-British trade was supposed to double in the following two years, said Minister of Foreign Trade Li Chiang, due to deals in several fields, such as energy, aeronautics, mining, telecommunications, information technology. To achieve this, China had to pay advanced technology by increasing exports making use of cheap labour.[36] Moreover, the Bank of China was expected to do everything possible to facilitate contracts negotiated by British industries in the PRC, while on the question of credits government departments were to instruct the Bank to make all necessary arrangements.[37] In order to understand how the British were eager to increase business with China, it is important to consider that members of the government were joined by industrialists in the discussions taking place in Beijing. In short, China's modernisation programme provided British firms with a special opportunity to supply highly advanced machine tools. Secondly, there was the chance to collaborate with the Chinese to licence the manufacture of certain machinery in China. Thirdly, it was imperative not only to modernise plants, but also production methods.[38] As for non-ferrous metals, Britain so far had been obliged to purchase such raw materials from politically unstable countries. Therefore, diversifying sources of supply was of paramount importance.[39]

In particular, non-ferrous metals were regarded as a pivotal area of collaboration, as China was rich in mineral resources and UK companies were ready to undertake mining and processing development for various projects. It is essential to notice the prediction that the estimated output was ten times the initial capital investment.[40] Furthermore, the exploitation of mineral resources and raw materials could be an opportunity for China to earn foreign currency useful to pay necessary imports.[41] The Asian country was also rich in coal resources, and therefore the PRC welcomed Britain's offer of assistance in the long-term development of that industry,[42] also highlighting that Chinese ministers had expressed their interest in joint collaboration ventures in many different fields. Therefore, it was possible to expect such enterprises to have been established in China by 1985.[43] Such optimistic outlook was due to the 14-billion-dollar-agreement signed during the talks, as well as a credit facility for another five billion dollars. A major theme the Chinese carried out during the negotiations dealt with their concern not to financially over-extend themselves in the modernisation drive. Loans were welcome, of course, but in order to repay them Beijing's exports had to be increased as much as possible.[44] As far as economic reform was concerned, Barry Naughton says that China's leaders had begun such a process without a road map or even a clear destination. At first they only aimed at reducing the power of planners, lowering entry barriers and giving ordinary people some decision-making authority.[45] However it was, the establishment of formal diplomatic relations between the People's Republic and the United States had set in motion a process of fruitful negotiations involving the world of business and the government of communist China, eager to join market forces to modernise the economy and thus play a major role on the regional and then global scenario. This was also shown by the interview that Han Gua, vice minister in charge of the State Capital Construction Commission, gave to the *Beijing Review* on the development of modern industry in China. To improve the ability to pay, he said, exports needed to be expanded, thus mainly relying on itself while making external assistance subsidiary.[46]

As regarded Soviet containment, the Middle East, the Persian Gulf and the Red Sea were the places were Moscow's contention was mostly perceived, as well as the area of Indochina, where the Soviets were accused of seeking military bases to expand their influence on the Pacific region and the Indian Ocean.[47] The People's Republic sought peace, said Deng Xiaoping addressing US organisations, in which each country had the chance to develop and make progress free from aggression, interference and bullying. China was also in favour of détente, provided it was not used as a pretext to carry out aggression and expansion.[48] As far as this is concerned, Alexander Pantsov thinks that it was possible for Deng to really fear the Soviet Union to encircle the PRC with military bases along the entire border. Probably, he also could not forgive Vietnamese leaders, who had been manoeuvring between the USSR and the

PRC and then gradually sided with the Soviets mainly because, according to the Chinese, during the Cultural Revolution Beijing could not provide them with substantial aid.[49] Such allegations described the so-called southward strategy (nanxia zhanlue) of Soviet hegemonism as a way to outflank Western Europe and disrupt energy supplies through the Middle East. This thrust was said to be focused on a secondary geopolitical offensive in the East-Asian area, nicknamed the dumbbell strategy, aiming at the Strait of Malacca as a mid-point of a strategic bar joining Soviet naval activities in the Indian and Pacific Ocean.[50] In virtue of that, Hua Guofeng stressed the importance for China of a stable and peaceful international environment. That was why Soviet hegemonism was accused to interfere in the economic development of Beijing and its trading relations with the West.[51]

3.2 Economic and Security Cooperation

What is essential to notice about the balance of power in the Far East, is that the Chinese invasion of Vietnam, begun on 17 February 1979, showed how poorly Beijing's armed forces were able to perform. Shortly afterwards, China withdrew from the neighbouring country, but nevertheless the Dragon had also demonstrated that the Soviet Union had not been able to protect its Vietnamese ally.[52] Furthermore, the Vietnamese invasion of its Cambodian neighbour had violated the unspoken norm of ASEAN members, opposing the invasion of one Southeast Asian State by another country of the region. Consequently, Hanoi had been isolated at the UN General Assembly.[53] On the other hand, the Socialist Republic of Vietnam believed that the People's Republic of China was pursuing a policy of expansionism against socialism, thus jeopardising stability in Southeast Asia and the world. However, as Sergey Radchenko says, China's punitive strike and veiled alliance with ASEAN had worked, since Vietnam gave up pursuing revolutionary dreams in the region in the following years.[54] At the same time, we must not ignore that Moscow was persuaded that the communist rival was about to join NATO in an attempt to encircle the Soviet Union. Therefore, in the first stage of the war Leonid I. Brezhnev informed the US president that the USSR could not remain neutral, thus ordering troop movements at China's northern border. As a matter of fact, the Cambodian crisis and the following Afghanistan counterpart drove the PRC further away from the USSR. As Lorenz Lüthi reports, a Chinese spokesman called on the world to stop appeasing the USSR as long as it was big and dangerous.[55]

Meanwhile, in order to highlight what sort of competition normalisation had provoked, suffice it to quote that American economic officers and government representatives had travelled to China in the same days as the British. In light of this, the White House had to decide whether MFN status for China should be extended, as well as ExIm Bank financing. Moreover, once Britain had signed the economic agreement with the PRC, a trade deal with the United States was desirable as well.[56] Such moves were even more urgent if we consider that in those days the PRC government had set up the new Finance and Economics Committee, with broad oversight of the economy, a step which within a few weeks led to the emerging of Special Economic Zones.[57] At the same time, the Sino-Vietnamese conflict, and the consequent further heightening of Sino-Soviet tensions, was said to have created a situation in which Moscow's feud with Beijing threatened to involve East Asian security matters of direct concern to American interests. Washington had already developed a sort of security relationship with the People's Republic. In the last two years, some more direct security dealings had been arranged, by exchanging views on a wide range of issues and providing the Chinese information on Soviet military capabilities, and not objecting to third country arms sales to China, as well as responding to Chinese requests of purchase of dual-use technology. However, American analyses estimated that gratifying somehow Beijing's interest in acquiring Western arms and advanced technology might affect US-Soviet relations and enhance concerns in Japan and Southeast Asia about the possibility of a Sino-Soviet confrontation. On grounds of that, American policy was to reconcile these conflicting tendencies, seeking to strengthen ties with the Chinese to inhibit Soviet actions, but avoiding gratuitously provoking Moscow or stimulating concerns on the part of Asian allies.[58] Therefore, it seemed there were two distinct reasons for seeking to improve security relations with communist China. First of all, security issues could be useful to improve bilateral relations and minimise the prospect of a Sino-Soviet reconciliation. Secondly, US-PRC security relations were likely to provide some leverage over Soviet behaviour, presuming the Soviets were sufficiently concerned about the future course of Sino-American developments.[59]

In the meantime, the Chinese approach to the economy was gradually developing towards a more balanced stance. Soon after the Third Plenum, in fact, Deng had ordered his managers to lower some planning targets in order to avoid large foreign trade debts and give priority to projects likely providing quick returns on investments, thus accumulating capital before undertaking any programme. In a few words, Deng had decided to back the advocates of a more balanced budget, therefore acknowledging the importance to put the economy on a solid base. As far as this was concerned, at the end of 1978 the Chinese State had only four billion dollars in foreign currency reserves, hence realising that the original goals for modernisation were too ambitious and that the details for implementing them were not so clear.[60] According to Ezra Vogel, the other reason influencing Deng's economic thinking was that the attack to Vietnam would be a further drain on the budget. As a matter of fact, by March 1979 enough data and analyses had been collected to present proposals for cutting back contracts to import foreign plants and lowering economic targets for the following years. In particular, a formal document was introduced to propose two or three years of readjustment, whose need was explained at the Politburo meeting of 21–23 March 1979. In short, balanced development was necessary, first of all considering agriculture and making sure to make the repayments for imported goods and technology.[61]

A few days later, on 30 March, Deng Xiaoping announced the so-called policy of adjustment in order for the economy to change from varying degrees of imbalance to relative balance. The new path aimed at laying a solid foundation for the four modernisations, though it was necessary to make a partial retreat. The party acknowledged some unrealistically high targets had been set, which needed to be resolutely lowered. At the same time, some ill-managed enterprises running at a heavy loss had to be consolidated or even temporarily shut down. Due to a low starting point, China was still regarded as one of the world's poor countries, with scientific and technological forces far from adequate. Secondly, arable land was not enough to produce for the whole population, thus posing serious problems with regard to food, education and employment. Furthermore, the territory was rich of natural resources, but many of them had not been surveyed and exploited yet. What Deng stressed was that socialism was not responsible for China's backwardness. Despite mistakes, he carried on, progress had been made in the previous decades on a scale which allowed the economy to attain a fairly high rate of growth. Now that experience had been summed up and errors corrected, development was expected to run more rapidly than any capitalist country in a steady and sustained way. Despite the superiority of socialism, the Chinese leader realised that capitalism had already a history of several hundred years, therefore it was normal for the Asian country to learn from the peoples of the capitalist nations. In a nutshell, whatever was progressive and useful in capitalist countries had to be introduced into China.[62] Deng Xiaoping was following the ideas of Chen Yun, who had been the architect of the second Five-Year Plan rejected by Mao in favour of the strategy of the Great Leap Forward. A key principle in both Chen's and Deng's thought was that the over-bureaucratised state machinery was simply not up to running the production process in a modernising economy. Instead, they proposed that production units should be given more autonomy in management. Even more important was the establishment of Special Economic Zones (SEZ), originally proposed at the major Central Work Conference to discuss economic reforms in April 1979, and designed as areas with an economic and fiscal environment advantageous to foreign entrepreneurs and that would attract foreign technology and investment. Deng proposed that they be set up in the Southern provinces of Guangdong and Fujian, not only because they were adjacent to Hong Kong and Taiwan respectively, but also because these were the provinces which had historically acted as China's gateways to the rest of the world.[63] The document giving birth to Special Economic Zones and issued by the Central Committee was classified as 1979.50. Such a record literally began experimentation with the policy of decentralisation and outward-oriented development. In particular, Lawrence C. Reardon says that Guangdong Party leaders had taken advantage of their personal connections with Deng in order to claim greater provincial authority over economic and foreign trade plans, thus hoping to harness overseas Chinese capital to build infrastructures and accelerate development.[64] As far as the relationship between Deng and Chen was concerned, Zhao Ziyang reminds that the latter had always objected to the idea of SEZs. Moreover, on the issue of foreign investments Chen was completely in conflict with Deng, who thought it was difficult for a developing economy like China's to take off without foreign investment. Instead, Chen Yun was very cautious about that, being persuaded that they were not the solution for the development of the Middle Kingdom.[65]

The Central Work Conference was particularly notable for canvassing other important reforms, such as financial decentralisation, enterprise autonomy and greater reliance on the market. The main source of contention, however, was readjustment, with supporters of heavy industry arguing that investment in that sector was necessary to underpin light industry.[66] The logic of the light industry programme was publicised by Dong Fureng, an economist of the PRC Academy of Social Sciences. Instead of plans decided on a political level, markets were thought to be much better allocators of goods and services. Moreover, he spelled out the appropriate foreign economic policy to carry out reforms, that is close economic relations with advanced industrialised countries, using foreign capitals, loans, aid, as well as setting up processing zones where imported goods were assembled or finished. Finally, China was supposed to restructure the economy with special attention to light industry and textiles where start-up costs were low, energy consumption was lower and quick returns were able to generate foreign exchange. In April 1979, Foreign Trade Minister Li Qiang said the PRC should seek technical help in heavy industrial sectors, while increasing export of light-industry goods, also by making use of joint ventures.[67] Recent historiography states there were manifold reasons why Deng accepted Chen's ideas. The most plausible motivation seems to be that, while the budget was in surplus at the end of 1978, payments for purchases of foreign technology and equipment could not be met. Other commitments would have also been major drains on the budget, for example the decision to increase the purchase price of agricultural products, as well as wage and defence spending increases. Perhaps there was also a political explanation, that is Deng may have decided to develop a tacit alliance with Chen against Hua Guofeng, as we must not forget that Chen had provided important support to Deng with regard to launching the war against Vietnam.[68] Advanced technology from foreign countries was always welcome, of course, but production had to be increased in order to implement the policy of exporting first and trying to achieve a balance between imports and exports. Cooperation with foreign companies could be undertaken in power industry, energy resources, communication and transport, raw materials processing, iron and steel industry.[69] In particular, by making use of technological achievements of others it was possible for China to bypass a good part of the process of research and experimentation, while at the same time raising technological level. The Asian country enjoyed a good potential of export commodities and many ways to accumulate hard currency were possible, such as exporting oil, coal and non ferrous minerals. Joint enterprises were also pivotal to introduce technology.[70] The main controversy occurred around the market issue, long been regarded as the antithesis of socialism. Some argued that planned economy and market economy should integrate with each other. Others held that socialist market economy constituted a new form of market economy based on public ownership of the means of production.[71]

According to Barry Naughton, reorientation of the economy was attractive because it provided a way to cope simultaneously with several problems, such as agriculture, energy and employment. China's leaders believed agricultural problems could be addressed through liberalising rural economic policy and releasing resources previously gone to heavy industrial development. Apart from that, it was necessary to shift the structure of industrial output away from energy intensive investment and towards labour-intensive and energy-frugal consumption goods. Finally, jobs had to be provided to millions and millions of young people who had been urbanised in the previous years, and the most effective way was through the rapid expansion of the labour-intensive light manufacturing and service sectors.[72] Though not directly related, this was accompanied by a shift in foreign policy, since the PRC was turning towards the United States as the main model and outside driving force of the modernisation process, thus reducing the importance of Sino-European relations for Beijing. Nevertheless, maintaining close ties with London, Paris and Bonn remained crucial for keeping up pressure on Moscow and tapping into the resources of the advanced economies of Europe.[73] As regarded foreign trade, Gregory C. Chow reminds that a certain number of institutional reforms was introduced, beginning with strict control for the purpose of providing exports to pay for the imports required under central planning. Provinces were given autonomy to promote exports, while trading companies were established in cooperation with industrial enterprises to facilitate decentralisation of trading activities. In addition, several coastal provinces established export-processing zones, where foreign investors were encouraged to set up factories, independently or jointly with Chinese enterprises.[74]

In those days, there was a debate in the United States whether the administration should complete the strategic relationship with China through any form of military collaboration. As far as arms sales were concerned, the White House did not want to supply either China or the Soviet Union, but there was no intention to institute an embargo against Beijing, once both France and Britain were in the business. In short, it seemed this issue depended on how much Moscow could be involved in the Far East.[75] How far the communist Asian country was interested in multilateral trading connections was also proved by the fact that Beijing had not interrupted commercial and technical relations with the Soviet Union, despite the lacking extension of the 1950 Treaty, even during the incursions in Vietnam. On the other hand, Britain shared the Western strategic and economic interest in a stable and prosperous China, of course well disposed towards the West and independent from the Soviet Union. Moreover, the Chinese had begun to talk about the purchase of nuclear power stations and cooperation on fast reactors, something economically very profitable for London, but at the same time this could cause some problems of non proliferation, especially with respect to India.[76] The establishment of Special Economic Zones allowed foreign companies to deal with single provinces, rather than with the central government. The British showed their interest in this proposal, so that the Department of Energy issued a report setting out the details to sell nuclear reactors and possibly their fuel. A preliminary agreement had already been signed in January and other powers like France, the Federal Republic of Germany and Japan had also offered the sale of pressurised water reactors. A full negotiating team was expected to go to China in the following Autumn in order to assess the possibility of such a contract. However, what the British government had to clarify first was its position within the COCOM, according to which nuclear materials and plants could not be exported towards communist bloc countries, unless specific approval. As a matter of fact, too many advanced industrial countries were involved in such deals, thus the Department of Energy thought COCOM interests could be met if members agreed to ask the Chinese to commit themselves not to use for military purposes any material supplied for civil nuclear programmes. Obviously, the Soviet reaction to sales of nuclear reactors to China was likely to be extremely critical, but it does not seem this was going to prevent London from having so profitable contracts with Beijing.[77]

What the Americans were also concerned about, was that China's potential membership at the World Bank and other international financial institutions inevitably involved the removal of Taiwan from those organisations, thus potentially undermining Congress support to several multilateral organisms. Therefore, the US approach reflected the concern of a lot of agencies that extending tariff preferences to the People's Republic would jeopardise the whole General System of Tariff Preferences. The point was that, since Beijing still defined itself as a developing country and claimed to give an example to Third World nations, the relationship with communist China was no longer an East-West problem *per se*, but it was beginning to affect North-South relations as well.[78] In the meantime, Secretary of Commerce Juanita Kreps's visit to China in May 1979 produced the frame of a trade agreement whose effective implementation depended on the successful conclusion of a textile accord. During the conversations, Deng asserted that the policy of opening up and absorption of large amounts of foreign capital and technology had not changed. However, it was necessary to readjust plans to take into account practical realities and limits to rapid development. Thus, while emphasis on agriculture and light industry remained unaltered, additional investment in power and transport was needed. Moreover, in order for China to attract foreign capital, some international practices had to be accepted, such as foreigners having a say in running joint venture factories.[79] Actually, China's economic and trade relations were expanding rapidly, that was why Secretary Blumenthal said that MFN treatment, following the signing of the Trade Agreement and its approval by Congress, was supposed to provide a boost to bilateral trade. Also, the administration was aware that China was interested in compensation-type agreements especially attractive in the energy and raw materials field. At the same time, Vice Premier Kang Shien highlighted that boosting China's ability to export required some shift from heavy towards light industry. In heavy industry, he added, emphasis was to be put on the development of energy.[80]

3.3 The Dawn of the Thatcher Era

The advent of Margaret Thatcher in May 1979 was quite welcomed in China, as the Labour government had not managed to fully develop relations with Beijing due to the will to compromise with the Soviet Union, thus harming trade relations in the defence field. As a consequence, the Chinese government hoped Tories would acquire a strong stance against the Soviets, therefore appreciating closer relations with the Dragon.[81] As far as defence sales were concerned, the Chinese policy was based on the acquisition of manufacturing licenses, while at the same time British authorities had never disguised that the purchase of technology had to be followed by hardware. In that period, British Aerospace was offering three different versions of Harrier aircraft, while the Americans had already observed they would not oppose British sales to China. Therefore, the new conservative executive hoped to pave the way to the sale of more contentious items and eventually to modify COCOM rules.[82] In the meantime, Downing Street had the intention to authorise the transaction of items such as image intensifier tubes, communication systems and radars, night vision equipment, artillery and mortar location equipment.[83] In the same days, a CIA report on China's new steel production programme was circulating within the Carter administration, stating that the Chinese were beginning to realise they lacked human and material resources to carry out the initial project lasting till 1985. Moreover, the huge scope of the plan was supposed to imply enormous investment resources needed much more urgently in light industry and agriculture. Apart from that, steel was the largest single category in China's import bill, having reached 1.5 billion dollars in 1977, while finished steel items accounted for about ninety per cent of Beijing's purchases, with Japan and West Germany as largest suppliers.[84] Since the Far Eastern country had to import steel products for several years to come, domestic output was expected to be insufficient. In order to boost output, new facilities were planned, while the old ones were going to be expanded and upgraded above all under Federal German contracts. In the longer run, it was estimated, with abundant raw materials and Western technology infusion the future of China's steel industry looked bright, but in the short term a high level of imports was necessary.[85]

Science and technology had no class nature, we can read in the *Beijing Review*. Importing advanced technology and equipment was regarded as a vital and complex task giving priority to what granted quicker results and profit at less cost. The final objective was making use of the latest techniques and technology from abroad in order to improve the ability to produce according to Chinese skills. Therefore, it was useless to import things which could be domestically made.[86] At the plenary meeting of the Second Session of the Fifth National People's Congress on 21 June, the minister in charge of the State Planning Commission, Yu Qiuli, delivered a speech highlighting that the 1979 national economic plan was focusing on developing agriculture and light and textile industries, strengthening also coal, petroleum and power. In particular, agricultural output was to increase by four per cent, industrial production by eight per cent, with an 8.3 per cent increase in light industry and 7.6 per cent in heavy industry.[87] The reasons why readjustment was necessary was given by Shi Zhengwen in an article published in the *Beijing Review* on 29 June 1979. Simply said, imbalances in the economy had surfaced in many ways, such as agriculture going up rather slowly. Another unbalanced situation was the relationship between light and heavy industry, the investment in the latter continuously going down and affecting market supplies. The third imbalance was within the heavy industry itself, as the development of energy and transport sectors had not kept the same pace as metallurgical and processing industries. In summary, the most important thing to do was to bring about a harmonious proportion among agriculture, light and heavy industry, with the former taking priority. As concerned imports, more technology and less equipment was to be purchased in order to improve machine-building capacity, at the same time balancing exports to guarantee payments.[88] More than 1,000 projects were cancelled in 1979 and 1980, more than 6,000 new ones were initiated, while the establishment of new funding agencies such as the People's Bank, the Construction Bank, the Bank of China, or joint ventures with foreign corporations meant that if one channel were closed to an enterprise, the manager would simply go to another until getting the necessary funding; once some funds were allocated and work started, funds and materials from the central government would be forthcoming. The result was that total state investment in 1979 was thirty-two per cent over the target.[89]

In light of all this, Hua Guofeng's 18 June report at the National People's Congress stated that the three years starting in 1979 would be committed to readjusting and improving the national economy in order to gradually bring it on the path of sustained and high-speed development. In short, the target for the following three years was (a) achieving a relative balance between the growth of grain and other sideline farm production on one hand and that of the population and industry on the other; (b) reaching a growth rate for light and textile industry equal or slightly higher than the heavy industry one; (c) increasing energy production; (d) narrowing the scope of capital construction; (e) increasing peasants' and non-agriculture workers' income. Within the same span of time, each enterprise was supposed to have a leading body strong enough to take responsibility for production. Finally, energetic steps had to be taken to develop foreign trade and expand technical cooperation with advanced industrialised countries, with the purpose to absorb funds from abroad as well.[90] Three days later, at the plenary meeting of the Second Session, Vice-Premier Yu Qiuli stated that commodity supply had to be augmented, as well as foreign trade, in order to cause a quick exchange between countryside and towns, and between China and other countries. As far as oil industry was concerned, geological survey and prospecting were to improve to make sure that more reserves be found as soon as possible. The plan for 1979, in addition, stipulated that exports were supposed to increase by 14.7 per cent over the previous year, while imports would be 32.4 per cent higher than 1978. Such a difference was due to the massive purchase of new technology and equipment, amounting to 220 per cent more than the previous year. Therefore, the only way to strike a balance in foreign exchange was increasing foreign currency earnings by every possible means.[91] To help implement such a plan, the Second Session of the Fifth National People's Congress adopted a law on joint ventures encouraging these companies to market their products outside China, after having opened an account with the Bank of China or any bank approved by the Bank of China.[92] To sum up, an overall balance had to be achieved in three aspects: (a) the scale of imports was to be tailored according to the ability to export and the capacity to pay in foreign currency; (b) imported projects had to be balanced with the building ability, as well as the capacity to provide ancillary equipment; (c) further balance between imported projects and the ability to assimilate new technologies was also necessary.[93] Once again, we can quote Barry Naughton to better understand Chinese economy's dynamics. One of the great achievements of the early reform period was to reduce imbalances slowing down investment rates, thus having productivity growth compensated. Fewer new assets were created, but the existing ones were used more efficiently. As a result, the economy was able to produce more consumption goods without sacrificing growth.[94]

To tell the truth, the new Chinese economic policy was so welcomed in the West that trade was regarded as one of the best ways to influence the Asian country. Commercial relations, therefore, did not have to be viewed just as a second front against the Soviet Union. Rather, it was a way to increase the PRC's interest in the stability and prosperity of the West. However, there was nothing the British produced that China was not able to get elsewhere, though almost entirely in Western advanced countries. Hence, London was supposed to be clever enough to make its interests accepted as the whole West's stake.[95]

With regard to the European Community, the Chinese saw Europe as a useful counterweight not only to the Soviet Union, but also to the United States on the global scene. As president of the European Commission, Roy Jenkins visited China in 1979 to pave the way for expanding trade with the EEC. On a conversation with Jenkins, Deng Xiaoping noted with interest the integration among the European continent, which was believed to become an important pole in balancing the division of power in the world. Jenkins, on the other hand, realised the future importance of China as a global power in terms of its nuclear capacity and economic potential, thus concluding that the self-interest of the West lay in assisting China's modernisation process.[96] At the same time, the Trade Agreement with the United States implied that Chinese exports to the North American country would be taxed at the lowest rate provided to other countries. Hence, such a decision set Beijing's entry into the world economy, so that two-way trade between the United States and the PRC increased from practically zero in 1971 to almost 13 billion dollars in 1988.[97] The Carter administration was by then prepared to offer a credit arrangement with the PRC to cover lending up to two billion dollars by the ExIm Bank, over a period of two to five years on a case-by-case basis, with the commitment to arrange additional funds to that amount. In a conversation with Deng Xiaoping on 27 August, Vice-President Mondale said the United States was ready to sell the most advanced and highly sophisticated jet aircraft produced by Lockheed. Such a license was historic, since it was the first time that an American administration had authorised the sale of such a technology to a communist nation. In a word, Mondale admitted the White House was beginning to differentiate between China and the Soviet Union. This concept was a sort of watershed in the relationship with Beijing, as it was underlined by Deng himself, who said that the attitude to lump all communist countries together as a whole needed to be changed.[98] On grounds of that, Deng Xiaoping also stressed the necessity to strengthen China's national defence capabilities implying the need of Beijing and Washington to cooperate in the sense of global strategy, with the latter selling aircraft, or at least not opposing the sale by allies.[99] On the other hand, Mondale said in a press conference that China should be able to take advantage of the expertise of American firms in the development of hydroelectric power and water resource projects. In particular, the government was supposed to encourage American corporations to invest in China by making available for them insurance and guarantee facilities of the Overseas Private Investment Corporation.[100] Tellingly, the stronger the bond between the two nations, the more stable international community was expected to be.[101]

The Americans were also concerned by the Soviet military presence in Vietnam, where they were making port calls and establishing military facilities. Therefore, the administration believed the interests of the region and of the United States and China would be best served if a search for a political settlement in Kampuchea were initiated, resulting in the removal of foreign troops and the installation of a genuinely non-aligned government. Concerning this question, Deng's opinion was even stricter, for he did not think that Vietnam was a threat only to China. Rather, it was thought to be an important part of the global strategy of the Soviet Union, compared with a barbell, with the Pacific and Southeast Asia as one hand, and the Middle East as the other, thus setting Moscow's drive towards the Indian Ocean. The bar linking the two ends of the barbell was the Malacca Straits. On grounds of that, China was in favour of the United States strengthening military facilities in the Pacific and Indian Ocean.[102] Such a theory was also reminded by Premier Hua, who said that the Soviets were trying to poke hands in the Middle East and the Persian Gulf, thus attempting to control production and transport of energy resources.[103] The relationship between the Anglo-Saxon power and the East Asian giant was becoming so collaborative that the secretary of defence suggested that the time had come to develop a strategic dialogue and military contacts to parallel arrangements the United States had with the USSR. In a few words, Carter's main advisers were proposing the China card as a form of leverage towards the Soviet Union, exactly what had been always denied. In fact, Brown added that Sino-US ties in the field of security would probably provide the Soviets a powerful inducement for greater restraint and sensitivity to US interests.[104]

On the contrary, Secretary Vance was worried that strategic policies would show a tilt towards China rather than maintaining an essential balance. According to the head of the State Department, Washington had a major interest in pressing forward vigorously with the bilateral relationship with the PRC and in broadening the areas of global cooperation. At the same time, there was an equally pivotal stake in seeing the Soviet Union contained in its efforts to gain strategic advantage in troubled areas. Hence, sooner or later the United States and China were expected to closely work together in pursuit of common objectives. However, this did not imply any military security relationship, for this was supposed to suggest that there was no more hope to improve relations with the USSR. As an alternative, Vance was proposing a triangular policy based on bilateral US relations with Moscow and Beijing better than the rapports between the two communist capitals. In substance, the administration did not have to preclude or reduce the chances of improved US-Soviet relations.[105] As usual, the national security adviser did not agree with the secretary of state, as Brzezinski did not believe that it was possible to have relations with the Soviet Union as friendly as those with the PRC. Moscow, reminded the Polish-American statesman, was a country militarily threatening the United States on a global scale, while China neither threatened Washington nor was involved in any anti-American activities. By virtue of that, it was unavoidable that the scale and warmth of the relationship with Beijing was going to be affected by the Soviet attitude towards the North American superpower.[106] What Brzezinski underlined was that there were several "Chinese cards" and the long-range strategic significance of a cooperative US-Chinese relationship stood on its own feet. Paradoxically, the Soviets were turning to the United States to balance what they perceived as a Chinese threat. Moreover, the Europeans were getting more aware of the importance to their own security of the forty-four Soviet divisions diverted to the Far East.[107] On the contrary, Vance of course did not deny the importance of the new relationship with China as an essential element in the global balance of power. The secretary of state, however, wanted to distinguish between the areas in which the relation with the PRC was to be pursued and those taking into account the likely reaction of allies, third countries, or the Soviet Union. China was extremely useful to the United States because it was a powerful country on the Soviet border with potential military ties with Washington. Such an ambiguity was an important factor in deterring Soviet adventurism, but developing a formal military collaboration with the Far Eastern country was unlikely to produce moderation in Soviet behaviour. Vance did not advocate an even-handed policy towards the two communist countries, for China was only a regional power, technologically and militarily backward, not directly threatening American security. Nevertheless, the state secretary said it was necessary to take full account of the way others assessed what Washington did with Beijing. That was why the administration was supposed to move very carefully and rule out export of any items destined for military use, especially as far as nuclear equipment and technology were concerned.[108]

Meanwhile, Moscow's Foreign Minister, Gromyko, had delivered a speech at the United Nations asking to submit a resolution against the policy of hegemonism in international relations. Through this initiative it was clear that the Kremlin was trying to overturn the allegation which Beijing had been addressing for several years. The purpose of such a draft resolution, said the Soviet representative, was that no states or group of states should claim, for any motives whatsoever, hegemony in regard to anyone. Hence, the intention was to have the Security Council expressing itself against hegemonism, in order for the major powers to reach a broad international agreement claiming the renunciation of that kind of policy in all its manifestations.[109] Maybe this position is easier to interpret if we read what the British secretary of state, Lord Carrington, said in a BBC interview broadcast just a few days after Gromyko's speech. The Conservative minister, in fact, stated that the relations with the two communist governments were on a slightly different footing. Succinctly, despite the will to always have a friendly attitude the Soviet Union remained a potential adversary. Instead China, though not a potential ally, shared at least a substantial community of interests with the United Kingdom. On the other hand, the secretary of state did not think it was possible to have an ordinary amicable relationship with Moscow until détente became a reality, with a significant decline of military spending in the Soviet Union. Different words, instead, were used to announce Hua's visit to the United Kingdom in November, as Carrington said that commercial contacts were expected from that diplomatic event.[110] Moreover, during the same UNGA session the chairman of the Chinese Delegation, Han Nianlong, delivered a vitriolic speech against the Soviet Union, accusing Moscow of being engaged in frenzied arms expansion unprecedented in scale and speed. Relying on military strength, the Kremlin was said to push a global offensive strategy with a view to encircle Europe, control strategic routes and increase influence in Africa, the Middle East and South-East Asia.[111] As far as relations with Western Europe were concerned, Nicola Casarini stresses that just a few years afterwards the Chinese began to put forward the idea that the US defence build-up had begun to stabilise the balance of power between the superpowers. Therefore, an increasingly multi-polar world order was to become the main feature of the international system. Hence, close alignment with the United States and NATO was not as necessary to Chinese security as had been in the previous decade. Accordingly, Western Europe could act as a counterweight not just against Moscow, but against the United States as well. Such a view responded to Beijing's desire for an international system in which regional powers such as China would play major roles. On grounds of all this, in order to diversify growing dependence on Japan and the United States, the Dragon began to increase commercial ties with Western Europe.[112] Indeed, in 1979 the European Commission signed an agreement on textile imports with the People's Republic doubling the share for textile exports, which was then one of Beijing's most competitive sectors. On the other hand, reaching an agreement on such a kind of commodity had not been easy, since the Commission was also worried about relations with Third World suppliers, who were going to be damaged by China's entry into the international textile market.[113] According to Laurens Hemminga, in those years China's antagonism towards the USSR and the consequent isolation within the communist bloc was one of the key reasons why Beijing decided to address Europe, though governments such as those of France and West Germany were quite prudent to develop ties with the Dragon until the PRC had moderated its posture towards the Soviets. However, Hemminga says that more than Moscow it was the United States to play a pivotal role in setting the main terms of Europe's relationship with the Far Eastern country.[114]

3.4 Hua Guofeng's Visit to Britain

At the celebrations of the thirtieth anniversary of the People's Republic, Ye Jianying stated that in order for socialism to replace capitalism, productive forces had to be liberated and labour productivity be achieved, with the aim of turning China into one of the main productive countries in the world.[115] This was also a way to raise national defence capabilities to resist and defeat foreign aggression in case of a modern war. As far as international relations were concerned, a peaceful environment was necessary to favour national construction.[116] On announcing his visit to Western Europe, Hua Guofeng said that the law on joint ventures was not enough to speed up international trade and investment, due to China's lack of experience. By virtue of that, supplementary laws and regulations had to be worked out in order to guarantee the rightful interests of foreign investors.[117] As a matter of fact, a strong China was believed to serve world peace and stability, that was why a good part of the technology and equipment imported was useful to generate export earnings. What the premier highlighted was that socialism and modernisation were not necessarily in contradiction. Although some Western influence was inevitable, it was something to watch out for.[118]

As regarded joint ventures in particular, Yasheng Huang states that the 1979 Equity Joint Venture Law established foreign-invested enterprises as independent legal persons separate from that of their shareholders and with a corporate structure broadly similar to that found in market economies, with a board of directors representing the interests of shareholders. Thus, these companies acquired a corporate form that state-owned enterprises did not achieve until the 1993 Company Law giving legislative recognition to their legal independence.[119] In addition, Ashley J. Tellis observes that China was able to grow not through an autarchic process, but rather being embedded in a larger liberal economic order supported by the United States, and therefore taking advantage of the interdependence arising from deliberate American investments in producing an open international trading system. This investment resuscitated Western Europe while creating the first wave of Asian success, thus contributing to advancing the most important American strategic objective of the time, that is containing the Soviet Union. On grounds of all this, in the last decade before Soviet disintegration, Washington took the first tentative steps towards integrating China into this containment system.[120] To tell the truth, the question of joint ventures was by then gaining the upper hand in the Chinese economic debate. As an evidence of this, suffice it to quote Deng Xiaoping who, in a meeting with a group of US governors, said that there were plans to adopt more joint venture companies, for example in the oil field, for American enterprises were in those days prospecting in the South China Sea. What the PRC government wanted, we can always quote the old leader, was the possibility to sell to the international market, thus being able to solve the payment problem, bringing money to China and therefore develop some domestic market. In order to achieve all this in the best possible way, the Chinese had first of all to learn handling the technology they were absorbing. This could be also achieved by sending students to the United States, which actually was encouraged by Deng's interlocutors.[121] As far as modernisation was concerned, for the energy industry the aim was to increase production at a time when oil output was beginning to stagnate. As a matter of fact, PRC oil production underwent three main stages: (a) discovery of oilfields in the late 1950s and early 1960s; (b) in 1979, when production slowed down unexpectedly; (c) output, almost as unexpectedly, showed signs of renewed strength in 1983. Tight government control over the oil sector gave little incentive to produce more and made the industry totally dependent on the executive for investment.[122] In a word, closer relations with the United States were dictated not by military imperatives, but by economic ones. To be fully effective, Deng's economic policies required access to international export markets, thus normalisation with Washington had had priority.[123]

Within this context, Downing Street's objectives in the Chinese Premier's approaching visit focused on the importance to appear as a major interlocutor on international issues and as a valuable trading partner. Despite huge differences, over a medium term British and Chinese interests coincided in sensitive areas and Britain had the chance to benefit from Beijing's involvement in the solution of global issues.[124] So confident felt the British government towards the new leadership of China, that Number Ten wanted to encourage Beijing to take an increasingly active part in multilateral discussions on the main international question dealing with East/West relations and other hot spots like Southern Africa.[125] On balance, Chinese initiatives at the United Nations were regarded as useful to British interests, since Beijing's main tactical task, despite some radical positions on particular Third World issues, was to seize opportunities to embarrass the Russians, rather than undermining the Western stance.[126] As far as international trade was concerned, major contracts were ready to be concluded on coal mining and mineral development in general, as well as steel plants, power generation equipment and railways. As a matter of fact, the trade balance was in favour of the United Kingdom for the first time since 1975, due to high technology goods and equipment. The pattern, however, was irregular and China was changing foreign trade policy and planning cycle in order to grant payments by augmenting exports and increasing domestic production after acquiring the necessary know-how.[127] Within the several trade agreements stipulated with the People's Republic, there were also certain types of military material. Bearing in mind that the Chinese wanted primarily new weapon systems in order to acquire manufacturing licenses and build up their own defence network, London had already pointed out that the willingness to transfer technology would be conditional to the volume of work involving the UK industry.[128]

By reading the transcripts of the talks between the two prime ministers, we assume that Margaret Thatcher had a vision of Soviet designs quite similar to that of the Chinese, as both heads of government thought that helping Vietnam to expand was serving Moscow's purposes, pushing the Russians forward about 4,500 km from Vladivostok, thus threatening Thailand and Malaysia to get control of the Malacca Strait. Moreover, Hua warned that in Afghanistan the Soviets had engineered a coup against President Daoud, who claimed more freedom of action to develop relationships with a wider selection of countries. Once got rid of him, Afghanistan had become a danger to Pakistan as well. Thatcher agreed with her Chinese counterpart's analysis, stating she was confident that the United States and Western Europe would hold fast in the West, while China and Japan would do the same in the East, consequently preventing the USSR from waging war on two fronts.[129] Obviously, this implied for the United Kingdom to be ready to assist China with a wide range of defence equipment, included Harrier aircraft.[130] Just to give evidence about that, the first two contracts for defence sales to China had already been signed, since the Chinese delegation had had very good discussions with Rolls Royce on Spey engine, and other fields such as marine turbines were going to be involved. In addition, Premier Hua said Beijing was interested in Britain's oil industry, especially as regarded BP operations in the Yellow Sea, agreements with American and French companies having already been reached. The same question could come out for coal, and there was no problem for China to repay, for the output would be simply divided according to contracts. Apart from that, the People's Republic had huge mineral wealth and proposals for extraction and processing had already been made by British companies.[131]

Actually, London was willing to undertake the development of Chinese coal mines with a full transfer of technology perhaps under joint ventures, as well as the construction of nuclear power stations able to produce electricity. Vice-Premier Yu Qiuli added that China needed also to buy know-how in order to renovate its industry as well as managing joint ventures.[132] As an evidence of this, on 29 November the government of the United Kingdom signed an Arrangement on Railway Scientific and Technical Cooperation with the People's Republic, which was the first outcome of the agreement on scientific and technological cooperation stipulated the previous year between the two countries.[133] Initial reform policies, reminds us Barry Nauhgton, drove transition through much of the 1980s in each of the three most important arenas of agriculture, rural enterprises, and opening to foreign trade and investment. Hence, the policies adopted by the government implied a gradual marketisation of the economy and managed to survive virtually unchanged until an even more thorough privatisation in the late 1990s.[134] Finally, Arthur R. Kroeber argues that Chinese economic development since 1978 is partly explicable by the model of the "East Asian Developmental State". This because the Chinese case differed in at least three important questions: (a) the task of building a modern industrial economy while maintaining the Communist Party's monopoly on political power; (b) China's enormous physical size and legacy of relatively autonomous local governments made it far more difficult to enforce national industry restructuring; (c) reforms took place during a time when international trade and investment rules were rapidly liberalised. Unlike Japan, South Korea and Taiwan, Beijing allowed a relatively high degree of participation in domestic market by foreign firms. Furthermore, until the end of the 1990s China deliberately avoided privatisation and focused on deregulating prices and creating competitive markets.[135]

Chinese authorities and press organs gave a very positive assessment of the premier's visit to Europe, stating that it had been very useful to boost the relationship with the West on anti-Soviet terms. Once back to China, in fact, Hua Guofeng said that an alliance against the Soviet Union was out of question, but an exchange of views on problems of common concern and cooperation was always welcome between China and the West.[136] The aim of the modernisation revolution, said Deng Xiapoing, was to liberate and expand productive forces, without which everything was just empty talk, though the state-owned sector and collectively owned sector were still the mainstay of the economy. The country was therefore believed to enjoy four favourable conditions for attaining the goal: (a) abundant energy and mineral resources, including almost all the ferrous, nonferrous and rare metals; (b) over the previous thirty years, the PRC had laid a preliminary material foundation for industry, agriculture, science and technology; (c) people were being encouraged to emancipate their minds, so as to create the necessary conditions for arousing initiative and bringing their intelligence and wisdom into full play; (d) opening to the outside world was the correct foreign policy to pursue, as it was impossible to achieve objectives without international cooperation.[137] Many experts emphasised the necessity of studying other countries working to establish socialism, while some voiced the opinion that the experiences in industrial development and modernisation of some Far-Eastern and Southeast-Asian nations were most relevant to China. As a result, the standpoint was adopted and officially approved that China had to implement modernisation setting out from the particular conditions of the country, but relying on socialist principles.[138] Deng Xiaoping had a TV interview on 15 October on a wide range of subjects, including socialist democracy, economic construction and relations with Third World countries, which were of paramount importance to Beijing's foreign policy, since China claimed to belong to the Third World and support liberation movements. In the international arena, however, the Asian country pursued good relations with many developed capitalist states in order to carry out the struggle against superpower hegemonism.[139] In a few words, the Chinese leadership wanted to grant more rights to private enterprises in order for them to draw their own plan based on market principles. The intention, tellingly, was to organise the economy in accordance with the conditions prevailing in China and based on foreign experience. The theory of class struggle was by then a thing of the past, while now the People's Republic needed stability and a peaceful international environment. Hence, the struggle to carry out was the one against hegemonism, which meant the Soviet Union, accused to pursue a policy of armaments within a favourable strategic platform in order to achieve its aims without a war or through a war from a standing start.[140] Since it was regarded as very unlikely for Moscow to launch an attack on two fronts in the East and the West, the Chinese thought in the near future the Soviets would increase efforts to expand southwards in Asia and Africa, where economic difficulties and internal conflicts provided them good opportunities to intervene.[141] On the other hand, the Russians accused the Asian communist government to seek the encirclement of the Soviet Union in a ring of hostile countries and political blocs. Hence, the opposition to détente and the recognition of inviolability of European frontiers.[142]

Meanwhile, the Americans had solidly included the new relationship with China in the global balance of power, as the secretary of defence wrote in a memorandum to the president, with a positive outlook for further development contributing to security and prosperity of both countries. The real issue at stake, we can always read in the document, was more sensitive forms of security cooperation implying a closer and more purposive alignment, even including arms sales. The Department of Defence wanted to make clear that Soviet conduct would affect the future pace of Sino-US security collaboration. Thus, the Soviets had to understand that if they engaged in aggressive or expansionist actions, it would become possible for Washington and Beijing to work together in the field of defence as well. As a consequence of that, a policy of even-handedness between the Soviet Union and the People's Republic of China, as advocated by Cyrus Vance, was not realistic. Actually, in deciding what "balance" was, it was pivotal to recognise that the USSR and China posed different problems and offered different opportunities. The Soviets, in fact, were viewed as the main strategic challenge to the United States, by piling up military capabilities far beyond their defensive require- ments, by threatening the security and even existence of free societies and values, and by showing opportunism in Third World disputes. On the other hand, Chinese strategic interests were largely convergent with those of the Americans, promoting a policy of balance to constrain Moscow's growing power. Such considerations, therefore, shaped Washington's approach to export controls and technology transfers without ruling out arms sales to China.[143] At this point, quoting Odd Arne Westad, we can say that the Chinese strategy was to get as much as possible out of the Americans by telling them what Beijing thought they wanted to hear, that is that the Soviet Union was a threat to world peace. Throughout the following years the United States treated China as a quasi-ally, with the purpose to turn China into a real threat to the USSR.[144]

Notes

1 Kissinger, *On China*, 336–337.
2 *British Embassy Peking Despatch: The Politburo and "Democracy Wall" – The Chinese Internal Situation*, 18 December 1978, in NA, FCO 28/3862, *Sino/ Soviet Relations*, Confidential.
3 Naughton, *Deng Xiaoping: The Economist*, 500.
4 Manfred Kulessa, 'Deng's Reforms 1976–1988', in Theodor Leuenberger (ed.), *From Technology Transfer to Technology Management in China* (Heidelberg: Springer-Verlag, 1990), 9.
5 *China: Annual Review 1978*, 4 January 1979, in NA, FCO 21/1685, *China Internal Political*, Confidential.
6 Wang Zhongchun, 'The Soviet Factor in Sino-American Normalization, 1969–1979', in Kirby, Ross and Gong (eds.), *Normalization of US-China Relations*, 172.
7 Telegram 040751Z from USLO Peking to SecState WashDC Priority 3389, *Conversation with Deng Xiaoping*, 4 January 1979, PEKING 00024, Confidential, Exdis, in NARA, RG 59, CFPF 1973–1979, Electronic Telegrams, https://aad.archives.gov/aad/createpdf?rid=129036&dt=2776& dl=2169, accessed 21 September 2021.
8 Telegram 140307Z from SecState WashDC to USLO Peking Immediate 010718, *Secretary's China Speech*, 14 January 1979, STATE 010718, Limited Official Use, in NARA, RG 59, CFPF 1973–1979, Electronic Telegrams, https://aad. archives.gov/aad/createpdf?rid=111090&dt=2776&dl=2169, accessed 21 September 2021.
9 *S. Pares to Mr. Ferguson: Chinese Views on the Inevitability of War*, 9 January 1979, in NA, FCO 28/3862, Confidential.
10 *US/China Economic Relations*, Washington, DC, 8 January 1979, 10:05–10:45 a.m., in JCPL, NSC Institutional Files (H-Files), Box 72, PRC 086, 1/8/79, US-China Economic Relations, Confidential.

11 'Vice-Premier Deng Xiaoping Interviewed by US Newsmen', 5 January 1979, *Beijing Review*, 22/2, 1979, 16–18, 24.

12 Wang Bingnan, 'Growth of the Friendship between Chinese and American People', *Beijing Review*, 22/4, 1979, 9–13.

13 Ross, 'From Lin Biao to Deng Xiaoping: Elite Instability and China's US Policy', *The China Quarterly*, 30/118/2, 1989, 292.

14 Western Europe had always been influenced by different international dynamics superseding Cold War developments. The imperial past and the process of de-colonisation deeply affected Cold War relations between the PRC and Britain, France and to a lesser extent West Germany. All three nations had acted as imperialist Powers in China in the nineteenth century, and these closer ties were undoubtedly a driving factor for their refusal to follow Washington's policy of non-recognition. Janick Marina Schaufelbuehl, Marco Wyss and Valeria Zanier, *Europe and China in the Cold War: Exchanges beyond the Bloc Logic and the Sino-Soviet Split* (Leiden: Koninklijke Brill NV, 2019), 3–4.

15 Izvestia Article, *New Aspects of Relationships*, 13 January 1979, quoted in British Embassy Moscow: *US/China Normalisation: Soviet Press Comment*, 17 January 1979, in NA, FCO 21/1693, *USA-China Relations*, Restricted.

16 *Address by the Honourable Cyrus R. Vance Secretary of State at the Briefing for Chief Executives and other Senior Officials from Member Firms of the National Council for US-China Trade and the USA/ROC Economic Council Department of State: Stability in East Asia: The US Role*, 15 January 1979, in NA, FCO 21/1693.

17 *Your Meeting with Deng Xiaoping*, Washington, DC, 25 January 1979, in JCPL, National Security Affairs, Brzezinski Material, VIP Visit File, Box 2, China: Vice Premier Deng Xiaoping, 1/28/79-2/1/79, 1/25/79 Briefing Book [I], Secret, Sent for Action.

18 Vitally Kozyrev, 'Soviet Policy toward the United States and China, 1969–1979', in Kirby, Ross and Gong (eds.), *Normalization of US-China Relations*, 280–281.

19 'An Interview with Brezhnev', *Time*, 22 January 1979.

20 *Scope Paper for the Visit of Vice Premier Deng Xiaoping of the People's Republic of China January 29-February 5, 1979*, Washington, DC, 26 January 1979, in JCPL, National Security Affairs, Brzezinski Material, VIP Visit File, Box 2, China: Vice Premier Deng Xiaoping, 1/28/79-2/1/79: 1/25/79 Briefing Book [I], Secret, Sensitive.

21 *R.C. Samuel to Mr. Scott: British Relations with China*, 25 January 1979, in NA, FCO 49/834, *British Relations with China*, RS 020/6, Confidential.

22 *R.Q. Braithwaite to Mr. Murray: Britain's Relations with China*, 31 January 1979, in NA, FCO 49/834, Confidential.

23 *Summary of the President's First Meeting with PRC Vice Premier Deng Xiaoping*, Washington, DC, 29 January 1979, 10:40 a.m.–12:30 p.m., in JCPL, National Security Affairs, Staff Material, Far East, Oksenberg Subject File, Box 57, Policy Process: 10-11/78, Top Secret, Sensitive, Eyes Only.

24 *Summary of the President's Meeting with the People's Republic of China Vice Premier Deng Xiaoping*, Washington, DC, 29 January 1979, 3:35–4:59 p.m., in JCPL, National Security Affairs, Staff Material, Office, Outside the System File, Box 47, China: President's Meeting with Vice Premier Deng: 1-2/79, Top Secret, Sensitive, Eyes Only.

25 *Secretary's Luncheon for PRC Vice Premier Deng Xiaoping*, Washington, DC, 29 January 29 1979, 12:45–2 p.m., in NARA, RG 59, Executive Secretariat Files: Lot 84 D 241, Box 9, Vance NODIS Memcons, 1979, Secret, Nodis.

26 British response to Chinese war against Vietnam was overwhelmingly hostile, and in all the invasion did considerable damage to the PRC's reputation. Tony Benn was told in 1980 that Beijing's actions had been punitive, damaging civilian facilities as well. It was only a few years later that China loyalists in Britain began to express support for its policy towards Vietnam and the remnants of the Khmer Rouges resisting to the new regime with China's backing. Buchanan, *East Wind*, 215.

27 *Memorandum of Conversation*, Washington, DC, 29 January, 1979, 5–5:40 p.m., in JCPL, National Security Affairs, Staff Material, Office, Outside the System File, Box 47, China: President's Meeting with Vice Premier Deng: 1-2/79, Top Secret.

28 *Summary of Cabinet Members' Meeting with Chinese Vice Premier Deng Xiaoping*, Washington, DC, 31 January 1979, 8–9 a.m., in JCPL, National Security Affairs, Staff Material, Office, Outside the System File, Box 47, China: President's Meeting with Vice Premier Deng: 1-2/79, Secret.

29 Joseph Lelyveld, 'Reporter's Notebook: For Teng, only Oblique Vision of America', *New York Times*, 2 February 1979.

30 Lu, 'Deng Plays the China Card', 80.

31 *Telegram No. 172 from Peking to FCO*, 7 February 1979, 070900Z: Washington Tel No. 490-Deng's Visit to the US, in NA, FCO 21/1693, Confidential.

32 Export-oriented light industry got priority, and this implied on one hand the advent of a domestic consumer culture, so that people would save less and buy more, while on the other hand a new campaign to conquer foreign markets was about to be launched, thus placing the Dragon in competition with other export-oriented economies with cheap labour markets, such as South Korea, Singapore, or Taiwan. Lowell Dittmer, 'China in 1980: Modernization and its Discontents', *Asian Survey: A Survey of Asia in 1980*, Part I, 21/1, 1981, 33–34.

33 *British Embassy Washington D.C. Despatch: The Visit of Teng Hsiao-P'ing to the United States*, 26 February 1979, FEC 020/3, in NA, FCO 21/1693, Confidential.

34 *Record of a Four-Power Meeting of Political Directors at 1 Carlton Gardens on 26 February 1979 at 11.00 AM: Relations with the Soviet Union and Eastern Europe, including the Effects of the China Factor*, 26 February 1979, in NA, FCO 21/1696, *Sino-Soviet Relations*, FEC 020/5, Secret.

35 *Note of Mr Varley's Opening Discussions with Vice-Premier Wang Zhen, Sunday 25 February 1979 at 8.30 AM*, February 1979, in NA, FCO 21/1710, *Visit by Mr Varley to China*, FEC 026/1, Confidential.

36 *Note of Mr Varley's Meeting with Mr Li Chiang, Minister of Foreign Trade, Sunday 25 February 1979 at 2.00 PM*, 28 February 1979, in NA, FCO 21/1710, Confidential.

37 *Record of Meeting between Mr Varley and Mr Chiao Pei-hsin Chairman, Bank of China, at the Head Office of the Bank of China, Sunday 25 February at 3.00 PM*, 26 February 1979, in NA, FCO 21/1710, Confidential.

38 *Note of Mr Varley's Meeting with Nr Chai Shu-Fan, Minister, Sixth Ministry of Machine Building, Tuesday 27 February 1979 at 8.00 Am*, in NA, FCO 21/1710, Confidential.

39 *Record of Meeting between the Secretary of State for Industry and Vice-Premier Li Xiannian at 1615 Hours on 1 March 1979*, in NA, FCO 21/1710, Confidential.

40 *Note of Mr Varley's Meeting with Mr Gao Yangwin, Vice-Minister, Ministry of Metallurgy, Saturday 3 March 1979, at 9.00*, 5 March 1979, in NA, FCO 21/1710, Confidential.

41 *Note of Visit to the Ministry of Communications, Peking Friday 2 March 1979,* March 1979, in NA, FCO 21/1710, Confidential.

42 *Note of Mr Varley's Meeting with Mr Xiao Han Minister of Coal Industry, Thursday 1 March 1979 at 5.30 PM,* 3 March 1979, in NA, FCO 21/1710, Confidential.

43 *Note of a Meeting with State Planning Commission and Ministry of Foreign Trade, Wednesday 28 February 1979,* in NA, FCO 21/1710, Confidential.

44 *Visit of the Secretary of State for Industry to China: 24 February–5 March 1979,* 20 March 1979, in NA, FCO 21/1710, FEC 026/1, Confidential.

45 Naughton, *The Chinese Economy,* 97.

46 'On the Development of Modern Industry', *Beijing Review,* 22/12, 1979, 9–13.

47 *Record of Meeting between the Secretary of State for Industry and the Chinese Minister of Foreign Affairs at 1640 Hours on 26 February 1979,* in NA, FCO 21/1710, Confidential.

48 'Vice-Premier Deng in Washington', *Beijing Review,* 22/6, 1979, 9–14.

49 Pantsov and Levine, *Deng Xiaoping,* 349.

50 Keith, 'The Origins and Strategic Implications of China's Independent Foreign Policy', *International Journal,* XLI, 1, 1985–1986, 120–121.

51 *Note of a Meeting between the Secretary of State for Industry and Premier Hua Guofeng at 1710 on 4 March 1979,* in NA, FCO 21/1710, Confidential.

52 Although Deng was not in the highest power position before the war, he wanted to teach Vietnam a lesson. The war became an index for the power struggle between Deng and Hua Guofeng. Deng won the support of the majority, and China decided to fight the Southern neighbour. Chih-Chia Hsu, 'Foreign Policy Decision-making Process in Deng's China: Three Patterns for Analysis', *Asian Perspective,* 23/2, Special Issue on the Dynamics of Northeast Asia and the Korean Peninsula, 1999, 213.

53 Yahuda, *The International Politics of the Asia-Pacific, Fourth and Revised Edition,* 46–47.

54 Sergey Radchenko, *Unwanted Visionaries* (Oxford: Oxford University Press, 2014), 127.

55 Lüthi, *Cold Wars,* 531.

56 *US-China Economic Relations,* Washington, DC, 13 March 1979, 3–3:50 p.m., in JCPL, Brzezinski Donated Material, Subject File, Box 25, Meetings, PRC 97: 3/79, Confidential.

57 Teiwes-Sun, 'China's New Economic Policy under Hua Guofeng', 22.

58 On 3 April 1979, the PRC announced that the Treaty of Friendship stipulated with the Soviet Union in 1950 would not be prolonged. On that circumstance, the Kremlin issued a statement accusing China not to be coherent with what declared about the readiness to maintain normal relations with Moscow. *Statement of Soviet Government,* 5 April 1979, in NA, FCO 28/3862, OPK11/V 7452.

59 *Memorandum from Secretary of Defense Brown to the President's Assistant for National Security Affairs (Brzezinski): Sino-American Relations – Attachment US-PRC Security Cooperation: Enduring Dilemmas and Present Choices,* Washington, DC, 23 March 1979, Secret, Sensitive, in FRUS 1977–1980, Vol. XIII, Doc. 226, 842–853.

60 Denis Fred Simon, 'China's Capacity to Assimilate Foreign Technology: An Assessment, Part 1', in *Selected Papers Submitted to the Joint Economic Committee: China under the Four Modernization,* Congress of the United States, Ninety-Seventh Congress, Second Session (Washington, DC: Government Printing Office, 1982), 523.

61 Vogel, 428–429.

62 Deng, 'Speech at a Forum on the Principles for the Party's Theoretical Work: Uphold the Four Cardinal Principles', 30 March 1979, in *The Selected Works of Deng Xiaoping*, Vol. II, https://dengxiaopingworks.wordpress.com/2013/02/25/uphold-the-four-cardinal-principles/, accessed 5 October 2021.

63 Goodman, *Deng Xiaoping and the Chinese Revolution*, 93–94.

64 Lawrence C. Reardon, 'Seven Policies that Opened China to the Outside World, 1979–1990', in Roberts (ed.), *Chinese Economic Statecraft*, 39–42.

65 Bao, Chiang and Ignatius (eds.), *Prisoner of the State*, 101–102.

66 Teiwes-Sun, 'China's Economic Reorientation after the Third Plenum: Conflict Surrounding "Chen Yun's" Readjustment Program', 1979–80, *The China Journal*, 35/70, 2013, 171–173.

67 Cumings, 'The Political Economy of China's Turn Outward', 244–245.

68 Teiwes-Sun, 'China's Economic Reorientation after the Third Plenum', 167–168.

69 'Minister Li Qiang on Expanding China's Foreign Trade to Speed up the Four Modernizations', 27 April 1979, *Beijing Review*, 22/17, 1979, 15–16.

70 'Interview with Zou Siyi, a Leading Member of the Export Bureau of the Ministry of Foreign Trade: Some Questions on Developing Economic and Technological Exchanges with Foreign Countries', 27 April 1979, *Beijing Review*, 22/17, 1979, 17–20.

71 Wei-Wei Zhang, *Ideology and Economic Reform under Deng Xiaoping, 1978–1993* (London-New York, NY: Routledge, 2010), 58.

72 Naughton, *Growing out of the Plan*, 76–79.

73 Albers, *Britain, France, West Germany*, 144.

74 Gregory C. Chow, 'Economic Reform and Growth in China', *Annals of Economics and Finance*, 5/1 2004, 131–132.

75 *US Security Policy in Asia*, 17 April 1979, in NA, FCO 21/1694, *USA-China Relations*, FEC 020/3, Confidential.

76 *Far Eastern Department Paper: China*, 26 April 1979, in NA, FCO 21/1690, *UK-China Relations*, FEC 020/1, Confidential.

77 *Department of Energy Draft Paper: Nuclear Cooperation with China*, 11 May 1979, in NA, FCO 28/3862, Confidential.

78 *China as a Developing Country*, Washington, 8 May 1979, in JCPL, National Security Affairs, Brzezinski Material, Country File, Box 9, China (PRC): 4-5/79, Confidential.

79 *Memorandum from the Under Secretary of State for Economic Affairs (Cooper) to Secretary of State Vance: Secretary Kreps' Mission to China*, Washington, DC, 18 May 1979, Confidential, in FRUS 1977–1980, Vol. XIII, Doc. 244, 878–880.

80 *Discussion of Chinese Economy and US-China Relations*, Washington, DC, 30 May 1979, 11:30 a.m., in JCPL, National Security Affairs, Staff Material, Far East, Oksenberg Subject File, Box 47, Meetings: 5/79, Confidential.

81 *Comments by Dong Xiang on the British Election and Song Zhihguang's Remarks on Hong Kong*, 25 May 1979, in NA, FCO 21/1691, *UK-China Relations*, FEC 020/1, Confidential.

82 *Memorandum by the Secretary of State for Foreign and Commonwealth Affairs – Defence Sales to China: Future Policy*, 6 June 1979, OD (79) 5, Confidential, https://c59574e9047e61130f13-3f71d0fe2b653c4f00f32175760e96e7.ssl.cf1.rackcdn.com/B36943923DB647559E1142F6AE4579EC.pdf, accessed 31 October 2021.

83 *Minutes of a Meeting Held at 10 Downing Street on Monday 11 June 1979, at 4.30 pm*, 13 June 1979, OD (79) 2nd Meeting, Secret, https://c59574e9047e61130f13-3f71d0fe2b653c4f00f32175760e96e7.ssl.cf1.rackcdn.com/8B882790B8ED43029 8D2F856C1232A96.pdf, accessed 31 October 2021.

84 Although the United States could not satisfy many of China's demands, it was pleased to see other Western partners deal with the PRC and even took advantage of such interactions. This wave of technology importation and the reality of other countries' technological advancement inspired enthusiasm within China to acquire the same technology to achieve that kind of modernisation sought since the mid-1960s but obstructed by the Cultural Revolution. Lei Liu, 'China's Large-Scale Importation of Western Technology', 819.

85 *Research Paper – China: The Steel Industry in the 1970s and 1980s*, May 1979, ER 79-10245, https://www.cia.gov/readingroom/docs/CIA-RDP86B00985R00030004 0017-8.pdf, accessed 9 October 2021.

86 'Policy on Importing Technology', *Beijing Review*,22/22, 1979, 11–13.

87 'China's National Economy (1978–79)', *Beijing Review*, 22/26, 1979, 8–12.

88 Shi Zhengwen, 'Readjusting the National Economy: Why and How?', *Beijing Review*, 22/26, 1979, 13–23.

89 Lowell Dittmer, 'China in 1981: Reform, Readjustment, Rectification', *Asian Survey*, 22/1, A Survey of Asia in 1981: Part I, 1982, 36.

90 Hua Guofeng, 'Report on the Work of the Government (Delivered at the Second Session of the Fifth National People's Congress on June 18, 1979)', *Beijing Review*, 22/27, 1979, 5–31.

91 Yu Qiuli, 'Arrangements for the 1979 National Economic Plan', *Beijing Review*, 22/29, 1979, 7–16.

92 'The Law of the People's Republic of China on Joint Ventures Using Chinese and Foreign Investment (Adopted by the Second Session of the Fifth National People's Congress on July 1, 1979)', *Beijing Review*, 22/29, 1979, 24–26.

93 'Plans Readjusted, Policy Unchanged', *Beijing Review*, 22/30, 1979, 9–11.

94 Naughton, 'Economic Rebalancing', in Jacques deLisle and Avery Goldstein (eds.), *China's Challenges* (Philadelphia, PA: University of Pennsylvania Press, 2015), 112–113.

95 *Western Leverage on the Soviet Union, Its Allies and China*, 2 August 1979, in NA, FCO 21/1691, FEC 020/1, Confidential.

96 Anna Michalski and Zhongqi Pan, *Unlikely Partners? China, the European Union and the Forging of a Strategic Partnership* (Singapore: Palgrave Macmillan, 2017), 42.

97 Schaller, *The United States and China*, 192.

98 During Deng's short war with Vietnam, General Zhang Aiping spoke to the visiting US Secretary of Defence, Harold Brown, saying that with American help Beijing would develop faster, perhaps also in the interests of the US. Odd Arne Westad, *Restless Empire: China and the World since 1750* (New York, NY: Basic Books, 2012), 374.

99 *Summary of the Vice President's Meeting with People's Republic of China Vice Premier Deng Xiaoping*, Beijing, 27 August 1979, 9:30 a.m.–12:10 p.m., in JCPL, National Security Affairs, Staff Material, Office, Outside the System File, Box 53, Chron: 8/2/79, Secret.

100 The Overseas Private Investment Corporation (OPIC) was a US development finance institution assisting private businesses that wanted to invest abroad. OPIC encouraged development in emerging markets by helping assess and manage risks.

101 *Vice-President Mondale's Press Conference on August 28 at 6.15 pm at Minzu Hotel, Beijing*, in NA, FCO 21/1694.

102 *Summary of the Vice President's Meeting with Deng Xiaoping*, Beijing, 28 August 1979, 9:30 a.m.-Noon, in JCPL, National Security Affairs, Staff Material, Office, Outside the System File, Box 53, Chron: 8/2/79, Top Secret, Sensitive, Eyes Only.

103 *Summary of the Vice President's Meeting with Premier Hua Guofeng*, Beijing, 28 August 1979, 3:30–5:30 p.m., in JCPL, National Security Affairs, Staff Material, Far East, Oksenberg Subject File, Box 47, Meetings: 8-9/79, Top Secret, Sensitive, Eyes Only.

104 *Trip to China*, Washington, DC, 16 September 1979, in JCPL, Brzezinski Donated Material, Geographic File, Box 9, China (People's Republic of), Alpha Channel: 12/78-1/80, Secret, Sensitive.

105 *Memorandum from Secretary of State to President Carter*, Washington, DC, 18 September 1979, in JCPL, National Security Affairs, Staff Material, Far East, Oksenberg Subject File, Box 25, Brown (Harold) 1/80 Trip: 8-9/79, Top Secret, Eyes Only.

106 *Secretary Brown's Visit to China: Conflicting Memoranda from Vance & Brown*, Washington, DC, 18 September, 1979, in JCPL, National Security Affairs, Staff Material, Far East, Oksenberg Subject File, Box 25, Brown (Harold) 1/80 Trip, 8-9/79, Secret.

107 *NSC Weekly Report 111*, Washington, DC, 5 October 1979, in JCPL, Brzezinski Donated Material, Subject File, Box 42, Weekly Reports [to the President], 102–120 [7/79-12/79], Top Secret, Codeword.

108 *Memorandum from Secretary of State to President Carter*, Washington, DC, 9 December 1979, in JCPL, National Security Affairs, Staff Material, Office, Outside the System File, Box 55, Chron: 12/11-20/79, Top Secret.

109 *Speech by Mr Gromyko*, in General Assembly Official Records, 34th Session: 7th Plenary Meeting, Tuesday, 25 September 1979, New York, https://digitallibrary. un.org/record/720391?ln=en#record-files-collapse-header, accessed 17 October 2021.

110 *Interview Given by the Secretary of State to Philip Short, for the BBC Radio 4 "Today" Programme to be Broadcast on 1 October*, 10 September 1979, in NA, FCO 21/1692, *UK-China Relations*, FEC 020/1.

111 'Han Nianlong's Speech at the U.N. General Assembly (Excerpts)', *Beijing Review* 22/41, 1979, 1321.

112 Casarini, *Remaking Global Order*, 28–29.

113 Harish Kapur, *China and the EEC: The New Connection* (Dordrecht: Kluwer Academic Publishers, 1986), 61.

114 Laurens Hemminga, 'Sino-European Relations in the 1980s: Increasing Engagement in the Shadow of the United States', in Roberts (ed.), *Chinese Economic Statecraft*, 290.

115 Robert McNamara, President of the World Bank, reminded Deng's enthusiastic acceptance of financial assistance. David M. Lampton, *Following the Leader: Ruling China, from Deng Xiaoping to Xi Jinping* (Oakland, CA: University of California Press, 2014), 27–28.

116 'Comrade Ye Jianying's Speech at the Meeting in Celebration of the 30th Anniversary of the Founding of the People's Republic of China (September 29, 1979)', *Beijing Review*, 22/40, 1979, 7–32.

117 'Premier Hua Guofeng Holds Press Conference', *Beijing Review*, 22/41, 1979, 8–11.

118 'Premier Hua Guofeng Interviewed by Felix Greene', *Beijing Review*, 42/22, 1979, 7–14.

119 Yasheng Huang, 'The Role of Foreign-Invested Enterprises in the Chinese Economy: An Institutional Foundation Approach', in Shuxun Zen and Charles Wolf, Jr. (eds.), *China, the United States, and the Global Economy* (Santa Monica, CA and Arlington, VA: Rand, 2001), 174.

120 Ashley J. Tellis, 'US-China Relations in a Realist World', in D. Shambaugh (ed.), *Tangled Titans: The United States and China* (Plymouth and Lanham, MD: Rowman & Littlefield Publishers, Inc., 2013), 78–79.

121 Telegram 180918Z from Embassy Beijing to SecState WashDC Immediate 9163, *Deng Xiaoping's Meeting with Governors' Delegation*, 18 October 1979, Beijing 7338, Confidential, in NARA, RG 59, CFPF 1973–1979, Electronic Telegrams, https://aad.archives.gov/aad/createpdf?rid=279327&dt=2776&dl=2169, accessed 21 October 2021.

122 Michal Meidan, *The Structure of China's Oil Industry: Past Trends and Future Prospects*, OIES Paper: WPM 66 (Oxford: Oxford Institute for Energy Studies, May 2016), 7–8.

123 Charles Chao Rong Phua, *Towards Strategic Pragmatism in Foreign Policy: Cases of United States of America, China and Singapore* (Abingdon and New York, NY: Routledge, 2022), 53.

124 *Visit of Premier Hua Guofeng of China 28 October – 3 November 1979: Steering Brief – Brief by Foreign and Commonwealth Office*, 17 October 1979, NMV(79)1, in NA, CAB 134/494, Confidential.

125 *Visit of Premier Hua Guofeng of China 28 October – 3 November 1979: Brief by Department of Foreign and Commonwealth Office; Annex E: UK Objectives*, 17 October 1979, NMV(79)1, in NA, CAB 134/494, Confidential.

126 *Visit of Premier Hua Guofeng of China 28 October – 3 November 1979: Brief by the Foreign and Commonwealth Office – China's International Role*, 17 October 1979, NMV(79)5, in NA, CAB 134/494, Confidential.

127 *Visit of Premier Hua Guofeng of China 28 October – 3 November 1979: Brief by Department of Trade – Bilateral Trade and Technological Cooperation*, 19 October 1979, NMV(79)8, in NA, CAB 134/494, Confidential.

128 *Visit of Premier Hua Guofeng of China 28 October – 3 November 1979: Brief by the Ministry of Defence – Defence Sales*, 18 October 1979, NMV(79)10, in NA, CAB 134/494, Confidential.

129 *Record of Discussion between the Prime Minister and Premier Hua Guofeng at No. 10 Downing Street on 29 October 1979 at 1530 Hours*, 30 October, 1979, in NA, FCO 21/1711, *Visit to the UK by Hua Kuo Feng*, FEC 026/2, Confidential.

130 At a 17 December meeting with President Carter, Thatcher said that Britain was ready to sell China Harrier aircraft. *Note of a Meeting Held in the Oval Office, White House, Washington D.C., Monday 17 December, 1979, 1230 PM*, in NA, FCO 21/1694, Secret.

131 *Record of a Discussion between the Prime Minister and Premier Hua Guofeng at 10 Downing Street on 1 November 1979 at 1600 Hours*, 5 November 1979, in NA, PREM 19 Volume 3, Confidential.

132 *Note of a Meeting with the Vice Premier of the People's Republic of China at Claridge's on Tuesday 30 October 1979*, in NA, PREM 19/3, Restricted.

133 *Department of Transport Press Notice: Anglo-Chinese Agreement Signed*, 29 November 1979, in NA, T 370/1501, *Nationalised Industries Trade Agreements with China*.

134 Barry Naughton, 'A Political Economy of China's Economic Transition', in Loren Brandt and Thoman G. Rawski (eds.), *China's Great Economic Transformation* (Cambridge: Cambridge University Press, 2008), 104.

135 Arthur R. Kroeber, 'Developmental Dreams: Policy and Reality in China's Economic Reforms', in Scott Kennedy (ed.), *Beyond the Middle Kingdom: Comparative Perspectives on China's Capitalist Transformation* (Stanford, CA: Stanford University Press, 2011), 44–51.

136 'Premier Hua's Visit to Britain: New Impetus for Closer Co-operation', *Beijing Review*, 22/45, 1979, 8–11.

137 Deng, *We Can Develop a Market Economy under Socialism: Excerpt from a Talk with Frank B. Gibney, Vice-Chairman of the Compilation Committee of Encyclopaedia Britannica, Inc. of the United States, Paul T. K. Lin, Director of the Institute of East Asia at McGill University of Canada, and others*, 26 November 1979, http://www.china.org.cn/english/features/dengxiaoping/103388.htm, accessed 26 October 2021.

138 Barna Talas, *Economic Reforms and Political Attempts in China 1979–1989* (Heidelberg: Springer-Verlag, 1991), 91–92.

139 'TV Interview with Deng Xiaoping', 15 October 1979, *Beijing Review*, 23/2, 1980, 18–23.

140 *Speaking Notes – Hua Guofeng's Visit to the Federal Republic of Germany from 21 to 28 October 1979*, 16 November 1979, in NA, FCO 21/1698, Restricted.

141 *Record of a Meeting in Peking on 27 November 1979 with the Chinese Foreign Minister and Institute for International Studies*, in NA, FCO 21/1692, Confidential.

142 *Izvestia Article: Peking's Flirt with Europe*, 10 November 1979, in NA, FCO 21/1698.

143 *US Policy toward China*, Washington, DC, 13 December 1979, in JCPL, National Security Affairs, Staff Material, Office, Outside the System File, Box 55, Chron: 12/11-20/79, Top Secret.

144 Westad, *Restless Empire*, 374–375.

4   Afghanistan and Arms Sales

4.1 Talks with the People's Republic on Afghanistan

In September 1979, President Carter asked his national security adviser to arrange contingency options in case of Soviet invasion of Afghanistan, where in the previous year a communist coup had taken place. However, Brzezinski had warned that Kabul's terror tactics to implement social lay reforms were proving counterproductive, and he informed the president that a direct Russian intervention was becoming more and more probable. On Christmas night, Soviet forces invaded the Western Asian country, thus installing a new president. According to Brzezinski, the Soviet action had initiated a regional crisis of strategic significance. Hence, he suggested the administration had to use the invasion of a strategically sensitive Asian country as a justification to pave the way to a defence relationship with China. As it had already happened so many times, the secretary of state did not agree, stating that such a step would set back relations with the Kremlin.[1] On the other hand, what seemed to be more worrisome according to the US Embassy in Moscow was that the Soviet action appeared to mark a major watershed in Russian policy, as this was the first time since the Second World War that the USSR had intervened militarily outside the Warsaw Pact area to install a regime of its own choice.[2] Despite Vance's opposition, the Chinese ambassador at Washington DC got involved in briefings with American officers on actions to be taken in response to the Soviet breakthrough. To tell the truth, at that point it was difficult to think that the Carter administration did not want to react by tightening the collaboration with Beijing. Actually, the Chinese had always been warning about what they regarded as a Soviet strategy to encircle the rivals in Asia and get control of the Malacca Strait and the Persian Gulf. As an evidence of that, the Chinese ambassador underscored the importance of taking concrete steps to strengthen Afghanistan's neighbours. What had happened in that country, he said, showed that the USSR was no one's natural ally but rather an international gangster. In a nutshell, the diplomat stressed that what had occurred in Afghanistan could not be regarded as a localised incident, but it was an event of global relevance.[3] This interpretation was very similar to what Secretary Brown said in the meeting

DOI: 10.4324/9781003390138-5

with Vice Premier Geng Biao, warning that the Americans were concerned about Soviet intervention in Afghanistan severely disturbing the regional balance in Southwest Asia, and consequently threatening to disrupt the global network of strategic relationships.[4] As Vitaly Kozyrev says, the invasion accelerated the PRC's (People's Republic of China) rapprochement with the Anglo-Saxon power. What worried the most, moreover, was the unpredictability of Moscow's foreign policy, due to the growing role of force the communist Euro-Asian country had acquired.[5] Such a rivalry was always considered as a dangerous situation, but the positive thing from the Western point of view was the Chinese interest in stability and integrity of ASEAN countries.[6] Once again, it is interesting to notice how different Cyrus Vance's opinion was from his own colleagues within the administration. In his memoirs, in fact, he tries to understand the Soviet point of view by writing that Moscow had acted for a number of reasons, such as the fear to have Amin's regime replaced by an Islamic fundamentalist government spreading religious fever along Russia's Southern borders. Others believed that the Kremlin had to seize the opportunity to enjoy better positions towards Pakistan and China. Moreover, the secretary did not rule out the idea that the downward spiral in US-Soviet relations had released the brakes on Russian international behaviour. In a few words, if the Soviets had felt that there was more to lose in their relationship with the United States, they would have been more cautious.[7]

As a matter of fact, President Carter told Margaret Thatcher that the Soviet intervention was an extremely grave development, similar in scope and permanent impact to what they had done in Czechoslovakia eleven years previously. Briefly, Moscow was accused to have changed a proper nation into a puppet state, with profound strategic consequences on the stability of the entire region. Therefore, the president thought it was essential to make this action as politically costly as possible to the Soviet Union. As far as the United Nations was concerned, the People's Republic of China was supposed to be one of the actors leading the counter measures to take.[8] It was clear that the West could now take advantage of the fact that throughout the decade China had been more vocal than the United States in warning on the danger of expansion by the Soviet Union, thus portraying Russian efforts to contain China in Asia – for example through military presence in Vietnam, ever-closer military relationship with India and growing involvement with Afghanistan – as part of a wider expansion and influence to be countered by a united international front. Chinese leaders began to recalculate their respective approaches to the Soviet Union and the United States, since the previously perceived danger that the United States would "appease" Moscow looked then remote.[9] Most importantly, on 24 January 1980 the Congress passed a trade agreement conferring MFN status on China, thus exempting Chinese exports to the United States from the high tariff rates stipulated in June 1930. Despite this move, under US law the People's Republic of China was placed within the purview of the Jackson-Vanik Amendment of 1974, linking trade benefits to the human rights policies of communist (or former Communist) countries, preventing them from participating in any US programme extending credits, or credit guarantees, or investment guarantees. This provided the legal grounds for the annual congressional renewal of China's MFN status until 2001, when the PRC joined the World Trade Organisation, whose rule prohibits members from imposing trade restrictions on other members.[10] As a matter of fact, Deng was simultaneously acting on three fronts, that is the West in general, Japan and international financial organisations, in order to achieve three objectives: (a) strengthening domestic reforms on the way to modernisation by acquiring external economic support; (b) reunion with Taiwan and other territories lost in the past; (c) containing Soviet strategic threats. In a few words, by getting full membership in the main international organisations, it would have been more likely for Beijing to obtain assistance, loans and technical expertise, while at the same time boosting its own international status and exercise greater global influence.[11]

Talking to Harold Brown, Deng Xiaoping was very caustic when he said that Afghanistan was to be turned into a quagmire bogging down the Soviet Union for a long time in a guerrilla warfare.[12] According to the Chinese, the southwards drive strategy of the Soviet Union aimed at seizing warm water ports along the Indian Ocean. Hence, Pakistan inevitably became the next target on the list.[13] As a consequence of that, Beijing reportedly told the Pakistanis that it was urging the United States to renew substantial arms shipments to Islamabad, fearing that a "partial" American response to Pakistan could be interpreted as a lack of determination to confront Soviet aggression. Over the longer term, the CIA thought Beijing might try to create a sort of regional alignment against Moscow, also hoping to reach increased cooperation with New Delhi.[14] After Afghanistan, said also Premier Hua, the Soviet Union was ready to a step further. As an outcome of that prediction, China was in favour of effective measures to punish the aggressor. The interesting thing at that point was that by and large the two powers saw international events in the same way. A strong NATO Alliance and a stable Northeast Asia, for example, were regarded as essential for the security of both nations. The events in Afghanistan, said on the other hand Secretary Brown, had heightened the sense of concern, extending it to many countries in the Middle East. In particular, the United States appreciated the Chinese to contain Moscow's influence due to the difficult situation with Iran, where American officers were being held as hostages after the assault against the embassy.[15]

From the Chinese point of view, reminds us Richard Evans, at the beginning of the 1980s the main threat to face was always the USSR, but it was a different kind of danger. Instead of invasion and nuclear attack, Beijing felt the risk of strategic encirclement, with the Soviets pursuing a policy to become the dominant Power in Asia by eliminating all positions of Chinese and also American strength.[16] As Ronald C. Keith says, Soviet invocation of the Brezhnev Doctrine to justify military intervention in Afghanistan was anathema to Beijing. Relations with the Soviet Union were particularly tense due also to Russian expansionism in Africa and Southeast and Central Asia.[17] As far as technology transfer was concerned, the American Executive by then believed that a new policy was to be established in order to distinguish between China and the Soviet Union preserving legitimate security interests.[18] The defence secretary openly stated that his department was increasing the budget and intended to widen military presence in the Middle East and Arabian Sea area, being more ready than ever to play a central role with partners and allies to organise opposition to Soviet expansion. Better words were not possible to Deng's ears, as the Chinese leader claimed that China had always pointed out explicitly that the Soviet Union was the source of international turbulence and a threat to peace and security in the world. In a word, Moscow was accused of having linked its strategy in the West to the one in the Asian and Pacific region, thus trying to increase naval strength in the Indian Ocean and form two edges of the same policy to control the Straits of Malacca. Hence, the only way Deng proposed to cope with the Bear was standing unite in an earnest fashion. As a consequence of this, Washington was not ready yet to sell arms to the People's Republic, but this did not mean that all military equipment was ruled out. On the contrary, Brown was drawing a distinction between dual use technology and military equipment, such as surveillance and warning devices.[19] In addition, Brown himself encouraged the Chinese to acquire the necessary projects and know-how to develop their own industry and machinery.[20] Therefore, Washington wanted to provide military equipment or sell technology in order for China to build up military capabilities on its own.[21]

On 16 January 1980, Deng delivered a speech at a meeting called by the Central Committee of the Communist Party, on the occasion of which he said the most recent events in Iran and Afghanistan proved that the incoming decade would be a dangerous era. Hence, the task of opposing hegemonism had to be on China's daily agenda. In addition, economic construction was to be stepped up. Without sound economic foundations, to put the matter in a nutshell, it was impossible to modernise national defence, and science and technology should primarily serve economic construction. In the previous year, the total volume of exports had increased by twenty-six per cent, with 140 contracts on medium and small compensatory trade, and more than 2,000 deals on processing materials provided by overseas customers. As far as agriculture was concerned, the value of output had augmented by 7.3 per cent over the previous year. New advances had been made by heavy industry in better serving agriculture and light industry to produce consumer goods.[22] As a matter of fact, the situation at the dawn of the 1980s was described as excellent, having paved the way for victorious advance in all spheres. However, and here lay the vice premier's innovative stance, modernisation could not be achieved merely by keeping to the socialist road. Rather, it was also necessary to master professional knowledge and skills.[23] Apart from that, as it was easy to realise, the Americans were not the only ones to approach China as an outcome of the situation in Afghanistan. The Foreign Office, in fact, studied quite a wide range of possible actions to take in response to the Soviet invasion. In other words, the China card had to be used in a more resolute way, for example by opening credit flows towards Beijing, though there was always a broad interest in keeping the door open to an improvement of Anglo-Russian relations.[24]

Unlike the USSR, China was not perceived as a threat to the West, at least over a medium term, also because in the foreseeable future reconciliation between the two communist leading countries was not in sight. On the contrary, China had embarked on a new relationship with the West for reasons of self-interest in order to modernise the country and develop a first class economy, whose process was predicted to be slow but at the same time it was a good reason to pursue the good relations which had been built up for a few years by then. Words like these cannot be surprising if we think that China was said to seek a strong NATO and a politically united Western Europe for anti-Soviet reasons. Hence, it was natural for the British and Western governments in general to encourage Chinese development for economic and strategic purposes. London was supposed to take advantage of this card against the Russians short of the point at which Moscow might see a threat to its vital interests. And that was why it was better to involve as many allies as possible in any deliberate strengthening of relations with Beijing in order to have as much impact as possible in the short term, but without tying hands. As concerned defence sales, it was important for British firms to get firmly into the market in the shortest possible way, with the aim to promote UK interests in a field which the Americans seemed about to open wide to their allies, to say the least.[25] In particular, the American announcement on 24 January about the readiness to sell carefully selected items of support military equipment, though not weapons yet, was considered as clearly relevant to start a new era of Sino-Western relations.[26] Just to be as clear as possible, the Soviet invasion of Afghanistan further contributed to a sense of shared strategic aims, which seemed to suggest that the prospects for increased collaboration in the sector of security and defence were substantially improving under the new British conservative government. Nevertheless, the Chinese were starting losing interest in spending large amounts of scarce foreign currency on military goods that were not going to pivotally change the immediate strategic situation of the People's Liberation Army. Secondly, from the early 1980s onwards Beijing was increasingly concentrated on maintaining stability at its borders in order to focus on economic reforms at home, thus reducing the need for high-profile military deals with the West.[27]

4.2 The Fifth Plenum: Deng Xiaoping Tightens the Rope

At the Fifth Plenum of the Central Committee of the Communist Party between 23 and 29 February, Deng Xiaoping gained another victory in his struggle to tighten his control over the party by managing to have his main opponents removed from their formal positions. Even more important, according to British reports, was the elevation of Hu Yaobang and Zhao Ziyang (Deng's twin heirs apparent) to the Standing Committee, since maybe for the first time there were coevals of Hua Guofeng in the highest party organ.[28] Such moves were said to be part of Deng's strategy to push forward with institutional and economic reforms while keeping a high degree of stability.[29] To be precise, as General Secretary Hu was now able to manipulate the party without any reference to Chairman Hua, while Zhao was in the front row to replace Hua as premier. In particular, the role of the secretariat was going to be the executive arm of the party, enabling the Politburo of the Central Committee and its Standing Committee to consider and take decisions on important issues of domestic and foreign affairs.[30] In order to fulfil the four modernisations and solve problems in the quickest possible way, the party decided to summon the twelfth National Congress to be held in 1982 to revise the Constitution and outline a new national economic plan.[31] It was obvious for Deng to try to ease Hua out of the chairmanship and replace him with his men, especially Zhao, who had experience as a highly pragmatic provincial official, with a very successful record as leader of Sichuan, China's most populous province.[32] Months later, at the third session of the Fifth National People's Congress in Beijing, Deng resigned his vice-premiership in order to force the "voluntary resignation" of several revolutionaries of the older generation. Such a move enabled Deng, who kept control of the Central Military Commission, to place his allies in power in party and state, thus removing any potential obstacle to reform.[33]

Meanwhile, the Americans were discussing the possibility for the People's Republic to seek to take over the China seat at the International Monetary Fund and the International Bank for Reconstruction and Development. The stance of the Carter administration was by then oriented to support that position, being in US long-term interest for a country as important as China to join such institutions.[34] As a matter of fact, Chinese government officers were turning towards the World Bank, which had been the most unwelcome institution in Mao's China, portrayed as an agent of American imperialism during the Cultural Revolution. Instead, Deng Xiaoping thought that global financial institutions were the key to provide technical and economic support.[35] The president of the World Bank, Robert McNamara, visited China and met Deng on 15 April 1980, when the Chinese leader said that the PRC would modernise with or without World Bank assistance. On this historic step we can quote Pieter Bottelier, according to whom McNamara realised that helping China reorient its development model would establish credibility for the World Bank as an independent multilateral agency very important to Beijing, closed to the outside world since the early 1950s and essentially a black box for the World Bank, which was joined on 15 May. Hence, the Bank not only was seen as a valuable source of technical advice, international experience and information on development, but also, being perceived as an independent and neutral organisation, as a sort of "air-lock" between China and the Western world during the initial stages of reform.[36] In light of this, the Bank describes the work with China in the first years as mainly a question of educating Chinese officials in new economic ideas and technical systems.[37]

As concerned the British, the secretary of defence visited China in March 1980, and this is evidence of how the invasion of Afghanistan had accelerated arms sales and talks. On that occasion, the Chinese explained their philosophy to first improve existing weapons and then acquire technology for the following generation, which Britain was ready to provide. Beijing did not want to over-extend and that was why the purchase of Harrier had been postponed. Nevertheless, the secretary of defence was optimistic about Chinese intentions, adding that his Asian counterparts really meant business. The key role remained British firms and their ability to get organised in order to deal with the Chinese defence market where European and American competition was expected to be resolute. At that point, it had become important to exploit Beijing's openings and plan long-term cooperation,[38] which as far as defence sales were concerned included refitting of F7 and F8 aircraft, Luda class destroyers and tank engine collaboration with Rolls Royce, as well as developing new air-to-air missiles and radar altimeters. Overall, the Chinese market potential was assessed to be a medium-sized one with substantial opportunities, especially in the Guangdong area, where massive projects were being in progress, such as development of oil fields, electricity supply, highway construction and a nuclear power station.[39] On the other side of the Atlantic, Carter emphasised to Geng Biao that the American unchanging opposition to Vietnam's invasion of Kampuchea and the Soviet Union's invasion of Afghanistan were very important factors in the cooperation with Beijing,[40] so that it was essential to look for ways to support each other at the United Nations and ASEAN.[41]

David Goodman defines Deng as a sort of conservative reformer, a traditionalist who wanted to restore what he considered had been the CCP's tradition, overturned during the Cultural Revolution. As he had stressed in January 1980, support for the party had to be renewed through economic growth.[42] To further widen cooperation, in China an economic debate was being held on competition in a socialist economy. Some argued that there should not be competition in a socialist system, as that meant capitalism, while others said that competition was the struggle waged by producers for their own interests. Under the conditions of socialism, the only way to give full play to workers' initiative was starting a socialist emulation under party leadership. Finally, there were those who admitted the benefits of competition, on condition that (a) market economy was to be expanded allowing not only consumer goods, but also means of production to access the market; (b) enterprises were supposed to have more power of decision and sell products directly on the market; (c) prices had to fluctuate within certain limits.[43] A very important step of such a debate was maybe the invitation following Chinese nomination to Milton Friedman to participate in a series of lectures within an exchange programme between the United States and China. As Julian Gewirtz reminds, Friedman had won the Nobel Prize in 1976, establishing himself as an advocate of a sort of free market radicalism. What the market did, he had written, was minimising the extent to which government participated directly in the economy, which he believed would end inflation and high taxes. At the sessions, the scholar confronted the idea that inflation was either a capitalistic, or a communist phenomenon. Instead, he said that government was the fundamental source of inflation. Such a radical stance was difficult to accept in post-Mao China, so that the Nobel Prize winner exclaimed that the Chinese officials he had met were profoundly ignorant about how a market or capitalist system worked. Indeed, Gewirtz's thesis is that interactions like that with Friedman heightened awareness by Chinese leaders of the limitations of their understanding of how markets operated. Hence, the new leadership team of Deng, Hu Yaobang and Zhao Ziyang backed off from ambitious reform plans, instead deferring to readjustment with the aim of rapidly bringing down the deficit and stabilising the economy.[44]

Concisely, the collaboration with the West had become so close that the United States was by then a central factor as a source of help in the modernisation of the country, as a facilitator in the increasing intimacy with Japan and Western Europe, and as at least an ambiguous deterrent in Soviet military calculations about China.[45] By reading records, it seems the Chinese were enthusiast about studying the procedures of capitalism, after having followed the over-centralised example of the Soviet Union too closely. The ten-year-plan for the 1980s was being drawn up, to be adopted the following year by the People's National Congress.[46] However it was, Deng said the target could not be too high, setting by the end of the century a *per capita* living standard comparable to that of Japan, West Germany and France in the 1950s.[47] In particular, energy was going to be identified as a key area, outlining plans in coal industry exploration and processing, as well as oil and hydro-power.[48] The energy sector offered relatively good opportunities for UK exports as China planned to expand coal production and required large imports of mining equipment. Apart from that, the British Petroleum was already carrying out seismic exploration work and hoped to win further contracts, thus opening opportunities for other offshore companies.[49] Another important form of cooperation was leasing, enabling British suppliers to export capital goods by selling them to an intermediary company which then leased them to Chinese trading organisations.[50] As far as foreign investment was concerned, important to remind is Zhao's comment on foreigners' fear that China might change and renounce previous agreements. Actually, the emerging leader denounced that there were too many demands put into the contracts due to Chinese suspicion of being exploited. The point was, quotes Zhao in his diary, that the Asian country had kept its doors closed for many years in the name of independence and self-reliance, thus imposing self-isolation. On the contrary, foreign trade and mutual exchange were regarded as a form of self-reliance, both in terms of raw materials market and as far as the real estate one was concerned, therefore attracting businesses from abroad for large-scale development and rapid urban growth.[51]

4.3 The Energy Network: Opportunities and Assessment

There is scarcely any doubt that the war in Afghanistan had enhanced the collaboration with the People's Republic of China. We also have to remind that the United States Embassy in reported that the Soviets suspected that Washington and Beijing would eventually be tempted to exploit a sustained anti-Soviet insurgency, thus leaving the USSR faced by a radical and unfriendly Islamic Southern neighbour, susceptible to potential overtures from the United States and China. Nevertheless, the Embassy saw no direct evidence that the Soviet move into Afghanistan was part of a larger design to expand military power to the Persian Gulf, or encircle China.[52] How irritating Sino-American rapprochement was to the Soviets was being clarified by Foreign Minister Gromyko himself, who added to his new American homologue, Edmund Muskie, that the very heart of China's policy led towards war, in their dreams even a conflict between the United States and the Soviet Union to take advantage from.[53]

By reading the available documentation, we notice that the Chinese always introduced the issue and were extremely strict in their assessment of Soviet policies. As an evidence of that, we can quote once again Hua Guofeng speaking to President Carter in Tokyo in July 1980, on the occasion of which the Chinese leader said that the attack to the central Asian country was part of a Soviet thrust to the South. If they were successful, he feared, they were expected to move on towards the Indian Ocean and the oil-producing regions of the Middle East. Hua also commented that the Vietnamese were like the Cubans in acting as Soviet proxies, and he believed that Moscow wanted to consolidate control on Cambodia in order to try to block the Strait of Malacca and turn it into the vital link between their strongholds in the Middle East and the Indian Ocean and the Pacific. In that case, Hua said that the West had no choice but to fight to prevent Europe from being outflanked.[54] Therefore, said also Vice Foreign Minister He Ying speaking to his British counterpart, it was important to take advantage at the United Nations and among Islamic countries.[55] On grounds of Soviet newspaper articles, these meetings incensed Moscow's authorities, who identified four Chinese aims: (a) to strengthen a Sino-US-Japanese axis; (b) to state that China ruled out the possibility of another military action against Vietnam; (c) to discuss with the Americans a common strategy towards the USSR; (d) to try to transform ASEAN into an organisation aimed against the Indochina area. In addition, according to Soviet analyses the Chinese had already decided to harm the Russians whenever and wherever they could.[56] As far as this question is concerned, Robert Ross is among those who do not think that the invasion of Afghanistan made Sino-American vision of the USSR further convergent. On the contrary, his position is that in the aftermath of the war the view of the two powers significantly started to diverge. Whereas the White House's perception of the "Red Threat" became as great as in the 1950s, on the other hand China's fear decreased. As a matter of fact, Carter's 1980 defence budget was much larger than that of the previous year, and his successor engaged the United States in a new stage of the Cold War by challenging the Soviet Union on all fronts. Hence, while the Americans perceived an increasing threat from Moscow during the late Carter administration and even more during Reagan's mandates, Chinese leaders felt a reduced Soviet menace and an improved security stance. After the invasion of Afghanistan, Beijing realised that the Atlantic superpower had by then adopted a series of measures to resist the Soviet Union, including promoting a new strategic relationship with China, which had therefore become a more valuable partner to the United States. In conclusion, now that Washington was finally meeting the Soviet challenge, the possibility for Moscow to expand in the Far East was reduced, since Russians were also on the diplomatic defensive and isolated like never before.[57]

Going back to business questions, in the Summer of 1980 the British government was working on the Guangdong nuclear project offering considerable opportunities with total costs set at 3.5 billion dollars and the UK industry share estimated at about one billion dollars. The development of projects like these in the Guangdong region was also regarded as a way to strengthen economic interdependence with Hong Kong, thus contributing to a mutual Sino-British interest in the stability of the colony and establishing business confidence in the territory.[58] According to British interpretations, the main Chinese motivation in pursuing such a project was to seek closer and closer relations between the People's Republic and Hong Kong. In a few words, Beijing was anxious for Britain to be involved in the Middle Kingdom's economic development in order to maintain the status quo when the lease for the colony ended in 1997.[59] Apart from this, the nuclear power plant project fostered competition within Western allies. Just to make an example, the French Embassy Trade Attaché in Beijing contacted the Ministry of Electric Power to enquire how French firms could take part in the works.[60] Tellingly, far from being only a commercial initiative, the Guangdong project had by then acquired considerable political importance as a pivotal element in the relationship between Beijing and Hong Kong. Hence, Mrs Thatcher was keenly interested in developing the nuclear power plant, acknowledging that in those circumstances it was important for British tenders to be supported at the highest political level.[61] Actually, Guangdong was among the first areas to undergo major economic reforms and was one of the first two provinces, including Fujian, to establish Special Economic Zones always in 1980. Located in Southern China opposite Hong Kong and with a deep-rooted tradition of emigration resulting in a large population of overseas Chinese, a rich source of investment from abroad, Guangdong became the best choice for opening up to the outside world.[62] The British negotiation stance was based upon the need for the power plant to be at least partially financed by the sale of electricity to Hong Kong, with French and American companies as partners, though Britain was always supposed to have the lion's share.[63]

Such a thrust to foreign trade and exports was also due to the slump of petroleum prices at the end of the 1970s, which stimulated PRC authorities to diversify export composition and promote products with a comparative advantage. Within this process, the new trade strategy was further institutionalised through the establishment of the Special Economic Zones and the incremental opening of coastal cities.[64] Once the wall between the international and domestic market began to be torn down, external price signals conveyed the message to domestic producers that Chinese products were extremely competitive in labour-intensive industries. Hence, promotion of local output and the attraction of foreign direct investment that conformed to this comparative advantage became top priority.[65] The clearest hint about the change taking place may have come from a February 1980 article by Deng Xiaoping explaining that China was by then at a turning point and needed learn to use the favourable international climate to accelerate modernisation availing itself of foreign funding. The adoption of the open door principle paved the way to China's joining the WBG (a collective term for International Monetary Fund, International Development Association and International Finance Corporation, affiliated agencies of the World Bank) in 1980, with the purpose to get access to a large pool of capital resources necessary to stabilise the monetary situation, expand foreign trade and finance infrastructure projects. Before providing any WBG funds to the People's Republic, an in-depth economic survey was conducted by a World Bank team, which in 1981 produced a nine-volume report examining five key sectors, such as human resources, agriculture, transports, energy and industry. The report concluded that future Chinese economic growth would depend on improved efficiency and resource use, skilled labour reallocation, increased foreign trade, greater freedom for importers, exporters, producers and consumers. Due to China's economic and technological lag, advanced technology imports were regarded as crucial to the development process and better competitiveness for Chinese manufactured exports in the world market. Moreover, the report also concluded that the Far Eastern power would need to borrow foreign funds at a level proportionate to the desired rate of growth.[66]

Meanwhile, economic debate carried on in the People's Republic, so that in September 1980 Xue Munqiao, adviser to the State Planning Commission and director of the Research Institute of Economics under the Commission gave an interview on economic reforms. According to him, in order to build a developed socialist economy various forms of management had to be allowed and, within certain limits, also the existence of other economic sectors, thus tolerating elements of individual ownership.[67] In the same days, Zhao Ziyang received a very positive assessment in London, as he was said to pursue maximum freedom to enterprises and, though in limited manner, scope for market forces to cooperate. In addition, Foreign Office officers recommended the government to give Zhao some time to win over conserv-ative forces within the Chinese Communist Party who might not politically accept the economic stimulus requested to galvanise China and get Hong Kong levels of productivity. Essentially, the pragmatism of the new administration was regarded to have left the party in something like an ideological vacuum.[68] In this regard, in a sort of farewell speech just before his removal from the premiership, Hua Guofeng claimed that the readjustment policy had marked the beginning of a pivotal change in China's economic construction, leaving behind over extension of investments and instead conforming to economic laws. In a few words, the general orientation was to transform public hyper-centralised management, extend the decision-making process of enterprises and transform regulation through planning into regulation through planning combined with the market. This did not mean that the delegation of power could weaken the necessary centralised control. Rather, such a control was supposed to be exercised mainly by using economic methods, instead of the mere administrative methods of the past.[69] In light of all that, in the future priority was going to be given to saving also through state investments in capital construction, bank credits and other forms of association. As regarded the petroleum industry, agreements on marine prospecting had been signed with foreign companies and other calls for tenders were necessary, as well as research and experiments in nuclear power, solar and other renewable sources of energy.[70]

The importance of these reforms was also testified by the reports presented before the Congress of the United States. In particular, Arthur G. Ashbrook, Jr. stated that Beijing did not view foreign trade only as an instrument to raise growth, but also as a way to see itself as a proud self-sufficient nation, with political relations with customer and supplier countries. On the export side, China was reported to have explicitly recognised the importance of identifying labour-intensive foodstuffs, manufacture and handicrafts with good world market potential. Foreign trade, therefore, was expected to support Chinese growth in the 1980s through supply of low-cost food to cities and provision of machinery and technology at the cutting edge of the modernisation effort.[71] Nevertheless, obstacles to reform always looked considerable, being also technical and bureaucratic more than ideological. A more rapidly growing China was regarded to become an attractive trading partner and a more stable member of the world community. Instead, Bruce L. Reynolds wrote that China had to further reform in order to maintain an acceptable rate of economic growth. Central planning was said to have been enormously successful in generating extensive growth in industry by adding to the stock of labour, capital and other productive factors. Shortly, with an industrial growth rate exceeding ten per cent per year, China was rapidly building up a large and comprehensive industrial structure.[72] As far as energy was concerned, the slowing and then the dramatic halt in the growth of crude oil output had been the major factor of the 1970s. As a matter of fact, production peaked in 1979. As regarded the future outlook, the American assessment was that in the 1990s

Beijing would be better equipped to absorb a whole array of new technologies. Coal was expected to remain the foundation of the Chinese economy, but coal conversion technologies were supposed to be used extensively. Finally, China was thought to continue to develop its immense hydroelectric resources and build at least some nuclear power plants, thus likely emerging in the late 1990s as one of the world's most extensive and lowest cost energy systems.[73] As Kazushi Minami stated, Beijing had tree options to deal with the oil peak crisis: (a) reducing domestic consumption, turning oil-burning boilers into coal-burning ones wherever possible; (b) slowing down the pace of industrial development by curtailing technology imports; (c) finding new sources of oil, especially offshore. This was the ideal solution, but it was expensive and required equipment and technology much more sophisticated than the outdated Soviet one being used to drill onshore. Hence, Beijing had little to do but call foreign oil companies. Japanese and French firms had gained their first offshore development contract in December 1979.[74] At the same time, Deng Xiaoping had found a paramount ally in Armand Hammer, chairman of Occidental Oil, which had developed coalmines and oilfields in the Soviet Union. The American tycoon decided to invest something like 100 million dollars in offshore fields around China, with even more attention towards coalmine development worth hundreds of millions.[75]

4.4 Close Contacts with the People's Republic

The foreign minister of China visited again the United Kingdom in October 1980 and from archival documentation we easily figure out how wide the division with the Soviet Union still was. According to the minister, the Russians had no intention to withdraw from Afghanistan, while Beijing's position could be summarised as follows: (a) Moscow had to unconditionally withdraw from Afghanistan in accordance with United Nations Resolutions; (b) Kabul had the right to self-determination without any interference; (c) the Asian country was supposed to be a non-aligned state again. Huang's words were very harsh, stating that it was impossible for Beijing to seek an accommodation with the Soviet Union on Afghanistan, for such a stance would be tantamount to legalisation of the occupation of a foreign country. In that case, the following step was supposed to be the invasion of Iran and Pakistan. Hence, it had become essential to rally diplomatic and economic pressure against Soviet expansionism. By reading these statements, it is rather difficult to assume that Sino-Soviet relations were improving, at least in the immediate aftermath of the invasion. Such a philippic towards the communist superpower had practically become a constant in every talk the Chinese had with any Western interlocutor.[76]

Furthermore, Soviet documents reveal an equally strict attitude towards the Asian power, stating that the partnership between American imperialism and Beijing's hegemonism not only was by then spreading to the military sphere, but it had become dangerous to mankind. In a few words, with the pretext to have a strong and stable China, Washington was being accused to expand the parameters for cooperation with Beijing in the military-technical sphere by affirming the readiness to deliver modern weapons and technology to China. As concerned the PRC's modernisation programme, the Central Committee of the Communist Party of the Soviet Union had reached the conclusion that such a plan had been projected above all to speed up the process of transforming China into a military superpower. In practice, unrestrained militarisation was thought to accelerate economic collapse and increased instability in China, thus leading to destabilisation of the international situation and the inflammation of international tension. What was most worrying according to Soviet analyses, was that China was probably tempted to develop expansionist plans to swallow up neighbouring countries. In conclusion, sooner or later the Dragon was supposed to stop behaving like an instrument in American hands, therefore acquiring the strength to even pursue an anti-US policy.[77] Just a few days before his visit to the United Kingdom, Huang Hua had addressed the General Assembly of the United Nations on the international situation. What we can perceive from this speech is that the Chinese felt a new stage of Soviet expansionism had begun with the invasion of Afghanistan. While in the past the USSR relied on proxy agents to wage military invasion or subversion in the Third World, warned the foreign minister, this time the Kremlin had dropped the mask and sent in its own troops. Moreover, the theory of the "hostile neighbour" was regarded as a pretext for all of Moscow's neighbours to show complete obedience to the Bear. In other words, while threatening the whole Asian-Pacific region, the Russians were also accused of seeking to outflank the Europeans and hasten completion of global domination. What was quite new this time was the fact that the Chinese government claimed to be ready to join other countries in an international guarantee that the territories of Afghanistan and Cambodia be no longer subject to foreign interference.[78] In a few words, the split between the communist powers was not really a question of ideology. Rather, China claimed to face a real threat from the Russians, as fifty-four divisions, that is a million men, were stationed along the border with the People's Republic, stated Deng Xiaoping in an interview to British journalists. On the contrary, the old revolution veteran observed that China would always be interested in pursuing good relations with the United States, also once having achieved development, since the two Pacific countries had a lot in common, having to cope with the Soviets, thus showing the strategic importance of the People's Republic.[79]

As we can realise from the old leader's words, trading and economic relations were not the only reason why Beijing had approached Washington. Moscow was the common enemy and at this point the collaboration with the West, as well as entrance into major capitalistic sanctuaries such as the International Monetary Fund and the World Bank, was regarded as the best way to win Soviet competition on the global chessboard. To tell the truth, a few months before these talks the CIA had issued a report summarising the

Soviet invasion of Afghanistan as an opportunity for China to advance three key foreign policy objectives: (a) discrediting détente choices in the West; (b) driving a wedge between the Third World and Moscow; (c) pushing the United States towards a tougher anti-Soviet stance. At the heart of Beijing's strategy, wrote American analysts, there was the effort to get the United States to renew its close ties with Pakistan, in order for Islamabad to resist firmly the Soviet presence in the region. Moreover, the PRC was thought to seek over the long term an informal, Western-backed alliance of Southwest Asian countries able to challenge further Soviet encroachment in the region, thus opposing any plan to neutralise Kabul and make Moscow pay the highest political price possible for its intervention.[80] Nevertheless, it was also easy to realise that in Beijing's view of "labour sharing" in the global anti-Soviet struggle, China's main effort was supposed to be focused on Southeast Asia, while the task of thwarting the Soviets in Afghanistan was left to the West and countries of Southwest Asia.[81]

As far as economic questions were concerned, the size of the modernisation task was such that the Europeans could also hope for a substantial share of orders. In particular West Germany, with its export-oriented manufacturing sector, could offer a lot of what China needed.[82] Paramount importance was given to the energy field as a common interest between China and Britain,[83] while London's major objective was first of all to gain Beijing's full support to the Guangdong project, seeking also to figure out whether the government of the People's Republic pursued equity participation by the United Kingdom and the Hong Kong government.[84] To tell the truth, Downing Street expected the Asian communist power to give particular encouragement to British participation, as a preponderant share of the non-nuclear hardware to be supplied by British companies, while it seemed no UK enterprise was in the market for the nuclear reactor.[85] Essentially, the project attracted London because this was supposed to increase China's interest in the stability of Hong Kong and improve Britain's position in the negotiations about the return of the colony to mainland China.[86] However, competition was so strong that the French in October 1980 had reached an agreement in principle with the Chinese to supply the first nuclear stations on advantageous financial terms. Despite the Hong Kong connection linking British interests with China's energy domestic requirements, what worried the British most what that the pressure for an all-French package could persuade the Chinese to take a decision excluding a substantial UK share. Therefore, in order to prevent Paris from carrying out such a move, an early initiative to the French was desirable, at the same time without closing the door to possible partnerships with the Americans. The Hong Kong issue was so pivotal to British interests that London wanted to work on the assumption that the project would go ahead, even though the suspension of a certain number of capital construction contracts suggested that the Chinese would approach the entire question with caution. On grounds of this, collaboration with both the French and the Americans was thought the best thing to do, especially because Britain was not able to supply the heart of the station, that is the pressurised water reactor and the remainder of the nuclear steam supply system.[87] The size of the whole plan meant that the Chinese government had to issue export guarantees going far beyond those for other big contracts. The point was that these loans would not have been repaid until 2005 and London had doubts about a pro-Western foreign policy being maintained for such a long time. Finally, British companies alone were unable to provide all the technology needed.[88] As a matter of fact, China's leaders had become increasingly concerned about loss of control over the economy. Like Barry Naughton writes, readjustment had reduced excess demand in the producer goods sector. Moreover, investment had not been reduced as rapidly as expected, for enterprise investment had increased nearly as quickly as government investment had declined. As a result of these concerns, the pace of reform was drastically slowed down.[89] Finally, in the same months there were also those who did not believe so much in the benefit for the United States to favour such ongoing trading relations with China. Gerald Curtis of Columbia University, for example, expressed his doubts on the opportunities offered by the PRC, as well as American leverage on Chinese policies. While Beijing could become a huge market over the long term, said the scholar, other countries in the same continent were growing faster and had more dynamic economies with a better promising immediate outlook. Therefore, he urged US choices in Asia to be more balanced, thus not ignoring that the modernisation process in China could be very slow, though it was impossible to acknowledge that China was on the path of deep antagonism towards America's worst antagonist in the world.[90]

Meanwhile, Beijing had also managed to get access to American credit through government programmes such as Eximbank, Commodity Credit Corporation, Trade and Development Program and the Overseas Private Investment Corporation. As a matter of fact, on 16–18 September 1980 the US-China Joint Economic Committee (JEC) held its first meeting in Washington, the culmination of which was the signing of bilateral textile, civil aviation, maritime and consular agreements. However, the Chinese underscored that the terms and amounts of US offers were less favourable than those advanced by the Europeans and Japanese, stressing that the world situation, and especially Sino-American relations, had changed dramatically enough to reconsider Washington's aid policy and legislation. Moreover, Beijing's representatives expressed concern about the growing trade deficit with the United States. In fact, in 1979 US exports had totalled approximately $1.7 billion, while Chinese exports had accounted for roughly 594 million. The third issue surfaced in the meeting dealt with the role American firms could play in China's modernisation drive, for this time it was Atlantic delegates complaining about the need to address problems of business facilitation, since lack of adequate commercial and banking conditions in China were hindering the expansion of business contacts.[91] The situation of the Chinese economy was certainly one of the major issues debated at the Congress, as shown by the hearings before the Subcommittee on Priorities and Economy in

Government. Just a few days after the afore mentioned meeting, Admiral Stansfield Turner, director of the Central Intelligence Agency, highlighted that Beijing was continuing to pour domestic and foreign capital into coal, oil and hydro-power sectors. However, many energy projects were not possible to complete until the second half of the decade. Until then, energy output was estimated to grow slowly, though it is important to notice that oil exports to the United States had been initiated, reaching 700,000 tons in 1979.[92]

What was maybe the most sensitive point for the Americans was the policy of reforming economic management pursued by the Chinese, with central control over commodity pricing and distribution being relaxed, as well as a substantial number of enterprises being allowed to keep part of their profits. As far as foreign trade was concerned, textiles and petroleum led the way, but in the last year the Dragon had run an $800-million trade deficit. The CIA estimated foreign exchange reserves, excluding gold, had reached about two billion dollars (equal to two months imports) by the end of 1979, while Beijing's imports of Western equipment and technology had shifted away from heavy industry to energy, transport and communications and light industry. Through the joint venture law, the establishment of special economic zones, and above all the membership in several international economic organisations, the People's Republic was showing the intention to expand its role in the world economy. As regarded the implications for US-China trade, in view of possible domestic energy shortages Admiral Turner renewed emphasis on oil exploration and sales of US oil drilling equipment. In conclusion, what the Americans showed some doubt about was Chinese capacity to face energy constraint and the ability to absorb new technology and investment. The Far Eastern country was still an exporter of energy, but those exports were not believed to increase in the following years. Rather, it was possible for them to be cut back.[93] Readjustment in certain fields was regarded as necessary because otherwise, said Deng Xiaoping on Christmas Day 1980, it would be impossible to ensure the steady growth of the economy. In the previous two years large financial deficit had been accumulated, too much currency had been issued and prices had steadily risen. Only by making sufficient cuts in some fields it was still likely to gain the initiative and achieve overall stability. The success of the policy to open up to the outside world was supposed to secure a peaceful environment necessary to Chinese stability and prosperity for a long period.[94]

Notes

1 Brzezinski, *Power and Principle*, 427–431.
2 *Telegram from the Embassy in the Soviet Union to the Department of State: Ramifications of the Soviet Move into Afghanistan*, Moscow, 28 December 1979, 1900Z, Secret, Niact Immediate, Nodis, in Adam M. Howard (gen. ed.) and Melissa Jane Taylor (ed.), FRUS 1977–1980, Vol. VI, *Soviet Union* (Washington, DC: United States Government Printing Office, 2013), Doc. 247, 713–715.

3 *Telegram 3285 from the Department of State to the Embassy in China: Consultations with China on the Afghan Situation*, Washington, DC, 5 January, 1980, 0313Z, Secret, Immediate, Sensitive, Nodis in Howard (gen. ed.) and David Zierler (ed.), FRUS 1977–1980, Vol. XII, *Afghanistan* (Washington, DC: United States Government Publishing Office, 2018), Doc. 141, 402–407.

4 *Memorandum of Conversation: Meeting between Secretary of Defense Harold Brown and Vice Premier Geng Biao, People's Republic of China*, Beijing, 7 January 1980, 9–11:45 a.m., Top Secret, Sensitive, in FRUS 1977–1980, Vol. XIII, Doc. 290, 1036–1049.

5 Kozyrev, Soviet Policy, 283.

6 *Diplomatic Report No. 19/80: Her Majesty's Ambassador at Peking to the Secretary of State for Foreign and Commonwealth Affairs: China – Annual Review for 1979*, 31 December 1979, in NA, FCO 21/1799, *China Internal Political*, FEC 014/1, Confidential.

7 Vance, *Hard Choices*, 388.

8 *Telephone Conversation between the Prime Minister and President Carter*, 28 December 1979, Prime Minister's Personal Message Serial No. THCR 3/1/4 (Personal Message T180A/79T), Secret, https://c59574e9047e61130f13-3f71d0fe2b653c4f00f32175760e96e7.ssl.cf1.rackcdn.com/7707F595FCB94F938D81316A12BEBF99.pdf, accessed 31 October 2021.

9 Sutter, *US-China Relations: Perilous Past, Uncertain Present* (Lanham, MD: Rowman & Littlefield, 2018), 80.

10 Dong Wang, *The United States and China: A History from the Eighteenth Century to the Present* (Lanham, MD: Rowman & Littlefield Publishers, Inc., 2013), 251–252.

11 Kai Yin Allison Haga, 'Deng Xiaoping's use of Positive Economic Statecraft: The Importance of Securing Long-Term Partnerships with Major International Financial Organizations (IFOs)', in Roberts (ed.), *Chinese Economic Statecraft*, 163, 180.

12 In the following years, the People's Republic and the United States worked closely together to help the Mujahidin in Afghanistan against Soviet forces. Moreover, the Chinese were declared eligible to purchase weapons directly from the US government with American Executive's financing. Cohen, *America's Response to China*, 229.

13 *Memorandum of Conversation: Meeting between Secretary of Defense Brown and Vice Premier Deng Xiaoping*, Beijing, 8 January 1980, 10 a.m., Top Secret, Sensitive, in FRUS 1977–1980, Vol. XII, Doc. 150, 435–439.

14 *Article in the President's Daily Brief: China-Pakistan Response to Invasion of Afghanistan*, Washington, DC, 12 January 1980, Top Secret, For the President Only, in FRUS 1977–1980, Vol. XII, Doc. 162, 464.

15 *Meeting between Secretary of Defense Brown and Premier Hua Guo-Feng*, Beijing, 9 January 1980, 5–6:50 p.m., in JCPL, National Security Affairs, Staff Material, Far East, Oksenberg Subject File, Box 26, Brown (Harold) 1/80 Trip Memcons: 1/80, Top Secret, Sensitive.

16 Evans, *Deng Xiaoping*, 261.

17 Keith, *Deng Xiaoping and China's Foreign Policy*, 185.

18 *Memorandum for the Record: Second Meeting between Secretary of Defense Harold Brown and Vice Premier Geng Biao, People's Republic of China*, Beijing, 7 January 1980, 4 p.m., Top Secret, Sensitive, in FRUS 1977–1980, Vol. XIII, Doc. 291, 1050–1055.

19 *Meeting between Secretary of Defense Brown and Vice Premier Deng Xiaoping*, Beijing, 8 January 1980, 10 a.m., in JCPL, National Security Affairs, Staff

Material, Far East, Oksenberg Subject File, Box 26, Brown (Harold) 1/80 Trip Memcons: 1/80, Top Secret, Sensitive.

20 Although the new economic development concept was based on more realistic assumptions, during the years 1979–1980 it was not being implemented effectively. Tellingly, government spending and deficit increased, while prices continued to soar. As a consequence of that, Deng Xiaoping persuaded central authorities to cut expenses and reduce basic construction projects. Hsi-Sheng Ch'i, *Politics of Disillusionment*, 17.

21 *Meeting between Dr. Harold Brown and Zhang Aiping, Director of the Chinese National Defense Science and Technology Commission*, Beijing, 8 January 1980, 8 p.m., in JCPL, National Security Affairs, Staff Material, Far East, Oksenberg Subject File, Box 26, Brown (Harold) 1/80 Trip Memcons: 1/80, Top Secret, Sensitive.

22 'Fulfilment of 1979 National Economic Plan', *Beijing Review*, 23/16, 1980, 17–18.

23 Deng, 'The Present Situation and the Tasks before Us: Speech at a Meeting of Cadres Called by the Central Committee of the Communist Party of China', 16 January 1980, in *The Selected Works of Deng Xiaoping*, Vol. II, https://dengxiaopingworks.wordpress.com/2013/02/25/the-present-situation-and-the-tasks-before-us/, accessed 1 November 2021.

24 *Soviet Actions in Afghanistan and Sino-British Relations*, 16 January 1980, in NA, FCO 28/3986, *British/Sino Relations Following Soviet Invasion of Afghanistan*, 020/9, Confidential.

25 *Policy towards China after Afghanistan*, 18 January 1980, in NA, FCO 21/1803, *Sino-UK Relations*, FEC 020/2, Confidential.

26 *Policy towards China after Afghanistan: Action*, 29 January 1980, in NA, FCO 21/1803, FEC 020/2, Confidential.

27 Albers, *Britain, France, West Germany*, 157–158.

28 *China: Fifth Plenum Party Congress*, 29 February 1980, in NA, FCO 21/1799, FEC 014/1, Confidential.

29 *Telegram 193 from Peking to FCO: The Fifth Plenum*, 3 March 1980, 030655Z, in NA, FCO 21/1799, FEC 014/1, Confidential.

30 *Results of the Fifth Plenum: The CCP Secretariat*, 24 March 1980, in NA, FCO 21/1799, FEC 014/1, Confidential.

31 'Resolution on Convening the Party's 12th National Congress (Adopted on February 29, 1980)', Beijing Review, 23/10, 1980, 11.

32 Parris H. Chang, 'Elite Conflict in the Post-Mao China, Revised Edition', Occasional Papers/Reprint Series in Contemporary Asian Studies, 55/2, 1983, 18.

33 Dillon, *Deng Xiaoping*, 258.

34 *US-China Economic Relations*, Washington, DC, 27 March 1980, 4:30–5:45 p.m., in JCPL, NSC Institutional Files (H-Files), Box 79, PRC 136, US-China Economic Relations, 3/27/80. Confidential.

35 Between 1979 and 1989, China's total trade increased by almost ten times, from 45.5 to 415.6 billion yuan, and as a percentage of GDP more than doubled, from 11.4 to 26.3 per cent. Mark Chi-kwan, *China and the World since 1945: An International History* (Abingdon-New York, NY: 2012), 98.

36 Pieter Bottelier, Stanford King Center on Global Development Working Paper No. 277, *China and the World Bank: How a Partnership Was Built*, April 2006, https://siepr.stanford.edu/sites/default/files/publications/277wp.pdf, accessed 6 November 2021.

37 Devesh Kapur, John P. Lewis and Richard C. Webb, *The World Bank: Its First Half Century, Volume 1* (Washington, DC: Brooking Institution Press, 1997), 24.

38 *Her Majesty's Ambassador at Peking to the Secretary of State for Foreign and Commonwealth Affairs, Visit to China by the Right Honourable Francis Pym MP, Secretary of State for Defence, March 1980*, 3 April 1980, in NA, FCO 160/72, Departmental Series UK Eyes 'B', Far Eastern Department DS No 4/80, DS (L) 1521, Confidential.

39 *China Working Group: Note of a Meeting Held in Room 180 1 Victoria Street 18 April 1980: Reports of Recent Ministerial Visits and SBAC Exhibition*, 25 April 1980, in NA, FCO 21/1803, FEC 020/2, Confidential.

40 On 17 March 1980, Brzezinski had a conversation with the Soviet Ambassador to the United States, Anatoly Dobrynin. What was interesting about the meeting was the American suggestion to set up an Afghanistan genuinely non-aligned and non-hostile to the Soviet Union, with international arrangements including some neutral forces from Muslim countries as a guarantee of neutrality. The national security adviser also said that communists could participate in such a government, though without becoming the dominant force. *Memorandum of Conversation*, Washington, DC, 17 March 1980, Secret, in FRUS 1977–1980, Vol. XII, Doc. 235, 631–633.

41 *Summary of the President's and Vice President's Conversation with Vice Premier Geng Biao*, Washington, DC, 28 May 1980, 1:45–2:15 p.m., in JCPL, National Security Affairs, Staff Material, Far East, Sullivan Subject File, Box 70, Geng Biao Visit: 5/23–31/80, Secret.

42 Goodman, *Deng Xiaoping and the Chinese Revolution*, 124.

43 'Discussion on Economic Theory: Should there Be Competition in Socialist Economy?', *Beijing Review*, 23/22, 1980, 19–22.

44 Gewirtz, *Unlikely Partners*, 83–87.

45 *National Intelligence Estimate: Sino-Soviet Relations in the Early 1980's*, Washington, DC, 5 June 1980, NIE 11/13–80, Secret, in FRUS 1977–1980, Vol. XIII, Doc. 312, 1116–1117.

46 By June 1980, 6,600 industrial enterprises allowed to make autonomous decisions produced about forty-five per cent of the total output of all State industrial enterprises. The second step was making them financially independent. The third one was introducing a responsibility system, under which a part of an enterprise was allowed to keep the remaining profit after surrendering a fixed amount to the company controlling it. Chow, 'Economic Reform and Growth in China', 130.

47 *Remarks Made by Deng Xiaoping to US and Canadian Journalists on 5 June 1980*, in NA, FCO 21/1799.

48 *Record of a Meeting with Vice-Premier Kang Shi'en of the People's Republic of China at 10 Downing Street at 11.15 am on Monday 9 June 1980*, 13 June 1980, in NA, PREM 19/3626, Sec Relations/Int Sit, Restricted.

49 *Visit to UK by Vice-Premier Kang Shien: UK/China Trade Prospects in Energy*, undated, in NA, PREM 19/3626.

50 *Leasing Information Note: Trade with China*, June 1980, in NA, FCO 21/1804, Sino-UK Relations.

51 Bao, Chiang and Ignatius (eds.), *Prisoner of the State*, 107–108.

52 *Telegram from the Embassy in the Soviet Union to the Department of State: Another Look at Soviet Motives and Objectives in Afghanistan*, Moscow, 18 March 1980, 1526Z, Secret; Priority; Exdis, in FRUS 1977–1980, Vol. XII, Doc. 237, 637–641.

53 *Memorandum of Conversation: Meeting between Secretary of State Muskie and Foreign Minister Gromyko*, Vienna, May 1980, in FRUS 1977–1980, Vol. VI, Doc. 278, Secret; Sensitive, 807–825.

54 *Memorandum of Conversation*, Tokyo, 10 July 1980, 9:15–10:15 a.m., in JCPL, National Security Affairs, Brzezinski Material, Subject File, Box 38, Memcons: President: 7/80, Secret.

55 *Call on Sir Ian Gilmour by Chinese Vice Foreign Minister He Ying, Wednesday, 6 August, 10 Am*, 8 August 1980, in NA, FCO 21/1812, *Visit to the UK by Chinese Vice Foreign Minister: He Ying*, FEC 026/9, Confidential.

56 *Sino-Soviet Relations*, 23 July 1980, in NA, FCO 28/3989, *Sino/Soviet Relations*, 020/301/1, Confidential.

57 Ross, *Negotiating Cooperation*, 164–172.

58 *Brief for the Prime Minister's Meeting with Sir Lawrence Kadoorie*, 28 July 1980, in NA, PREM 19/255, *Correspondence with Sir Lawrence Kadoorie on UK/ Chinese Trade: Contracts for Castle Peak A & B Power Stations; Guangdong Nuclear Power Plant*, Confidential.

59 *Meeting with Sir Lawrence Kadoorie: Note of a Meeting Held in Room 11.01 Ashdown House at 11.30 am on 28 July 1980*, 4 August 1980, in NA, PREM 19/ 255, Confidential.

60 *Points Raised during an Informal Discussion between Mr. W.F. Stones and Mr. Chen Gang at a Dinner Party in Hong Kong on 22nd July, 1980*, 23 July 1980, Annex A, in NA, PREM 19/255, Confidential.

61 *Call by Sir Lawrence Kadoorie*, 30 July 1980, in NA, PREM 19/255, Confidential.

62 Joanna Z. Li and David C. Yang, 'Guangdong: China's Economic Powerhouse: The Past, the Present and the Future', in Tung X. Bui, David C. Yang, Wayne D. Jones and Joanna Z. Li (eds.), *China's Economic Powerhouse: Reform in Guangdong Province* (Basingstoke and New York, NY: Palgrave Macmillan, 2003), 208.

63 *Guangdong Nuclear Power Station Project*, undated, in NA, PREM 19/255, Confidential.

64 Four special economic zones were set up in 1979–1980, the largest of which, Shenzhen, was adjacent to Hong Kong to attract spill-over investments. Besides, the Zhuhai SEZ was set up across the Pearl River next door to the then Portuguese colony of Macau. Up the coast, the Shantou SEZ was established in the Chaozhou ethnic homeland to attract investment from this group, economically important in Southeast Asia. Finally, the Xiamen SEZ was designed to revive overseas links among the south Fujian people, whose dialect of Chinese is spoken also throughout Southeast Asia, as well as in Taiwan. Naughton, *The Chinese Economy: Adaption and Growth*, 34.

65 Hui Feng, *The Politics of China's Accession to the World Trade Organization: The Dragon Goes Global* (Abingdon and New York, NY, 2006), 47.

66 William Feeney, 'Chinese Policy in Multilateral Financial Institutions', in Kim (ed.), *China and the World*, 271–276.

67 'Special Interview: More on Economic Reform', *Beijing Review*, 23/36, 1980, 18–23.

68 *Telegram No. 598 from Peking to FCO: Your Visit to China*, 180756Z, 18 September 1980, in NA, PREM 19/2597, *China: Internal Situation*, Priority, Confidential.

69 'Hua Guofeng's Speech at the Third Session of the Fifth National People's Congress, September 7 1980', *Beijing Review*, 23/38, 1980, 12–29.

70 'Report on the Arrangements for the National Economic Plans for 1980 and 1981', *Beijing Review*, 23/38, 1980, 30–43.

71 Arthur G. Ashbrook, Jr., 'China: Economic Modernization and Long-Term Performance', in *China under the Four Modernizations*, 109.

72 Bruce L. Reynolds, 'Reform in Chinese Industrial Management: An Empirical Report', in *Ibidem*, 119–121.

73 Robert Michael Field and Judith A. Flynn, 'China: An Energy-Constrained Model of Industrial Performance through 1985', in *Ibidem*, 337–357.

74 Minami, 'The Bottleneck of Reform: China's Oil Policy in the 1980s', in Roberts (ed.), *Chinese Economic Statecraft*, 301–304.

75 Armand Hammer, 'On a Vast China Market', *Journal of International Affairs*, 39/2, 1986, 19–25.

76 *Record of a Conversation between the Secretary of State and the Chinese Foreign Minister at the Foreign and Commonwealth Office on 1 October 1980 at 11:30 am*, 6 October 1980, in NA, FCO 21/1816, *Visit by Chinese Foreign Minister (Huang Hua) to the U.K.*, FEC 026/14, Confidential.

77 *CPSU CC Politburo Directive to Soviet Ambassadors and Representatives: Carrying out Additional Measures to Counter American-Chinese Military Cooperation*, 2 October 1980, History and Public Policy Program Digital Archive, TsKhSD, F. 89, Per. 34, Dok. 10, No. P217/57, Top Secret, https://digitalarchive.wilsoncenter.org/document/117008, accessed 18 November 2021; *Sino-Soviet Relations*, 15 October 1980, in NA, FCO 3989, Confidential.

78 'Huang Hua on International Situation', 24 September 1980, *Beijing Review*, 23/40, 1980, 12–14.

79 *Telegram 769 from Peking to FCO: Deng Xiaoping on China's Foreign Policy*, 26 November 1980, 260820Z, in NA, FCO 21/1808, FEC 021/6, *Chinese Foreign Policy*, Restricted.

80 *Paper Prepared in the Central Intelligence Agency: China and Southwest Asia - The Challenge of Afghanistan*, Washington, DC, May 1980, Top Secret, in FRUS 1977–1980, Vol. XII, Doc. 261, 704–706.

81 *Paper Prepared in the Central Intelligence Agency: Chinese Aid to the Afghan Insurgents - Why So Little*, Washington, DC, undated, Top Secret, in *Ibidem*, Doc. 296, 786–787.

82 Albers, *Britain, France, West Germany*, 174–175.

83 *Record of a Conversation between the Prime Minister and the Foreign Minister of China, Vice Premier Huang Hua at 10 Downing Street on 2 October at 0900*, 2 October 1980, in NA, FCO 21/1816, FEC 026/14, Confidential.

84 Britain was unique among the trading partners of China due to Hong Kong, whose commercial relations with both the UK and China greatly exceeded the ones between London and China. US Congress, Office of Technology Assessment, *Technology Transfer to China*, OTA-ISC-340 (Washington, DC: US Government Printing Office, 1987), 128.

85 *Talks with Chinese Foreign Minister: 1 and 2 October 1980: Brief no 7 (h): Guangdong Nuclear Project*, undated, in NA, FCO 21/1816, FEC 026/14, Confidential.

86 During the 1980s, the Guangdong economy became a microcosm of the fast-changing economy, with entrepreneurs from Hong Kong moving their manufacturing businesses to the neighbouring province due to cheaper labour. Jacques, *When China Rules the World*, 181.

87 *Guangdong Nuclear Power Station Project*, 19 December 1980, in NA, PREM 19/255, Confidential.

88 Albers, *Britain, France, West Germany*, 187–188.

89 Naughton, *Growing out of the Plan*, 119.

90 Roberts, 'Orchestrating and Mediating New China's International Reintegration: The US Think Tank China Cluster in the 1980s', in Roberts (ed.), *Chinese Economic Statecraft*, 422.

91 *US-China Joint Economic Committee and Recommended Next Steps in the US-China Economic Relationship*, Washington, DC, 27 October 1980, in JCPL, National Security Affairs, Brzezinski Material, Country File, Box 10, China (PRC): 10/80-1/81, Confidential.

92 Between 1979 and 1983, the Chinese government set up an organisational and legal apparatus to deal directly with foreign oil companies. The China National Offshore Oil Company was formally established on 15 February 1982. Joint ventures were necessary because Chinese firms lacked the technology and experience to bid on service contracts. Finally, a legal regime had to be formed to persuade foreigners to form partnerships on Chinese soil. The outcome was that by 1984 several coastal cities were enjoying an oil boom. Lieberthal and Oksenberg, *Policy Making in China*, 257–258.

93 'Statement of Adm. Stansfield Turner, Director, Central Intelligence Agency', in *Allocations of Resources in the Soviet Union and China, 1980: Hearings before the Subcommittee on Priorities and Economy in Government of the Joint Economic Committee*, Congress of the United States, Ninety-Sixth Congress, Second Session, Part Six, Executive Sessions, 30 June and 25 September 1980 (Washington, DC: US Government Printing Office, 1981), https://www.jec. senate.gov/reports/96th Congress/Allocation of Resources in the Soviet Union and China - 1980 Part VI (1033).pdf, accessed 21 November 2021.

94 Deng, 'Speech at a Central Working Conference: Implement the Policy of Readjustment, Ensure Stability and Unity', 25 December 1980, in *The Selected Works of Deng Xiaoping*, Vol. II, https://dengxiaopingworks.wordpress.com/ 2013/02/25/implement-the-policy-of-readjustment-ensure-stability-and-unity/, accessed 23 November 2021.

Conclusions

In January 1981, the Reagan administration came to power with a hawkish conservative agenda claiming to build up America's defence system, re-invigorating the country's alliances and challenge the Soviet Union all over the world. The newly elected president appointed Alexander M. Haig Jr. as secretary of state, being sure that the invasion of Afghanistan, the Soviet-Cuban interventions in Angola and in the Horn of Africa, as well as Vietnam's occupation of Cambodia, had made a new geopolitical activism possible. However, Reagan did not immediately realise that he had chosen the person who most strongly believed in China as the key to a global American strategy to contain the Soviets. The secretary wanted to move quickly to transform the tacit alliance between China and the United States into a "strategic association", under which Washington was expected to treat China as a friendly non-allied country.[1] To tell the truth, Reagan's views on China were rooted in the old days. As a matter of fact, he criticised his immediate predecessor's concept of ethical foreign policy based on human rights, as well as Nixon and Kissinger's realistic view of international relations, responsible to have accepted too many compromises with the communist counterpart. The neo-president had campaigned on the issue of selling weapons to the Republic of China, and he deeply admired nationalist leaders who had stood with America against communism and who still harboured the dream that they might someday return to the mainland. As far as this was concerned, in a 1989 interview Ambassador John H. Holdridge recalled that the inaugural ceremony of the new administration seemed rather awkward, as it had been made public that an official representation from Taiwan would attend. Chai Zemin, the Chinese ambassador, warned that if these people were present at the ceremony, he would not go. The last thing needed in the world to start the Reagan administration, said Holdridge, was such a diplomatic incident over China policy.[2] The new administration increased defence spending and pursued a hard line Soviet policy, proclaiming the objective to develop a programme to eliminate the Soviet system of government. In spite of that, such a point in common with Beijing did not initially produce consensus on the strategy towards China. On the contrary, Haig believed

DOI: 10.4324/9781003390138-6

that, in the context of heightened US-Soviet relations, Chinese participation was imperative in terms of American interests. In a word, the People's Republic could be the most important country to Washington's global position.[3] For Haig, the Chinese civil war was over and the Kuomintang had lost. Like Kissinger, the new secretary believed that America's strategic interests were on the mainland. Actually, Reagan's statements in the election campaign had disturbed Beijing's authorities and only by settling the Taiwan question could the two countries establish new relations and continue to develop them. Apart from that, shortly before Inauguration Day, Deng Xiaoping stated that if the US government adopted a hard-line policy towards the Soviet Union, China was not absolutely supposed to set aside questions such as the one concerning Taiwan.[4]

To tell the truth, during Reagan's hard-line administration, the Chinese message was even more welcomed than it had been to Jimmy Carter. In those years, in fact, Washington treated China as a de facto ally, even giving access to technology sometimes unavailable to others, as reminded by Westad, with the purpose to turn the PRC into a real threat to the Soviet Union. Beijing never became a big importer of US weapons, as what the People's Republic wanted was access to American military technology, including aviation and missiles. In a few words, Deng's plan was to make China one of the world's top military powers by producing its own weapons after acquiring the necessary technology and learning how to exploit it.[5] As far as foreign policy was concerned, according to the available documentation the Chinese were doing a lot to persuade the Americans to collaborate against the Soviets. Actually, both China and the United Stated had some common objectives in Southwest Asia, the most important of which was of course opposing Soviet actions in Afghanistan and prevent further destabilisation of the area. In a report issued by the Bureau of Intelligence and Research, we may also read that the White House had agreed that the Chinese should encourage Pakistan and Iran to coordinate their efforts to face Moscow's presence in Afghanistan, as well as advising the countries of the area to compose their differences and move towards regional security cooperation. In spite of that, the Americans themselves recognised that the People's Republic displayed a stricter confrontationist style towards the Soviet Union than did the United States. Moreover, Beijing was making clear that Washington's inaction in Afghanistan would encourage Soviet aggression, thus putting pressure for the United States to militarily support Afghan resistance, something American Intelligence itself regarded as unwise.[6] Finally, the Carter administration ended its term with a CIA research paper claiming that American actions had become central to the Chinese foreign policy equation. In a nutshell, having closely identified himself with the US connection over the past several years, Deng had now to demonstrate that the benefits of such a choice were outweighing the costs of ongoing hostility towards the USSR.[7] In the first year of the Reagan administration, in fact, the British got access to an internal document which had been only given restricted circulation on the origins of Soviet hegemonism. The lecture stated that such a policy was not linked to any particular leader in Moscow. Rather, it was a long-term strategy.[8] In addition, the Chinese foreign minister's words were quite similar to those of the Carter Doctrine when he said to his British counterpart that the presence of Soviet troops 400 miles from the Strait of Hormuz was an unacceptable destabilisation of the region. Therefore, the first line of resistance against the Soviet southward-driven policy into the oil producing area had to be set in Afghanistan and Cambodia, which were not at all to be regarded as local conflicts.[9] According to Lorenz Lüthi, the roaring years 1979 and 1980, facing structural changes in the international system in Asia and the Middle East, as well as wars among non aligned countries, left Non-Alignment weakened. As revealed by strategic divisions surfaced at the 6th Conference on non-aligned countries held in Havana in 1979,[10] pro-Soviet forces from within and outside undermined Non-Alignment as an alternative vision to the Cold War, thus setting up the conditions under which Asia helped end the global Cold War in the following decade.[11]

Nevertheless, at the beginning of the Reagan era the portrait of the Chinese economy seen by the British point of view was rather gloomy, due to a state of crisis caused by planning mistakes, lack of deficit reduction and monetary expansion. As a result of overspending, China had an overall financial deficit which in 1980 would be higher than predicted.[12] Thus, it was time for overall spending to be brought down to the level of necessity. What is important to underline, however, is that the British diplomats on the spot did not expect Chinese leaders to revert to radical policies, while exports continued to grow. Therefore, commitment to reforms was not supposed to be abandoned, but the new phase of readjustment affected trade balance and London's hope of defence sales, as these could now only rise in line with economic conditions. Despite this, China's international influence was supposed to grow, with the Far Eastern market likely to become more and more rewarding, while Beijing was thought to become even more insistent in requests especially for favourable treatment, whether in the context of commercial or financial exchanges. By virtue of this, the temporary phase of crisis did not have to dissuade the British to expand political relations with the Dragon. As a matter of fact, British strategic interests in cooperating with China and encourage Beijing in outward-looking and broadly pro-Western policies had not changed,[13] and Deng was always very optimistic about the prospects for bilateral trade. In particular, heavy industry was to take into account the needs of light industry and agriculture. At the same time, industrial enterprises had to be reorganised and technical innovations introduced to allow telecommunications and energy facilities to be strengthened. The fact that certain contracts already being negotiated might be affected by cuts did not imply that the two countries should not explore further ways of cooperation. In a few words, Britain was always regarded as a major trading partner in Europe.[14] Once again, it is important to highlight Zhao Ziyang's words when he states that in 1980 industrial output had grown 8.1 times, GDP had grown 4.2 times and industrial fixed assets had grown 26 times. Despite all this, average consumption had only doubled. The rise in living standards was also significantly lower than GDP growth, thus improvement in living standards was not commensurate with what people had contributed with their work. In a few words, Zhao realised that the key problem was a question of efficiency and not the nominal speed of production growth. Hence, the system had to be transformed into a market economy resolving the problem of property rights, therefore finding a way for the Chinese people to receive concrete returns on their work.[15] In order to pursue such a task, in 1980 Zhao collaborated also to establish the Sino-Japanese Economic Knowledge Exchange, whose purpose was borrowing from advanced foreign experiences to serve the People's Republic's reform programme and economic development.[16]

Arranging the foreign secretary's visit to China a few months after the launch of the new economic conservative phase bore the clear message that the Asian communist country had acquired importance on a global scale as a never-ending market, a partner in world financial institutions and an anti-Soviet stronghold in the Indo-Pacific area. The most important resolution approved by the Communist Party of China in 1981 proved British predictions right. In fact, the document adopted by the Sixth Plenary Session of the 11th Central Committee on 27 June marked another pivotal passage towards China's entry into the world's leading powers by repudiating "ultra-leftism" as seen in Mao-led movements. The most impressing passage was certainly the one criticising the Cultural Revolution, blamed as responsible for the most severe setback and heaviest losses since the founding of the People's Republic, though the erroneous left wing theses were said to have been inconsistent with the system of Mao Zedong Thought, defined instead as the integration of the universal principles of Marxism-Leninism with the concrete practice of the Chinese revolution. Furthermore, practice was thought to have shown that the previous period of extreme left wing policies had not constituted a revolution or social progress in any sense. The resolution repudiated Mao's conduct as follows: (a) there were no facts to prove the takeover of the country by capitalists and revisionists; (b) the Cultural Revolution had purged those who were actually the leading cadres of the Party; (c) the same movement had deviated from the masses and the Party; (d) the extremist era had not brought any social progress. As a matter of fact, it was China itself to have been thrown into disorder, and the Great Helmsman in person was accused of having become arrogant, gradually divorcing himself from practice and the masses. Obviously, the principle of readjustment and improving the economy as a whole was confirmed in conformity with economic and natural laws within the limits of domestic resources. The other milestone of the resolution dealt with the international posture of China, stating that revolution and national construction could not be carried on in isolation from the rest of the world, even the richest and most industrialised one.[17]

The British realised that Deng needed an orthodox cloak on reformist policies, thus preserving the image of the Communist Party as the only hope for economic and social salvation, as well as maintaining the status of Mao's thought as the correct way to implement socialist doctrines to China' special situation. Such orthodoxy was believed to be of great importance in order to give ideological impetus to reforms.[18] In a nutshell, implementation of the four modernisations required a drastic change of attitude towards Mao's ideology to open up the country to foreign technology and capital investment. As already said, Deng needed an orthodox shield to convince more people of his genuine devotion to go a long way in reforming the political system and the economy.[19] As Michael Dillon says, the only way to reverse Maoist policies with mild opposition was by preserving Mao's historical status. Therefore, it was necessary to praise the Helmsman's positive contribution to the development of the nation, avoiding both rightist analyses of cancelling everything about the founder of the People's Republic and the leftist attitude refusing to debate on any serious criticism.[20] Socialism alone remained China's goal, but now the Party had the task to build up economic construction. Economic practice and theory were given equal importance in order to determine how to achieve the goal of wealth and power. It was clear to everybody that there was no turning back from the path taken.[21]

Meanwhile, in June 1981, in the same days as the presentation of the Resolution, Haig flew to Beijing to carry out the first high-level talks between Chinese leaders and the Reagan administration. The neo-secretary of state publicly reminded the White House's commitment to closer and more cooperative relations with the People's Republic, while privately he offered access to American military technology,[22] though Beijing did not want to purchase weapons from the United States as long as Washington continued to supply Taiwan.[23] Haig told his interlocutors that the administration was ready, on a case by case level, to take into consideration the possibility to sell lethal weapons systems to China. However, the secretary revealed this pivotal change in American arms policy at a press conference in the Chinese capital by proclaiming that his trip had marked the beginning of a new era of security co-operation. Despite the irritated replies by Department of State officers and President Reagan himself, Haig seemed persuaded that the People's Republic did not care about American military support to Taiwan, as long as Beijing had its share.[24] As we can realise from these episodes, both Atlantic powers did not want to lose ground towards China's leadership, thus increasing state visits and talks with the highest members of the PRC government. One more curious thing to notice by reading available records is that, despite readjustment spending cuts, both London and Washington were making pressure to sign arms deals with the Dragon, which hoped to keep foreign trade in balance over the following years.[25]

China's new foreign policy was framed by Deng Xiaoping in 1982, when he stated that Beijing could be trusted as a permanent member of the Security Council. Such confident stance marked a breakthrough with the past, showing how the People's Republic felt by then a global actor able to affect the international balance of power, whose foreign policy could be summed up in three sentences: (a) opposition to hegemonism; (b) safeguarding world peace; and (c) eagerness to strengthen unity and co-operation with Third World countries. Beijing had not ruled out the idea to lead developing countries against the superpowers, though it is clear that this position had by then become the façade in public *fora*, where the Dragon could blame both the Soviet Union and the United States.[26] Like Deng himself said, Third World member countries at the United Nations had increased and their international political influence had consequently augmented considerably.[27] Nevertheless, the government of the People's Republic had become one of the main trading partners of the West, while the Third World was a little more than a slogan to play the role of advocate of decolonisation. Just to give an example about this attitude, we can quote Hennie Van Vuuren, according to whom in the 1980s China enjoyed very good trading relations with apartheid South Africa, and the main driver of that was arms. Chris Thirion, former Military Intelligence Chief, in a 2015 interview said that Hansa was the codename used by the South Africa Defence Forces for China. This was due to Hansa Pilsener beer, which in those times had the tagline "The one that refreshes". For much of that decade, China had become "the one that refreshed" Pretoria's arms supply.[28] As a matter of fact, Westad reminds how disappointed Third World socialists were while watching China itself embracing market economy with overwhelming enthusiasm. It was by then clear that the relations with America and the decoupling from the Soviet Union had produced a brand system accepting market values while keeping the one-party regime.[29] The new policy agenda for the decade was finally set at the 12th National Congress, on the occasion of which Deng said that by economic construction the new leadership referred to policies designed to promote rapid economic growth. As far as foreign policy was concerned, China's national interest could not be fully pursued in separation from the overall interests of mankind.[30]

As we can see, the new leadership of the Asian communist giant alternated revolutionary language, full of old slogans dealing with solidarity throughout the Third World, to very pragmatic statements such as the impossibility to export revolution and instability. Capitalistic financial institutions could have only welcomed the intention to respect the status quo, and this was the reason why an everlasting market like that of China was always more attractive than business with the USSR. According to Henry Kissinger, the Reagan administration and the Chinese leadership had roughly similar assessments of Soviet problems and weaknesses, but drew out different observations on the policies to carry out. As a matter of fact, the Americans perceived Russian difficulties as an opportunity to go on the offensive, seeking to put pressure on the enemy both financially and geopolitically. On the other hand, the Chinese saw the same situation as a way to recalibrate global balance. They had no interest in the triumph of American and Western liberal values; rather, the time had come for the Dragon to gain freedom of manoeuvre on the international chessboard.[31] The balance of power of the Cold War had given the Middle Kingdom the chance to modernise its system and the post-Mao leadership had chosen to rely on the West to break isolation and play as an active protagonist. Such a "globalist" position got enshrined in the new Constitution of the People's Republic of China, stating that the achievements in revolution and construction were inseparable from support by the people of the world. Beijing adhered to an independent foreign policy, thus marking its distance from both super-powers, as well as to the principles of mutual respect for sovereignty and territorial integrity, non-aggression, non-interference in each other's internal affairs. At the same time, China kept the role of opposition to imperialism, hegemonism and colonialism. As concerned private economic initiative, Article 17 of the Chart said that collective economic organisations had decision-making power in conducting independent economic activities, on condition that they obeyed relevant laws.[32]

To conclude this reconstruction, it is quite easy to state that within a relatively short span of time the balance of power in the Indo-Pacific area had been reversed. First of all, the Nixon administration's policy to rely on China to weaken the Soviet Union and oblige Moscow to take a milder stance on the Cold War global front had been successful. Despite Russian overstretching commitments, the Soviets had become much more diplomatically isolated and it was now clear that the communist bloc was not united at all. Regional rivalries were consequently exploited by Western powers to better contain the USSR and make profits more and more. Overall, in both Atlantic countries there was not so much difference between progressive and conservative governments as far as the attitude towards the PRC was concerned. Deng's opening up to the market was welcome everywhere and to tell the truth it does not seem that human rights had priority in the Western political agenda once the balance of payments was at stake. Simply said, Beijing's market was too big to be ignored and the Anglo-Saxon allied collaborated, sometimes even competing with each other, to make the Dragon get access to the temples of world finance. Strategically, the Asian country was the perfect counterbalance towards Soviet aspirations or perceived threats. Chinese comments whenever there was the opportunity to meet Western interlocutors, in fact, were so sharp that ironically it was London and Washington sometimes to advice a more prudent and diplomatic attitude. Tellingly, Chinese authorities exaggerated the Soviet threat in order to gain more leverage on the West with the aim of favouring modernisation and acquiring the necessary technology to gain a better posture in the international competition. Hence, the post-Mao age marked the end of thirty years of isolation. About five years after the death of the Founding Father, the People's Republic of China had started the long journey in the world of capitalism. Having become therefore a large importer, especially of raw materials, China turned itself into the world's largest customer of world's iron ore, copper and oil. In a word, trade was the most important of Beijing's global economic interactions. Hence, while in the early 1980s the People's Republic's GDP growth made up about seven per cent of the world's total, after less than forty years China accounted for twenty-eight per cent of

global GDP growth.[33] Deng understood that the old Chinese order had collapsed about a century and a half previously, giving way to the one moulded by
the West first through colonialism and then after the second global conflict.
Such a balance managed world economy according to Western interests and
needs. Practically, all former vassal states of China were by then bound
somehow to the United States. On grounds of this, for a few years Beijing
was obliged to join the train of development, before setting its own path.
Consequently, the resurrection of China had to take place within the world as it
was and taking advantage of American collaboration. Paradoxically, the pov-
erty of China was useful to technological innovation. Actually, due to faster
means of transport and communication, as well as cheaper workforce and
infrastructure costs, enterprises were able to more easily produce in different
areas of the planet. In a word, the age of off-shoring had begun, and the Asian
country offered millions of blue collars willing to work at the assembly line for
much lower wages than their Western colleagues. This was the first step to build
up China's leading role on the global scenario and the two main Western
powers looked enthusiastic to be helpful.[34]

After all, as General Secretary Hu Yaobang stated, in modern times economic issues were no longer merely domestic questions, but had become
inseparable from international relations, thus foreign trade was to be redefined
as a significant part of foreign policy, promoted through economic diplomacy.[35] Through acknowledgement of post-Second World War order, the new
Chinese leadership was trying to gain credit as a moderate and responsible
partner of the international governance, thus accepting rules and procedures
dealing with a more and more globalised economy.[36] As acknowledged by Lee
Kuan Yew at the dawn of China's modernisation process, regionalism was no
longer the solution to achieve a balanced governance of international order. As
a matter of fact, globalisation meant that all nations, even the ones which had
written the rules of the system, had to get used to living in a competitive
scenario. There was just one world and inter-dependence was the new
reality.[37] What Western Capitals had not realised was that Beijing would never
pursue alignment with the Atlantic Alliance. On the contrary, having increased
trading and financial linkage with capitalistic countries gave the Asian giant a
lot of room to manoeuvre, thus being able to play interlocutors off against each
other. The Cold War was practically over in the Far East and the People's
Republic of China was on the right side of world governance. In short,
Western allies had pulled the trigger of a ruthless competition with a never
ending market whose rulers had been looking forward to regaining a dominant position for more than a century.

Notes

1 Patrick Tyler, *A Great Wall: Six Presidents and China, an Investigative History*
(New York, NY: Public Affairs, 1999), 296.

2 *Interview with John H. Holdridge*, 14 December 1989, in Frontline Diplomacy: The Association for Diplomatic Studies and Training Foreign Affairs, Oral History Project, https://memory.loc.gov/service/mss/mfdip/2004/2004hol02/2004hol02. pdf, accessed 25 November 2021.

3 Ross, *Negotiating Cooperation*, 168–169.

4 Deng, 'Our Principled Position on the Development of Sino-US Relations: Excerpt from a Talk with Theodore Fulton Stevens, a Republican and Assistant Leader of the US Senate, and Anna Chennault, Vice-Chairman of the Presidential Export Committee', 4 January 1981, in *The Selected Works of Deng Xiaoping*, Vol. II, https://dengxiaopingworks.wordpress.com/2013/02/25/our-principled-position-on-the-development-of-sino-u-s-relations/, accessed 25 November 2021.

5 Westad, *Restless Empire*, 374–375.

6 *Report No. 1453 Prepared in the Bureau of Intelligence and Research: Chinese and US Objectives in Southwest Asia*, Washington, DC, 8 September 1980, Secret, Exdis, in FRUS 1977–1980, Vol. XII, Doc. 314, 844.

7 *Research Paper Prepared in the Central Intelligence Agency: Sino-Soviet Relations and the Impact of the Invasion of Afghanistan*, Washington, DC, January 1981, Secret, in FRUS 1977–1980, Vol. XII, PA 81–10001, 901–903.

8 *The Origins of Soviet Hegemonism*, 4 November 1981, in NA, FCO 21/1912, *Sino-Soviet Relations*, FEC 020/7, Confidential.

9 *Record of Talks between the Secretary of State and the Chinese Foreign Minister at the Diaoyutai State House, Peking, on Wednesday 1 April 1981 at 3.00 PM*, in NA, FCO 21/1920, *Visit of Lord Carrington to China: 1–5 April 1981*, FEC 026/4, Confidential.

10 *6th Summit Conference of Heads of State or Government of the Non-Aligned Movement*, Havana, 3–9 September 1979, http://cns.miis.edu/nam/documents/Official_Document/6th_Summit_FD_Havana_Declaration_1979_Whole.pdf, accessed 26 December 2021.

11 Lüthi, *Cold Wars*, 537.

12 *Foreign and Commonwealth Office, Background Brief: China's Economic and Political Course*, January 1981, in NA, FO 973/136.

13 *British Embassy Peking Despatch: Modernisation in the Doldrums*, 23 March 1981, in NA, FCO 21/1905, *China Internal Political*, FEC 014/1, Confidential.

14 *Record of Conversation between the Foreign and Commonwealth Secretary and the Prime Minister of the People's Republic of China in Peking on Thursday, 2 April 1981 at 4.00 PM*, in NA, FCO 21/1920, FEC 026/4, Confidential.

15 Bao, Chiang and Ignatius (eds.), *Prisoner of the State*, 112–113.

16 Wendy Leutert, 'Reimagining the Chinese Economy through Sino-Japanese Engagement in the 1980s', in Roberts (ed.), *Chinese Economic Statecraft*, 219–220.

17 *Resolution on Certain Questions in the History of Our Party since the Founding of the People's Republic of China* (Adopted by the Sixth Plenary Session of the 11th Central Committee of the CCP), 27 June 1981, https://digitalarchive.wilsoncenter.org/document/121344.pdf?v=d461ad5001da989b8f96cc1dfb3c8ce7, accessed 28 November 2021.

18 *British Embassy Peking Despatch: The Sixth Plenum and the Fall of Hua Guofeng*, 31 July 1981, in NA, FCO 21/1905, FEC 014/1, Confidential.

19 Wen-Chang, 34–37.

20 Dillon, *Deng Xiaoping*, 262.

21 Gewirtz, *Unlikely Partners*, 97.

22 The honeymoon in Sino-American relations in the 1980s dissipated as interests of the two powers diverged over issues like the Persian Gulf. In fact, Beijing became a major weapons merchant in the mid-1980s supplying both sides in the Iran-Iraq

War. Of greatest concern to the US, China sold Iran "Silkworm" anti-ship missiles capable of striking Kuwaiti oil tankers under American protection. Eden Y. Woon, 'Chinese Arms Sales and US-China Military Relations', *Asian Survey*, 29/6, 1989, 612.

23 Cohen, *America's Response to China*, 227.

24 Mann, *About Face*, 121–122.

25 *Foreign and Commonwealth Office, Background Brief: China's Economy and Foreign Trade in 1980*, July 1981, in NA, FO 973/183.

26 On 24 March 1982, Leonid Brezhnev gave a speech in Tashkent indicating that it was time to relax Sino-Soviet tensions. Acknowledging that China was a socialist country, he disavowed any claim on its territory and suggested negotiations. The related response reiterated the importance of foreign policy revision, claiming that Beijing had by then "four aspirations", namely to realise Sino-Japanese and Sino-US normalisation, to solve the question of Hong Kong's return to China and to implement Sino-Soviet normalisation. The point was that improving relations with China would have been greatly beneficial to Moscow's need to refocus on the economy at home. Keith, *Deng Xiaoping and China's Foreign Policy*, 186.

27 Deng, 'Excerpt from a Talk with Javier Perez de Cuellar, Secretary-General of the United Nations: China's Foreign Policy', 21 August 1982, in *The Selected Works of Deng Xiaoping*, Vol. II, https://dengxiaopingworks.wordpress.com/2013/02/25/chinas-foreign-policy/, accessed 4 December 2021.

28 Hennie Van Vuuren, *Apartheid Guns and Money: A Tale of Profit* (London: Hurst & Company, 2018), 392–393.

29 Westad, *The Global Cold War: Third World Interventions and the Making of Our Times* (Cambridge: Cambridge University Press, 2007), 362.

30 Dittmer, 'The 12th Congress of the Communist Party of China', *The China Quarterly*, 24/93/1, 1983, 115–116.

31 Kissinger, *On China*, 388–389.

32 *China (People's Republic of)'s Constitution of 1982 with Amendments through 2004*, https://www.constituteproject.org/constitution/China_2004.pdf?lang=en, accessed 5 December 2021.

33 Naughton, 'China's Global Economic Interactions', in Shambaugh (ed.), *China & the World* (New York, NY: Oxford University Press, 2020), 114.

34 Michael Schuman, *L'impero interrotto: la storia del mondo vista dalla Cina* (Milano: DeA Planeta Libri S.r.L., 2021), 359–360.

35 Shu Guang Zhang, *Beijing's Economic Statecraft*, 267.

36 Antonio Fiori, Marco Milani and Andrea Passeri, *Asia: storia, istituzioni e relazioni internazionali* (Milano: Mondadori Education S.p.A., 2022), 372.

37 Kissinger, *Leadership*, 406–407.

Bibliography

Primary Sources NA (The National Archives) KEW, London

Papers of Prime Minister

PREM 13/255 – *Correspondence with Sir Lawrence Kadoorie on UK/Chinese Trade: Contracts for Castle Peak A & B Power Stations; Guangdong Nuclear Power Plant Oil Prices*, 1979–1980.

PREM 16/890 – *The Visit of the Federal German Chancellor, Herr Schmidt, to China, October/November 1975*, 1976.

PREM 16/1533 – *The Visit to the UK by Mr. Li Ch'iang, the Chinese Minister of Foreign Trade*, 1977.

PREM 16/1534 – *The Visit to the United Kingdom by Mr Huang Hua, the Chinese Foreign Minister*, 1978.

PREM 16/1949 – *Possible Visit to the UK by Chinese Vice-Premier Wang Chen*, 1978.

PREM 19/3 – *Visit to UK by Premier Hua Guofeng: meetings with Prime Minister, part 1*, 1979.

PREM 19/127 – *Visit to USA by PM on 16–19 November 1979: Policy*, 1979.

PREM 19/2597 – *China: Internal Situation*, 1979–1989.

PREM 19/2921 – *Sino-Soviet Relations: Visit by Mr Heath*, 1979.

PREM 19/3626 – *Sec Relations/Int Sit*, 1980.

Cabinet Papers

CAB 128/59 – *Cabinet Meetings*, April-August 1976.

CAB 128/60 – *Cabinet Meetings*, September-December 1976.

CAB 128/63 – *Cabinet Meetings*, January-May 1978.

CAB 128/64 – *Cabinet Meetings*, June-December 1978.

CAB 128/65 – *Cabinet Meetings*, January-March 1979.

CAB 129/205 – *Cabinet Memoranda*, January-March 1979.

CAB 134/494 – *Visit of Premier Hua Guofeng of China*, 28 October–3 November 1979.

Ministry of Defence Papers

DEFE/5/195/18 – *Defence Implications of the Sale of Harrier Aircraft and Spey Aircraft Engines to China*, 1973.

Department of Treasury Papers

T 370/1501 – *Nationalised Industries: Trade Agreements with China*, 1978–1980.
T 439/142 – *International Monetary Fund (IMF): People's Republic of China*, 1981–1983.

Foreign and Commonwealth Office – Research Department Later Research and Analysis Department

FO 972/14 – *China: National People's Congress*, 1978.
FO 973/22 – *Wider Options in China's Foreign Policy*, 1978.
FO 973/136 – *China's Economic and Political Course*, 1981.
FO 973/183 – *China's Economy and Foreign Trade in 1980*, 1981.
FO 973/284 – *China's Course for the 1980s*, 1983.

Foreign and Commonwealth Office Papers

FCO 21/1610 – *Political Relations between China and UK*, 1978.
FCO 21/1611 – *Political Relations between China and UK*, 1978.
FCO 21/1616 – *Visit of Huang Hua, Chinese Foreign Minister to UK*, 1978.
FCO 21/1685 – *Internal Political Situation in China*, 1979.
FCO 21/1688 – *UK Policy towards China: Response to British Ambassador's Despatch*, 1979.
FCO 21/1690 – *Relations between China and the UK*, 1979.
FCO 21/1691 – *Relations between China and the UK*, 1979.
FCO 21/1692 – *Relations between China and the UK*, 1979.
FCO 21/1693 – *Relations between China and the USA*, 1979.
FCO 21/1694 – *Relations between China and the USA*, 1979.
FCO 21/1696 – *Relations between China and the Soviet Union*, 1979.
FCO 21/1697 – *Relations between China and the Soviet Union*, 1979.
FCO 21/1710 – *Visit of Eric Varley, Secretary of State for Industry, to China, February-March 1979*, 1979.
FCO 21/1711 – *Visit of Premier Hua Guofeng of China to the UK, October-November 1979*, 1979.
FCO 21/1712 – *Visit of Premier Hua Guofeng of China to the UK, October-November 1979*, 1979.
FCO 21/1799 – *Internal Political Situation in China*, 1980.
FCO 21/1803 – *Relations between China and the UK*, 1980.
FCO 21/1804 – *Relations between China and the UK*, 1980.
FCO 21/1805 – *Relations between China and the Soviet Union*, 1980.
FCO 21/1808 – *Foreign Policy of China*, 1980.
FCO 21/1812 – *Visit by He Ying, Chinese Vice Foreign Minister, to the UK, August 1980*, 1980.
FCO 21/1816 – *Visit by Huang Hua, Chinese Foreign Minister, to the UK, October 1980*, 1980.
FCO 21/1905 – *Internal Political Situation in China: Including Despatch "The Sixth Plenum and the Fall of Hua Guofeng"*, 1981.
FCO 21/1912 – *Relations between China and the Soviet Union*, 1981.

FCO 21/1917 – *Foreign Policy of China: "The Domestic Context of Chinese Foreign Policy: The Politics of Sovereignty", by Kennet G. Lieberthal*, 1981.

FCO 21/1920 – *Visit by Lord Carrington, Secretary of State for Foreign and Commonwealth Affairs, to China, April 1981*, 1981.

FCO 21/1922 – *Visit by Lord Carrington, Secretary of State for Foreign and Commonwealth Affairs, to China, April 1981: Briefing*, 1981.

FCO 21/1924 – *Visit by Huang Hua, Chinese Foreign Minister, to the UK, November 1981*, 1981.

FCO 21/2038 – *Internal Political Situation in China*, 1981.

FCO 21/2053 – *Relations between China and the Soviet Union*, 1982.

FCO 28/3459 – *Political Relations between Soviet Union and China*, 1978.

FCO 28/3460 – *Political Relations between Soviet Union and China*, 1978.

FCO 28/3461 – *Political Relations between Soviet Union and China*, 1978.

FCO 28/3862 – *Relations between the Soviet Union and China*, 1979.

FCO 28/3863 – *Relations between the Soviet Union and China*, 1979.

FCO 28/3986 – *Relations between the UK and China Following the Soviet Invasion of Afghanistan*, 1980.

FCO 28/3989 – *Relations between the Soviet Union and China*, 1980.

FCO 28/4061 – *Visit by Lord Carrington, Secretary of State for Foreign and Commonwealth Affairs, to Peking, October 1980: Note on China and Eastern Europe*, 1980.

FCO 46/1713 – *China and NATO*, 1978.

FCO 49/782 – *Planning Paper on UK Policy towards China*, 1978.

FCO 49/783 – *Planning Paper on UK Policy towards China*, 1978.

FCO 49/834 – *Relations between the UK and China: Anglo-Chinese Planning Talks*, 1979.

FCO 69/837 – *Western Economic Relations with China*, 1981.

FCO 160/31 – *Diplomatic Despatches, 1975–1976 (Described at Item Level)*, 1975–1976.

FCO 160/72 – *Diplomatic Despatches, 1980 (Described at Item Level)*, 1980.

JCPL (Jimmy Carter Presidential Library), Atlanta, GA

Office of Staff Secretary

Series: *1976 Campaign Transition File*, 11/76-1/77, Container 1.

National Security Affairs

Brzezinski Material, Country File, Box 8, *China (People's Republic of)*: 77–78.

Brzezinski Material, Country File, Box 9, *China (PRC)*: 4-5/79.

Brzezinski Material, Country File, Box 10, *China (PRC)*: 10/80-1/81.

Brzezinski Material, Subject File, Box 38, *Memcons: President*: 7/80.

Brzezinski Material, VIP Visit File, Box 2, *China: Vice Premier Deng Xiaoping*, 1/28/79-2/1/79, 1/25/79 Briefing Book [I].

Staff Material, Far East, Oksenberg Subject File, Box 24, *Arms Sales*: 4-11/78.

Staff Material, Far East, Oksenberg Subject File, Box 28, *Brzezinski 5/78 Trip to China*: 2-12/77.

Staff Material, Far East, Oksenberg Subject File, Box 25, *Brown (Harold) 1/80 Trip*, 8-9/79.

Staff Material, Far East, Oksenberg Subject File, Box 26, *Brown (Harold) 1/80 Trip*, Memcons: 1/80.

Staff Material, Far East, Oksenberg Subject File, Box 43, *Meetings*: 77–78.

Staff Material, Far East, Oksenberg Subject File, Box 47, *Meetings*: 5-9/79.

Staff Material, Far East, Oksenberg Subject File, Box 47, *Policy Review Committee on PRM 24*: 6-7/77.

Staff Material, Far East, Oksenberg Subject File, Box 47, *Presidential on Cyrus Vance Trip to China*: 4-8/77.

Staff Material, Far East, Oksenberg Subject File, Box 49, *Mondale 8/79 China Trip: Briefing Material*: 3/78-8/79.

Staff Material, Far East, Oksenberg Subject File, Box 55, *Policy Process*: 10/76-4/77.

Staff Material, Far East, Oksenberg Subject File, Box 56, *Policy Process*: 77–78.

Staff Material, Far East, Oksenberg Subject File, Box 57, *Policy Process*: 10-11/78.

Staff Material, Far East, Sullivan Subject File, Box 70, *Geng Biao Visit*: 5/23-31/80.

Staff Material, Office, Institutional File, Box 26, *INT Documents: 1500s–1800s*: 2-4/77.

Staff Material, Office, Outside the System File, Box 46, *China: Brzezinski, May, 1978, Trip*: 77–78.

Staff Material, Office, Outside the System File, Box 47, *China: President's Meeting with Vice Premier Deng*: 1-2/79.

Staff Material, Office, Outside the System File, Box 51, *Chron*: 10/1-7/78.

Staff Material, Office, Outside the System File, Box 53, *Chron*: 8/2/79.

Staff Material, Office, Outside the System File, Box 55, *Chron*: 12/11-20/79.

Brzezinski Donated Material

Geographic File, Box 9, *China (People's Republic of), Alpha Channel*: 12/78-1/80.

Subject File, Box 25, *Meetings, PRC 97*: 3/79.

Subject File, Box 42, *Weekly Reports [to the President]*, 102–120, 7/79-12/79.

National Security Council Institutional Files (H-Files)

Box 42 *(PRC China)*, PRM-24 [1].

Box 62, PRC 019, 6/27/77, *(PRC China)*-PRM 24.

Box 72, PRC 086, 1/8/79, *US-China Economic Relations*.

Box 79, PRC 136, *US-China Economic Relations*, 3/27/80.

NARA (National Archives and Records Administration), College Park, MD

Department of State

Record Group 59, Central Foreign Policy Files 1973–1979, Electronic Telegrams, https://aad.archives.gov/

RG 59, American Embassy Beijing, 1979 Central Subject Files, Lot 82 F 82.

RG 59, Executive Secretariat Files: Lot 84 D 241, Box 9, Vance NODIS Memcons, 1979.

Published Documents

Brezhnev, Leonid I., *Our Course: Peace and Socialism – A Collection of Speeches Delivered in 1978* (Moscow: Novosti Press Agency Publishing House, 1979).

Burr, William (ed.), *The Kissinger Transcripts: The Top-Secret Talks with Beijing & Moscow* (New York, NY: The New Press, 1998).

Kissinger, Henry A., *Crisis: The Anatomy of Two Major Foreign Policy Crises* (London and New York, NY: Simon & Schuster, 2003).

"The Department of State Bulletin", 1976–1982.

Triangle Paper 13: Collaboration with Communist Countries in Managing Global Problems: An Examination of the Options (Tokyo, Paris and New York, NY: The Trilateral Commission, 1977).

Triangle Papers 15: An Overview of East-West Relations (Tokyo, Paris and New York, NY: The Trilateral Commission, 1978).

Office of Technology Assessment Archive

Technology Transfer to China, OTA-ISC-340 (Washington, DC: US Government Printing Office, 1987).

The Selected Works of Deng Xiaoping

Vol. 2 (1975–1982), https://dengxiaopingworks.wordpress.com

Documents of the People's Republic of China

First Session of the Fourth National People's Congress of the People's Republic of China, https://www.marxists.org

DBPO (Documents on British Policy Overseas)

Hamilton, Keith A. and Gill Bennet, (eds.), DBPO, Series III, Vol. III, *Détente in Europe, 1972–1976* (London and Portland, OR: Frank Cass, 2001).

Smith, Richard, Patrick Salmon and Stephen Twigge (eds.), DBPO, Series III, Vol. VIII, *The Invasion of Afghanistan and UK-Soviet Relations, 1979–1982* (Abingdon and New York, NY: Routledge, 2013).

UK Parliamentary Debates

House of Commons Debates, https://hansard.parliament.uk
House of Lords Debates, https://hansard.parliament.uk

FRUS (Foreign Relations of the United States)

Howard, Adam M. (gen. ed.) and David P. Nickles (ed.), FRUS 1977–1980, Vol. XIII *China* (Washington, DC: United States Government Printing Office, 2013).

Howard, Adam M. (gen. ed.) and David Zierler (ed.), FRUS 1977–1980, Vol. XII, *Afghanistan* (Washington, DC: United States Government Publishing Office, 2018).

Howard, Adam M. (gen. ed.) and Kristin L. Ahlberg (ed.), FRUS 1977–1980, Vol. I, *Foundations of Foreign Policy* (Washington, DC: United States Government Printing Office, 2014).

Howard, Adam M. (gen. ed.) and Melissa J. Taylor (ed.), FRUS 1977–1980, Vol. VI, *Soviet Union* (Washington, DC: United States Government Printing Office, 2013).

Keefer, Edward C. (gen. ed.) and David P. Nickles (ed.), FRUS 1969–1976, Vol. XVIII, *China 1973–1976* (Washington, DC: United States Government Printing Office, 2007).

Keefer, Edward C. (gen. ed.) and Steven E. Phillips (ed.), FRUS 1969–1972, Vol. XVII, *China 1969–1972* (Washington, DC: United States Government Printing Office, 2006).

Congress of the United States

Ninety-Fifth Congress, First Session, Part One, Executive Sessions, June 23, 1977 (Washington, DC: US Government Printing Office, 1977), https://www.jec.senate.gov/

Ninety-Fifth Congress, First Session, Part Three, 23 and 30 June (Executive Sessions), and 6 July 1977 (Washington, DC: US Government Printing Office, 1977). https://www.jec.senate.gov/

Ninety-Sixth Congress, Second Session, Part Six, Executive Sessions, 30 June and 25 September 1980 (Washington, DC: US Government Printing Office, 1981).

Ninety-Seventh Congress, Second Session, China under the Four Modernizations, Part 1 Selected Papers, Submitted to the Joint Economic Committee, Congress of the United States (Washington DC: US Government Printing Office, 1982).

Library of Congress

Frontline Diplomacy: *The Association for Diplomatic Studies and Training Foreign Affairs*, Oral History Project. https://memory.loc.gov

United Nations General Assembly

General Assembly Official Records, 34th Session: 7th Plenary Meeting. https://digitallibrary.un.org

Public Papers of the Presidents of the United States

Public Papers of Jimmy Carter, 1977–1981.

Memoirs, Autobiographies, Diaries

Bao, Pu, Renee Chiang and Adi Ignatius (eds.), *Prisoner of the State: The Secret Journal of Zhao Ziyang* (New York, NY: Simon & Schuster, 2009).

Benn, Tony, *Against the Tide: Diaries 1973–76* (London: Hutchinson, 1989).

Brzezinski, Zbigniew, *Power and Principle: Memoirs of the National Security Adviser 1977–1981* (New York, NY: Farrar Straus Giroux, 1983).

Carter, Jimmy, *Keeping Faith: Memoirs of a President* (Toronto, Sidney, London and New York, NY: Bantam Books, 1982).

Carter, Jimmy, *White House Diary* (New York, NY: Farrar, Straus and Giroux, 2010).

Kissinger, Henry A., *Years of Renewal: The Concluding Volume of His Memoirs* (London: Weidenfeld & Nicolson, 1999).

Thatcher, Margaret, *The Downing Street Diaries* (London: Harper Collins Publishers Ltd., 1993).

Vance, Cyrus, *Hard Choices: Critical Years in American Foreign Policy* (New York, NY: Simon and Schuster, 1983).

Conference Proceedings

Fardella, Enrico, Christian F. Ostermann and Charles Kraus (eds.), *Sino-European Relations during the Cold War and the Rise of a Multipolar World: A Critical Oral History* (Washington, DC: Woodrow Wilson International Center for Scholars, 2015).

Secondary Sources

Books

Albers, Martin, *Britain, France, West Germany and the People's Republic of China, 1969–1982: The European Dimension of China's Great Transition* (London: Palgrave Macmillan, 2016).

Ash, Robert, David Shambaugh and Seiichiro Takagi (eds.), *China Watching: Perspectives from Europe, Japan and the United States* (Abingdon and New York, NY: Routledge, 2007).

Baum, Richard, *Burying Mao: Chinese Politics in the Age of Deng Xiaoping* (Princeton, NJ: Princeton University Press, 1994).

Bernkopf Tucker, Nancy (ed.), *China Confidential: American Diplomats and Sino-American Relations, 1945–1996* (New York, NY: Columbia University Press, 2001).

Bianchini, Stefano and Antonio Fiori (eds.), *Rekindling the Strong State in Russia and China: Domestic Dynamics and Foreign Policy Projections* (Leiden and Boston, MA: Brill, 2020).

Brandt, Loren and Thoman G. Rawski (eds.), *China's Great Economic Transformation* (Cambridge: Cambridge University Press, 2008).

Buchanan, Tom, *East Wind: China and the British Left, 1925–1976* (Oxford: Oxford University Press, 2012).

Bui, Tung X., David C. Yang, Wayne D. Jones and Joanna Z. Li (eds.), *China's Economic Powerhouse: Reform in Guangdong Province* (Basingstoke and New York, NY: Palgrave Macmillan, 2003).

Cannadine, David, *Margaret Thatcher: A Life and Legacy* (Oxford: Oxford University Press, 2017).

Casarini, Nicola, *Remaking Global Order: The Evolution of Europe-China Relations and its Implications for East Asia and the United States* (Oxford: Oxford University Press, 2009).

Chang, David Wen-Wei, *China under Deng Xiaoping: Political and Economic Reform* (New York, NY: Palgrave Macmillan, 1991).

Chao, Charles Rong Phua, *Towards Strategic Pragmatism in Foreign Policy: Cases of United States of America, China and Singapore* (Abingdon and New York, NY: Routledge, 2022).

Chen, Jian, *From Mao to Deng: China's Changing Relations with the United States*, Cold War International History Project, Working Paper 92 (Washington, DC: Woodrow Wilson International Center for Scholars, 2019).

Chen, Jian, *Mao's China and the Cold War* (London and Chapel Hill, NC: University of North Carolina Press, 2001).

Chi-kwan, Mark, *China and the World since 1945: An International History* (Abingdon and New York, NY: Routledge, 2012).

Chow, Gregory C., *Interpreting China's Economy* (Singapore: World Scientific Publishing Co. Pte. Ltd, 2010).

Cohen, Warren I., *America's Response to China: A History of Sino-American Relations* (New York, NY: Columbia University Press, 2010).

De Freitas, Marcus Vinicius, *Policy Paper 19/05: Reform and Opening-Up: Chinese Lessons to the World* (Rabat: Policy Center for the New South, 2019).

deLisle, Jacques and Avery Goldstein (eds.), *China's Challenges* (Philadelphia, PA: University of Pennsylvania Press, 2015).

Dillon, Michael, *Contemporary China: An Introduction* (Abingdon and New York, NY: Routledge, 2009).

Dillon, Michael, *Deng Xiaoping: The Man who Made Modern China* (London and New York, NY: I.B. Tauris, 2015).

Dong, Wang, *The United States and China: A History from the Eighteenth Century to the Present* (Lanham, MD: Rowman & Littlefield Publishers, Inc., 2013).

Evans, Richard, *Deng Xiaoping and the Making of Modern China* (London: Penguin Books, 1995).

Fenby, Jonathan, *The Penguin History of Modern China: The Fall and Rise of a Great Power, 1850 to the Present* (London: Penguin Books, 2019).

Fiori, Antonio, Marco Milani and Andrea Passeri, *Asia: storia, istituzioni e relazioni internazionali* (Milano: Mondadori Education S.p.A., 2022).

Fiori, Antonio and Matteo Dian, (eds.), *The Chinese Challenge to the Western Order* (Trento: FBK Press, 2014).

Garthoff, Raymond L., *Détente and Confrontation: American-Soviet Relations from Nixon to Reagan* (Washington, DC: Brookings Institution, 1985).

Gewirtz, Julian B., *Unlikely Partners: Chinese Reformers, Western Economists, and the Making of Global China* (London and Cambridge, MA: Harvard University Press, 2017).

Goldstein, Avery, *Rising to the Challenge: China's Grand Strategy and International Security* (Stanford, CA: Stanford University Press, 2005).

Goodman, David S.G., *Deng Xiaoping and the Chinese Revolution: A Political Biography* (London and New York, NY: Routledge, 1994).

Hsi-Sheng Ch'i, *Politics of Disillusionment. The Chinese Communist Party under Deng Xiaoping, 1978–1989* (London and Armonk, NY: M.E. Sharpe, Inc., 1991).

Hui, Feng, *The Politics of China's Accession to the World Trade Organization: The Dragon Goes Global* (Abingdon and New York, NY: Routledge, 2006).

Jacques, Martin, *When China Rules the World: The End of the Western World and the Birth of a New Global Order* (London: Penguin Books, 2012).

Kapur, Harish, *China and the EEC: The New Connection* (Dordrecht: Kluwer Academic Publishers, 1986).

Keith, Ronald C., *Deng Xiaoping and China's Foreign Policy* (Abingdon and New York, NY: Routledge, 2018).

Kelly, Jason M., *Market Maoists: The Communist Origins of China's Capitalist Ascent* (London and Cambridge, MA: Harvard University Press, 2021).

Kennedy, Scott (ed.), *Beyond the Middle Kingdom: Comparative Perspectives on China's Capitalist Transformation* (Stanford, CA: Stanford University Press, 2011).

Kim, Samuel S. (ed.), *China and the World: Chinese Foreign Policy in the Post-Mao Era* (London and Boulder, CO: West View Press, 1984).

Kirby, William C., Robert S. Ross and Gong Li (eds.), *Normalization of US-China Relations: An International History* (London and Cambridge, MA: Harvard University Asia Center, 2005).

Kissinger, Henry A., *Leadership: sei lezioni di strategia globale* (Milano: Mondadori Libri S.p.A., 2022).

Kissinger, Henry A., *On China* (London: Allen Lane, 2011).

Kissinger, Henry A., *World Order: Reflections on the Character of Nations and the Course of History* (London: Penguin Books, 2015).

Lai, David, *The United States and China in Power Transition* (Carlisle Barracks, PA: The Strategic Studies Institute, 2011).

Lampton, David M., *Following the Leader: Ruling China, from Deng Xiaoping to Xi Jinping* (Oakland, CA: University of California Press, 2014).

Leuenberger, Theodor (ed.), *From Technology Transfer to Technology Management in China* (Heidelberg: Springer-Verlag, 1990).

Lieberthal, Kenneth and Michel Oksenberg, *Policy Making in China: Leaders, Structures, and Processes* (Princeton, NJ: Princeton University Press, 1988).

Lieberthal, Kenneth, Tong James and Sai-cheung Yeung, *Central Documents and Politburo Politics in China* (Ann Arbor, MI: University of Michigan Press, 1978).

Lüthi, Lorenz M., *Cold Wars: Asia, the Middle East, Europe* (Cambridge and New York, NY: Cambridge University Press, 2020).

Malik, Hafeez (ed.), *The Roles of the United States, Russia, and China in the New World Order* (New York, NY: St. Martin's Press, 1997).

Mann, James, *About Face: A History of America's Curious Relationship with China, from Nixon to Clinton* (New York, NY: Alfred A. Knopf, 1999).

Meidan, Michal, *The Structure of China's Oil Industry: Past Trends and Future Prospects*, OIES Paper: WPM 66 (Oxford: Oxford Institute for Energy Studies, May 2016).

Michalski, Anna and Zhongqi Pan, *Unlikely Partners? China, the European Union and the Forging of a Strategic Partnership* (Singapore: Palgrave Macmillan, 2017).

Naughton, Barry, *Growing out of the Plan: Chinese Economic Reform, 1978–1993* (Cambridge: Cambridge University Press, 1996).

Naughton, Barry, *The Chinese Economy: Adaption and Growth* (London and Cambridge, MS: The MIT Press, 2018).

Naughton, Barry, *The Chinese Economy: Transition and Growth* (London and Cambridge, MS: The MIT Press, 2007).

Pantsov, Alexander V. and Steven I. Levine, *Deng Xiaoping: A Revolutionary Life* (New York, NY: Oxford University Press, 2015).

Pomeranz, Kenneth, *The Great Divergence: China, Europe, and the Making of the Modern World Economy* (Princeton, NJ: Princeton University Press, 2000).

Radchenko, Sergey, *Unwanted Visionaries* (Oxford: Oxford University Press, 2014).

Rato, Vasco, *Dragon Rejuvenated: Making China Greatest Again* (Lisbon: Instituto da Defesa Nacional, 2020).

Roberts, Priscilla (ed.), *Chinese Economic Statecraft from 1978 to 1989: The First Decade of Deng Xiaoping's Reforms* (Singapore: Palgrave Macmillan, 2022).

Roberts, Priscilla and Westad Ode Arne (eds.), *China, Hong Kong, and the Long 1970s: Global Perspectives* (Cham: Palgrave Macmillan, 2017).

Ropp, Paul S., *China in World History* (New York, NY: Oxford University Press, 2010).

Ross, Robert S., *Negotiating Cooperation: The United States and China 1969–1989* (Stanford, CA: Stanford University Press, 1995).

Ross, Robert S. and Øystein Tunsjø, (eds.), *Strategic Adjustment and the Rise of China: Power and Politics in East Asia* (London and Ithaca, NY: Cornell University Press, 2017).

Schaller, Michael, *The United States and China: Into the Twenty-First Century* (New York, NY: Oxford University Press, 2002).

Schaufelbuehl, Janick Marina, Marco Wyss and Valeria Zanier (eds.), *Europe and China in the Cold War: Exchanges beyond the Bloc Logic and the Sino-Soviet Split* (Leiden and Boston, MA: Brill, 2019).

Schuman, Michael, *L'impero interrotto: la storia vista dalla Cina* (Milano: DeA Planeta Libri S.r.L., 2021).

Seldon, Anthony and Kevin Hickson (eds.), *New Labour, Old Labour: The Blair, Wilson and Callaghan Governments, 1974–1979* (London and New York, NY: Routledge, 2004).

Shambaugh, David (ed.), *China & the World* (New York, NY: Oxford University Press, 2020).

Shambaugh, David (ed.), *Power Shift: China and Asia's New Dynamics* (London, Berkeley and Los Angeles, CA: University of California Press, 2005).

Shambaugh, David (ed.), *Tangled Titans: The United States and China* (Plymouth and Lanham, MD: Rowman & Littlefield Publishers, Inc., 2013).

Shambaugh, David, Eberhard Sandschneider and Zhou Hong (eds.), *China-Europe Relations: Perceptions, Policies and Prospects* (Abingdon and New York, NY, 2008).

Shambaugh, David and Yahuda, Michael (eds.), *International Relations of Asia* (Plymouth: Rowman & Littlefield Publishers, Inc., 2008).

Shuxun, Zen and Charles Wolf, Jr. (eds.), *China, the United States, and the Global Economy* (Santa Monica, CA and Arlington, VA: Rand, 2001).

Sutter, Robert G., *Chinese Foreign Relations: Power and Policy since the Cold War*, Third Edition (Plymouth and Lanham, MD: Rowman & Littlefield Publishers, Inc., 2012).

Sutter, Robert G., *The United States in Asia* (Lanham, MD: Rowman & Littlefield Publishers, Inc., 2009).

Sutter, Robert G., *US-China Relations: Perilous Past, Uncertain Present* (Lanham, MD: Rowman & Littlefield Publishers, Inc., 2018).

Sutter, Robert G., *US-Chinese Relations: Perilous Past, Pragmatic Present* (Lanham, MD: Rowman & Littlefield Publishers, Inc., 2013).

Talas, Barna, *Economic Reforms and Political Attempts in China 1979–1989* (Heidelberg: Springer-Verlag, 1991).

Tung, X. Bui, David C. Yang, Wayne D. Jones and Joanna Z. Li (eds.), *China's Economic Powerhouse: Reform in Guangdong Province* (Basingstoke and New York, NY: Palgrave Macmillan, 2003).

Tyler, Patrick, *A Great Wall: Six Presidents and China, an Investigative History* (New York, NY: Public Affairs, 1999).

Vaïsse, Justin, *Zbigniew Brzezinski: America's Grand Strategist* (London and Cambridge, MA: Harvard University Press, 2018).

Van Vuuren, Hennie, *Apartheid Guns and Money: A Tale of Profit* (London: Hurst & Company, 2018).

Vogel, Ezra F., *Deng Xiaoping and the Transformation of China* (London and Cambridge, MA: The Belknap Press of Harvard University Press, 2011).

Wang, Gungwu and Yongnian Zheng (eds.), *China and the New International Order* (Abingdon and New York, NY: Routledge, 2008).

Wei-Wei Zhang, *Ideology and Economic Reform under Deng Xiaoping, 1978–1993* (London and New York, NY: Routledge, 2010).

Wen, David and Wei Chang, *China under Deng Xiaoping: Political and Economic Reform* (New York, NY: Palgrave Macmillan, 1988).

Westad, Odd Arne, *Restless Empire: China and the World since 1750* (New York, NY: Basic Books, 2012).

Westad, Odd Arne, *The Global Cold War: Third World Interventions and the Making of Our Times* (Cambridge: Cambridge University Press, 2007).

Yahuda, Michael, *The International Politics of the Asia-Pacific, Second and Revised Edition* (London and New York, NY: Routledge Curzon, 2005).

Yahuda, Michael, *The International Politics of the Asia-Pacific, Fourth and Revised Edition* (Abingdon and New York, NY: Routledge, 2019).

Yahuda, Michael, *Towards the End of Isolationism: China's Foreign Policy after Mao* (Salisbury: Macmillan Press Ltd., 1983).

Yu, Guangyuan, *Deng Xiaoping Shakes the World: An Eyewitness Account of China's Party Work Conference and the Third Plenum* (Manchester: Eastbridge Books, 2017).

Zhang, Shu Guang, *Beijing's Economic Statecraft during the Cold War, 1949–1991* (Washington, DC and Baltimore, MD: Woodrow Wilson Center Press and Johns Hopkins University Press, 2014).

Zhou, Yi, *Less Revolution, more Realpolitik: China's Foreign Policy in the Early and Middle 1970s*, Cold War International History Project Working Paper 93 (Washington, DC: Woodrow Wilson International Center for Scholars, 2020).

Zweig, David and Chen Zhimin, *China's Reforms and International Political Economy* (Abingdon and New York, NY: Routledge, 2007).

Articles and Essays

Bachman, David, 'Differing Visions of China's Post-Mao Economy: The Ideas of Chen Yun, Deng Xiaoping, and Zhao Ziyang', *Asian Survey*, 26/3, 1986.

Chang, Parris H., 'Elite Conflict in the Post-Mao China, Revised Edition', Occasional Papers/Reprint Series in Contemporary Asian Studies, 55/2, 1983.

Chih-Chia, Hsu, 'Foreign Policy Decision-Making Process in Deng's China: Three Patterns for Analysis', Asian Perspective, 23/2, Special Issue on the Dynamics of Northeast Asia and the Korean Peninsula, 1999.

Chow, Gregory C., 'Economic Reform and Growth in China', *Annals of Economics and Finance*, 5/1 2004.

Dittmer, Lowell, 'China in 1980: Modernization and its Discontents', *Asian Survey: A Survey of Asia in 1980*, Part I, 21/1, 1981.

Dittmer, Lowell, 'China in 1981: Reform, Readjustment, Rectification', *Asian Survey: A Survey of Asia in 1981*, Part I, 22/1, 1982.

Dittmer, Lowell, 'The 12th Congress of the Communist Party of China', *The China Quarterly*, 24/93/1, 1983.

Fardella, Enrico, 'The Sino-American Normalization: A Reassessment', Diplomatic History, 33/4, 2009.

Fontana, Dorothy Grouse, 'Background to the Fall of Hua Guofeng', *Asian Survey*, 22/3, March 1982.

Gurtov, Melvin, 'China: The Politics of the Opening', *Asian Perspective*, 12/1, 1988.

Hammer, Armand, 'On a Vast China Market', Journal of International Affairs, 39/2, 1986.

Hilton, Brian, 'Maximum Flexibility for Peaceful Change: Jimmy Carter, Taiwan, and the Recognition of the People's Republic of China', Diplomatic History, 33/4, 2009.

Keith, Ronald C., 'The Origins and Strategic Implications of China's Independent Foreign Policy', *International Journal*, 41/1, 1985–1986.

Kuisong, Yang and Xia Yafeng, 'Vacillating between Revolution and Détente: Mao's Changing Psyche and Policy toward the United States, 1969–1976', Diplomatic History, 34/2, 2010.

Lee, Lai To, 'Deng Xiaoping's ASEAN Tour: A Perspective on Sino-Southeast Asian Relations', *Contemporary Southeast Asia*, 3/1, 1981.

Lei, Liu, 'China's Large-Scale Importation of Western Technology and the US Response, 1972–1976', *Diplomatic History*, 45/4, 2021.

MacFarquhar, Roderick, 'Deng Xiaoping's Reform Program in the Perspective of Chinese History', *Bulletin of the American Academy of Arts and Sciences*, 40/6, 1987.

Min, Song, 'A Dissonance in Mao's Revolution: Chinese Agricultural Imports from the United States, 1972–1978', *Diplomatic History*, 38/2, 2014.

Minami, Kazushi, 'Oil for the Lamps of America? Sino-American Oil Diplomacy, 1973–1979', *Diplomatic History*, 41/5, 2017.

Mirsky, Jonathan, 'China's 12th Party Congress', *The World Today*, 38/12, 1982.

Naughton, Barry, 'Deng Xiaoping: The Economist', *The China Quarterly* (Special Issue: *Deng Xiaoping: An Assessment*), 34/135/3, 1993.

Ross, Robert S., 'From Lin Biao to Deng Xiaoping: Elite Instability and China's US Policy', *The China Quarterly*, 30/118/2, 1989.

Russo, Alessandro, 'How Did the Cultural Revolution End? The Last Dispute between Mao Zedong and Deng Xiaoping, 1975', *Modern China*, 39/3, 2013.

Schram, Stuart R., 'Economics in Command? Ideology and Policy since the Third Plenum, 1978–84', *The China Quarterly*, 99/3, 1984.

Teiwes, Frederick C. and Warren Sun, 'China's Economic Reorientation after the Third Plenum: Conflict Surrounding Chen Yun's Readjustment Program', 1979–80, *The China Journal*, 35/70, 2013.

Teiwes, Frederick C. and Warren Sun, 'China's New Economic Policy under Hua Guofeng: Party Consensus and Party Myths', *The China Journal*, 33/66, 2011.

Tianbiao, Zhu, 'Nationalism and Chinese Foreign Policy', *China Review*, 1/1, 2001.

Walker, Breck, 'Friends, but Not Allies: Cyrus Vance and the Normalization of Relations with China', *Diplomatic History*, 33/4, 2009.

Woon, Eden Y., 'Chinese Arms Sales and US-China Military Relations', *Asian Survey*, 29/6, 1989.

Xin, Zhan, 'Prelude to the Transformation: China's Nuclear Arms Control Policy during the US-China Rapprochement, 1969–1976', *Diplomatic History*, 41/2, 2017.

Yahuda, Michael, 'Deng Xiaoping: The Statesman', *The China Quarterly*, 34/135/3, 1993.

Periodicals/Newspapers

«Peking/Beijing Review»
«The New York Times»
«The Times»
«Time»

Web Sites

https://www.cia.gov
https://www.jimmycarterlibrary.gov
https://aad.archives.gov
http://trilateral.org
https://digitalarchive.wilsoncenter.org
https://www.presidency.ucsb.edu
https://ia800809.us.archive.org
https://marxists.org
https://www.nytimes.com
http://www.china.org.cn
https://www.margaretthatcher.org
https://dengxiaopingworks.wordpress.com
https://siepr.stanford.edu
https://www.jec.senate.gov
https://ota.fas.org
https://www.loc.gov/collections/
https://www.constituteproject.org
https://www.govinfo.gov
https://hansard.parliament.uk
https://www.un.org/en/ga/
http://cns.miis.edu/nam/

Index

9781032486611